DREAMING BASEBALL

WRITING SPORTS SERIES

Richard "Pete" Peterson, Editor

DREAMING BASEBALL

by James T. Farrell

Edited by Ron Briley, Margaret Davidson,
and James Barbour

Foreword by Eliot Asinof

THE KENT STATE
UNIVERSITY PRESS
Kent, Ohio

© 2007 by The Kent State University Press, Kent, Ohio 44242
All rights reserved.
Library of Congress Catalog Card Number 2006037402
ISBN: 978-0-87338-897-9
Manufactured in the United States of America
11 10 09 08 07   5 4 3 2 1

Library of Congress Cataloging-in-Publication Data
Farrell, James T. (James Thomas), 1904–1979.
Dreaming baseball / by James T. Farrell ; edited by Ron Briley,
Margaret Davidson, and James Barbour ; foreword by Eliot Asinof.
      p.   cm. — (Writing sports series)
ISBN-13: 978-0-87338-897-9 (alk paper) ∞
ISBN-10: 0-87338-897-6 (alk paper) ∞
1. Chicago White Sox (Baseball team)—Fiction.
2. Baseball—Corrupt practices—United states—Fiction.
I. Briley, Ron, 1949– II. Davidson, Margaret, 1936–
III. Barbour, James, 1933– IV. Title.
PS3511.A738D74 2007
813'.52—dc22   2006037402

British Library Cataloging-in-Publication data are available.

FOREWORD

Eliot Asinof

In 1960 I began researching *Eight Men Out* at the same time that James T. Farrell was finishing his novel about the 1919 World Series fix. Oddly enough, nothing had been published about the Black Sox scandal—as if it had never happened. Celebrated though he was, Farrell could not find a publisher for his novel. When I went to see him as part of my research about the scandal, he offered to show me his manuscript. "It's a morality tale," he said. "How a young boy's love for baseball is also threatened by the corruption of his heroes." During my visit, Farrell supplied a fund of names, events, and dates from his amazing baseball memory, but he also encouraged me to focus my own story on the lives of the eight men who betrayed baseball.

Fifty years later, Farrell's novel is finally to be published.

Mickey Donovan, Farrell's narrator and lead character, is, like Farrell himself, a working-class Chicagoan with a passion for baseball and a dream of someday playing in the major leagues for the hometown White Sox. (Farrell once said that he would rather play second base for the White Sox than write his novels.) Unlike Farrell, though, Donovan lives his dream and makes it to the White Sox, but just before they move into the 1919 World Series.

At that time playing on a major league ball club was an exciting experience—trips to big cities, hotel rooms, first-class dinners, and rides to the ballpark in taxis. But it was also a world shadowed by gamblers and rumors of fixed games. At the beginning of the 1919 World Series, such rumors spread like wildfire. By the time Chicago White Sox traveled to Cincinnati for the first two games of a nine-game World Series against the Reds, the 5-1 odds favoring the White Sox had shifted to even money.

When White Sox ace Eddie Cicotte, winner of twenty-nine games during the regular season, pitched poorly in an opening game for a 9-1 loss, and Lefty Williams, winner of twenty-three games, had uncharacteristic control problems in losing game two, it became clear that something was wrong. After rookie Dickie Kerr pitched a shutout for the White Sox in game three, Cicotte and Williams lost the next two games under suspicious circumstances to give the Reds a commanding 4-1 lead. With its bribed players performing better because they had not received all of the money promised to them by gamblers for fixing the World Series, the White Sox bounced back to win the next two games. But Lefty Williams, after a threat on his life, surrendered four runs in the first inning of game eight on the way to a 10-5 loss that gave the Cincinnati Reds a tainted world championship.

It was a time when every baseball fan suffered from the pain of baseball corruption. In F. Scott Fitzgerald's *The Great Gatsby*, Nick Caraway is shocked when Gatsby tells him that Meyer Wolfsheim, modeled after the real-life gangster Arnold Rothstein, had played with the faith of millions of Americans by fixing the 1919 World Series. James T. Farrell, a fifteen-year-old fan at the time, knew how much it had hurt. After the game at Comiskey Park in 1920, as the scandal was becoming public knowledge, Farrell waited outside the clubhouse for his fallen heroes. He heard what was said and remembered the exact words that summed up the ethical dilemma of that tragic time in baseball history. Kids, following the great Shoeless Joe Jackson, hollered plaintively, "It ain't so, Joe, it ain't so." Farrell would never forget the scene and those words.

Farrell's Mickey Donovan, while only a marginal player for the White Sox in 1919, narrates the circumstances surrounding the World Series fix and the character of the eight Black Sox players. It's Donovan's reaction to the growing scandal, the subsequent trial, and the banishment of the infamous "eight men out" that gives *Dreaming Baseball* its moral center. While Farrell is sympathetic to the players caught in the scandal and sees them as working-class victims exploited by their owner, his main concern in his "morality tale" is Donovan's struggle to hold on to his dream in the face of the betrayal of baseball by his own teammates.

While Mickey Donovan turns to his wife and family and his boyhood friends to gain a perspective on the scandal and restore his faith in the game, Farrell uses the fate of Buck Weaver, the one Black Sox player who proclaimed his innocence to his dying day, to transform the scandal into a tragic event. Weaver is indicted and banned with the others, but he played so well in the World Series that it was hard to believe that he was in on the fix. Weaver is Mickey Donovan's favorite teammate, the greatest third baseman of his time, the one Black Sox who forever appealed to Commissioner Landis for reinstatement and was forever denied. Though Weaver never took a dime from gamblers and played his heart out in the World Series, Judge Landis ignored Weaver's pleas for fairness and justice because Weaver, who admitted knowing about the fix, had failed to "rat" on his friends and teammates. Obsessed with the dream of someday being reinstated and even elected into the Hall of Fame, Weaver spent his aging years in Chicago running a girl's softball team, working at a pari-mutuel window, and writing futile letters to Commissioner Landis. In 1956 he died of a heart attack on the streets of Chicago.

Shortly thereafter James T. Farrell began his novel on the Black Sox, which in many ways is a testimonial to his boyhood idol Buck Weaver, who was broken by the 1919 World Scandal and became its ultimate victim.

The heart of Farrell's baseball novel, however, is the story of a young boy who dreams of playing one day for his hometown team and lives that dream, only to see it ruined by the social realities and personal failure that often shadow the dreamer. For Farrell, baseball is where youthful dreams begin, but it's also a test of character when the dream-come-true becomes a nightmare. In *Dreaming Baseball*, we learn if a love of baseball is strong enough to survive the game's darkest betrayal.

DREAMING BASEBALL

CHAPTER ONE

I

It was so cold that night at the ballpark in Sunnyside, Florida. I don't remember what the temperature was but it must have been 50 to 55 degrees. It seemed so cold that it would freeze 'em right off you, and Hank Space Patrol, one of the kids at Horace Stanton's Baseball School, kept trying to get a laugh by asking everybody, "Say, is this Florida or is it Alaska?"

That wind was like ice, and I had to stay there, keeping score in the book while our kids played the local Sunnyside team. Seeing ball games is my business, since I'm a scout for the White Sox, and I never tire of saying that every ball game is different and interesting and that you can always stand a chance of learning something. I mean it. But that game seemed longer than a double header, the way they play them in the American League nowadays. And I was depressed, the way I sometimes used to be in a slump during my days as a player. No, it was not depression. Maybe it was moodiness. It was something I'd never quite felt before.

There I was sitting on the open bench on the first base side of the fenced-in ball field, in front of wooden stands with a few of the hardier townsfolk watching the ball game because they must have had nothing else to do, keeping score, and it seemed to me as if I was living my whole life over again. That's a sad thing to do when you're fifty-six, an old ballplayer. It wasn't only sad. It was like everything, all of your life was only yesterday, so near that you were still living what you know

3

is gone and long ago in the past. It was a strange feeling I had. Before the game, I had been standing by the gate and a couple of the kids were talking. One of them was the oddball, Hank Space Patrol. He comes from Jersey, and even if he wasn't already twenty-six, he'd still be wasting his time thinking that he could ever become a ballplayer. He was nicknamed Hank Space Patrol because he wears a steel helmet at bat and when he goes out to left field, or even when he catches fungo flies.

You never know when you can have a disaster, he explained to me, although I didn't care what he wore on his head. He doesn't have the marbles inside it in the right order, and he was too pitiful for me to laugh at him. He brought his own bat down with him to Horace Stanton's Baseball School, and he guarded it like it was gold. But he was plate shy, and most of the time he was afraid even to take a swing at a pitch. One of the kids said to Space Patrol, "You're dreamin.'"

"We're all dreamin'," Space Patrol says.

"Wake up, Superman," another kid said to Hank Space Patrol.

"We're all dreamin'. We're dreamin' baseball," Hank Space Patrol said.

Funny, but that rang a bell in me. All of us, dreaming baseball. Then there was that sixteen-year-old kid they nicknamed "Young Stanky," breaking his leg when he broke his stride by hesitating on a slide into home plate. I saw it happen. The moment he hesitated for that fraction of a second, I knew he was going to break a bone. I wanted to yell to him but it was too late. He suffered a bad break, a compound fracture in his left ankle. The kid was in pain, in agony, but he had guts, and he bit his lip and fought not to moan. I'd had my eye on Stankowsky and I thought he might be a prospect, the only one among the forty-one at the baseball school that I'd buy as a prospect. Watching him, especially that night before the game got under way, I'd idly begun to think about myself when I was sixteen and seventeen, playing ball for St. Basil's, my high school team, and with the Rocks out in Washington Park on the South Side of Chicago. I'd been full of beans and fight and piss and vinegar then, crazy for baseball. That's one of the things I look for in a prospect. Is he crazy for baseball? I was like that. I was thinking about the Rocks, and especially Joe Hines, when Young Stanky had sustained his totally unnecessary injury and maybe ruined any chance he had of ever making it. It was a mean compound fracture. I was real sorry about it, real sorry.

And then, the game was proceeding, with that bitter wind and the cold nipping and clawing you. Right behind me was one of the local folks watching the Sunnyside boys play ball like nobody should play the game, and he had a portable radio going. I was not listening, only half-listening, the way you do when you're driving alone, or have coffee on—that's coffee and pie—and I heard the news about Buck Weaver on a news broadcast. The newscaster said that he had dropped dead from a heart attack on a street near his home on the South Side of Chicago. It was like I did not hear this news immediately. It was something like seeing the ball come breaking away from you and you swing too late. It was like a slow reflex. And then, I thought I had dreamed that I heard it and it wasn't true. It was a dream. And then, it hit me. All of this took only a couple of seconds. I just told myself, "Buck Weaver is dead."

That hit me. Buck Weaver had been my idol since he came up to the White Sox in 1913. I used to imagine that one day Mickey Donovan would be a greater ballplayer than Buck Weaver.

And then, I heard the news on a raw night in Sunnyside, Florida, where I was working as a baseball instructor.

"We're dreamin' baseball," the oddball, Hank Space Patrol, had said.

I was dreaming baseball. And that was my life.

II

It was Billy Ebert who suggested that I take a job with Horace Stanton, teaching the kids baseball. Billy and I played together on the White Sox in the 1920s, and we broke in together in 1918, during the War. You can't find a grander guy than Billy, and he was one hell of a ballplayer—fast, a good arm, a good leadoff man, and he pulled the ball nicely into left field for base hits. Billy is assistant farm director of the White Sox and he brought me back into baseball. A couple of years ago, I sat at the same table with him at the Annual Veterans Dinner in the Shrifton Hotel in Chicago. I wasn't doing so well, just getting by on a political job, and Billy asked me how I'd like to get back into baseball as a scout. Baseball's the only trade I ever learned, and I was born far too soon for the big money the boys make today and the nice cozy pensions they get. That's how I became a scout covering the Middle West. Billy told me before last Christmas that Horace Stanton needed another instructor and that he'd suggested me. I liked the idea, January in Florida and it meant $500. My first White Sox contract in 1918 called for $150 a month and a $50 bonus giving the club an option on my services for the next season.

And you never know where you'll find a kid who can make it. Most baseball men are dead set against private baseball schools and all of the men in the front offices would like to see these schools go out of business. Many of the scouts won't look at the kids in these schools, or if they do come around, it's merely to see their friends or to do a favor for a friend running a school. Of course, they are mainly right, and nowadays the kid who's any good doesn't have to go to the club. We'll find any prospect if he's anywhere in this country or even in Latin America. I just heard that one club sent a scout overseas to look at the soldiers playing ball in the army in Germany. But I'll look at any ball game. A good prospect can always slip through your fingers. And there's a future for any scout if he can deliver the goods. The ball clubs are organizations now, not one-man shows the way they were when I broke in and the Old Roman was living and he ran the club. The only man like him who's still active in baseball is Mr. Griffith.

I'm still dreaming baseball. I'm hoping to find some kid who'll one day be in the Hall of Fame. The name of Mickey Donovan will never be on a plaque in Cooperstown, but if I discover a future great, they'll write in the books about how Mickey Donovan the old White Sox all-around man discovered the Second Ty Cobb. Someday, they'll put Paul Kritchell in Cooperstown for finding Lou Gehrig, Rizzutto, a whole line of Yankee greats.

But there's plenty of dreaming here. Most of the kids who go to private baseball schools, they're dreaming pipe dreams. You feel sorry for them. At Horace's school, the kids came from all over the country. One lanky southpaw named Hazelton rode by bus all the way from Alaska to Sunnyside, Florida. He saved his money for months, working nights in a hotel. He was a nice kid, but plenty mixed up. I got to know him and all of the kids pretty well because I stayed at the camp with them, an old camp with a mess and recreation hall and cabins by a lake. Once it was used for revival meetings, I believe.

This wasn't living in the big league style, but it was interesting. The kids would mostly hang around at night, talking about baseball and themselves. Most of them didn't have much dough to spend on girls, and we also had to have a curfew. We couldn't give the school a bad reputation. Horace owns a home in Belleville, a city of 10,000 near Sunnyside. Old Matt Jones, former catcher, is one of the teachers. He bought a home in Orlando and drives over every day. Matt is a White Sox scout, too. I was asked to keep an eye on the kids in camp.

"I had a bad year last summer," Hazelton explained to some of the kids one night at supper.

"What happened, Lefty, did you lose all your juices, shacking up with squaws?" Potasky asked. He's a West Side Chicago kid who wants to be a catcher.

"The wolves kept him awake all night, howling," Hinton said. He's an outfielder from Columbus, Ohio, and I was afraid the other day that he'd get hit on the head and suffer a concussion when I was rapping out fungo flies to the outfielders.

"I just didn't have a good year. My curveball was breaking sharper than the summer before."

"You got good ballplayers in Alaska? I thought there was only Eskimos livin' there."

"I had to know if I can become a pitcher or not. I had to find out," Hazelton said, and you could tell he meant it.

There was a writer from a magazine around and he sat down and talked with the kids. He comes from Chicago and people say his books are the real stuff and others that they're dirty. He talked with Hazelton and some of the other kids.

"Why did you come?" he asked Smith, the kid with glasses who wants to be a catcher.

"We want to learn all we can. This is our big chance," Smith said.

"Yeah, we want to learn from the horse's mouth," Hank Space Patrol said.

"Do you like it here?" O'Neill, the writer asked.

"Do we like it here? This is our life. This is our future," Smith answered.

"That's how I think. I got to find out if I got a chance, or I don't know what I'll do. I'm twenty-one. I don't know what class of ball I'm ready for," Hazelton said.

"Alaska," Hank Space Patrol told him.

"You couldn't play ball in Alaska," Hazelton said.

"What do you mean, Lefty? Do they take their bats off their shoulders and hit the ball in Alaska?" one of the kids asked.

"Hell, when we think in $5, big leaguers think in $5,000," another of the kids said.

There have always been kids like that, ever since baseball became the national game, and there always will be. But at a school you get them all together, and nearly all of them are desperate to become big leaguers. That makes it so pathetic. Because most of them aren't even Class D. I was like that when I was their age, only we must have been shy. We didn't talk the way these kids do about making the big leagues. Other fellows would have laughed at us if we did. At least we'd have been afraid they would. And we wouldn't have had the dough to go to school in Florida to be taught. There wasn't anybody to teach you, even when you got to the big leagues. The veterans didn't want any bushers to take their livelihood away from them. But most of these kids aren't even bushers.

III

We work the kids out from about eleven until about four or four-thirty every day. There's a break for lunch, and they have a sandwich and soft drink. This was rough on me, because I'm not in too good of shape and I've taken on a lot of weight. My playing weight was 170 to 175 after I attained my full development, and now I'm 225 or thereabouts. But I'd give anything to be doing this sort of thing for keeps, in spring training. What man doesn't want to be young again? If you've been a ballplayer, you feel it. You know you can't do what you used to, and what else is there for you? A lot of old timers I know are alcoholics or almost that.

These kids don't think of things like that, but who does when he's young? I never did. Every day, they are like colts. And that kid Stankowsky, he never let up. Just warming up, he'd talk it up like he was in a World Series. He'd race around the field, doing his lap before practice started. He kept up a constant chatter in infield practice. Shortstop is his position. He's well built, and had a good, big pair of hands. He's fast, a switch-hitter, and takes a good cut at the ball. He's got the spirit and fight you need to make the big leagues.

Horace liked him, too. "You got to watch that kid, Mickey," he said.

"Yeah—what do you think of him, Horace?" I asked.

"He might be a good prospect. Hell, he's the kind of kid you can't keep away from a baseball diamond."

Matt Jones joined us, pounding his fist into a catcher's mitt. "It's good to have one of these on my hand and be in uniform."

Horace, of course, is still active, and although he's thirty-five, he looks good for a few more years, maybe five or six. He wasn't an old-timer like Matt and me. Not yet. Matt broke into the National League in 1920, and I might have played in a World Series against his club, if we'd won those three games in St. Louis.

"I was thirty-seven years in uniform," Matt said, proud of it, too.

"This kid they call Young Stanky, Matt," Horace said.

"He looks like a good boy, better'n any of my catchers."

"Can't keep a kid like that in high school, or on a job. I know how it is. I felt just the same as he. All I wanted to do was to throw a ball, and I'd throw a baseball through a brick wall. I damn near could do that," Horace said.

"How old is the boy?" Matt asked.

"He's only sixteen," I said.

"He's a prospect. I've been noticing him. He's got the attitude," Matt said.

Stankowsky couldn't sit down and watch others with a bat and ball. His old man, I found out, could hardly speak English. It was a big family with not much dough. Stankowsky had worked as a messenger boy and a pin boy and on a truck. He'd borrowed some dough from an older brother who had wanted to be a ballplayer and had come down, hoping that a scout would see him and sign him up. He didn't expect to do better than Class D, but he was only sixteen.

Charlie Allison joined us. He was big and looked young, young enough to play if he got himself in condition, but he was overweight. He's a handsome guy, with black curly hair, the kind of a guy the babes go for. But his walk was lazy and his look was lazy.

"Gentlemen," he said.

"It isn't often that old-timers like Mick and me are called 'gentlemen.'" Charlie smiled and yawned.

The kids were all around, taking infield practice. An outfielder named Chapp was hitting grounders for me because I had gotten calluses on my left hand gripping a bat. Chapp had played Class D in Georgia the season before, but the Senators, who had his contract, dropped him when he broke his left wrist. He came to "school" hoping it would help him get a contract. I rated him strictly Class D but perhaps fair or fair-to-middling in Class C.

Charlie Allison stood looking out on the field with his hands on his hips. He looked doggy, wearing shorts and a Bali-print sport shirt. A number of the kids in the infield or catching flies in the outfield looked toward us from time to time. Some of them were glancing at Charlie. He was like a miracle to them and a damned fool. For Charlie, as everybody knows who follows baseball, signed with Detroit for a $50,000 bonus. He had a good year or two, and the son-of-a-gun could hit, too, but he was just too lazy and didn't care. He demanded about $22,000 or $23,000 when he was traded to the White Sox, and when they wouldn't pay him, he didn't report. My highest salary was $13,500.

I looked at him and then at the kids, thinking that they'd break a leg and a neck to get the chance he'd thrown away. It's like that often enough.

"That Stanky kid has the spirit, all right," Matt said.

"He's trying to get his throws off too fast," Horace said.

"Yeah, I've been telling him that. He's just too goddamned anxious. Every time he fields a ball in infield practice, he acts like he was trying to throw Ty Cobb out at first," I said.

"He's worth working on," Horace said.

"Yeah, Horace, that's my opinion," I said.

"They're all pissy-assed to have a scout sign 'em up," Charlie said.

And they were. Every time a stranger stopped to watch the practice sessions, the kids kept wondering if he was a scout.

"There's no scout going to take you by surprise, Charlie," Horace said.

"I'd sign a contract if they'd give me enough," Charlie said.

"How much is that belly worth?" Horace kidded.

"You're only twenty-five gallons of beer overweight yourself," Charlie told Horace.

"I'll be in shape when the season opens. I'm getting my legs in good condition."

"Horace," said a big kid named Woytinsky, "can I throw today?"

"Just warm up. Don't throw any curves."

"Okay."

"Can he throw curves?" asked Charlie.

"Yes, they curve everywhere but on the ground. He's wilder than a March hare," Matt said.

"We'll let 'em have a game now. Charlie, how about umpiring along with Matt?"

"Why not, Horace?"

"You and I, Mickey, we'll manage the teams."

I walked toward home plate with Horace. The sun was warm enough to start taking all the kinks out of my muscles. There's something very soothing about the sun in Florida in winter. And the sound of the batted ball, the kids yelling, peppering it up, and wearing a uniform again, seeing all those kids, healthy as horses, too full of their beans—all this was in my memory, and in me. I had a good feeling of contentment. But I wished like all hell that I could be young again, that I was one of those kids beginning to fight my way up, with my head full of baseball.

We picked the sides, and Stankowsky was on my team. I told him he was batting first and noticed that he had a blob of tobacco in his jaw. He spat out a gob as expertly as Nellie Fox ever did. I would have done that, too, in Washington Park if I hadn't been afraid that I'd have had my pants kidded clean off me.

"Hey, Donovan—see that guy over there, is he a scout?" Henschel asked. He was a nineteen-year-old pitcher, but a hitter could read the trademark on his fastball while waiting to hit it.

"No, he sells sporting goods," I said.

Henschel looked disappointed. He was one of my pitchers and expected to work a couple of innings.

"Just my luck. And I won't get a chance to throw tomorrow night in the game," he said, real down in the mouth.

"You can't give up that easy, stick to it," Hank Space Patrol said.

IV

I did not mention Klingman. He ran the school with Horace and did all the work to keep the school running, buying supplies, cooking the meals, janitoring, counting the balls so nobody stole any, and whatever else had to be done. He was a tall fellow, thirty-six or thirty-seven, and looked like a ballplayer, but the best he ever did was about Double

A or maybe Triple A, catching a few games as a left-handed catcher. Most ballplayers didn't like Klingman, and I didn't either, but he was beginning to make a good thing out of the school. He advertised how many contracts were signed by those who came to his school, made speeches, wrote letters all over the country, kept records of all the boys, and didn't care who he took.

He had six or seven different spiels. Baseball was good for America and democracy, and that's why America wasn't like Russia. Sometimes he started on that line, but he always ended up with the value of going to his school. He talked about Yogi Berra's salary and pointed out how Yogi never went to college but still he was more famous than most college graduates and made more dough and so a kid ought to go to school, baseball school in Florida at the Horace Stanton School. I couldn't stomach hearing him, but he was only making his living, after all. Sometimes, I wished I would have had the idea fifteen or twenty years ago to start a baseball school. Then, I could have lived in Florida all the year around, and gotten a good setup, building a neat and cozy business. If Klingman can do this and was never even a big leaguer, why couldn't I have done so myself? I was twelve years in the American League and wound up with a lifetime batting average of .300.

Klingman roped me into speaking at a couple of Elks and Rotary Club lunches. I don't like that either, and I never learned to do it too well, like a lot of players and old-timers can. If I could, I'd clean up something, because there's good dough for players and old timers, even has-beens like myself, making personal appearances and saying a few words. Hell, I should have learned to do that, too, and gotten me a manager. I could have learned to give a talk about the stars I played with and against. The public is interested in that, but mostly in the stars. That's what's the matter with baseball. It's a game for the stars. You got a player making $60,000 or $80,000 a year and the rest of 'em are getting so much less, how can they feel? You might pretend to feel all right, but in your heart you don't. And that's what was eating up my old team, the White Sox. Goddamn it, that was the greatest team there was. But I couldn't talk about that team in public. I still don't like to think about it but I do, often. I've been thinking about it for years. But why did those players do it? It was money. And why am I down in Florida? Money. And why are the kids? Isn't it money, too?

When I was a kid, it wasn't the money so much as the fame, as the idea of becoming Mickey Donovan, a great star, greater than Buck Weaver. These kids feel the same, don't they? But they talk about money, salaries, the big dough they want to make. They'll play for anything, take a lousy job in Class D ball for $150 a month, just for the chance to play and to be seen by scouts. I was the same, wasn't I? I'd have risked my life to get a chance to show my stuff when I was sixteen years old. I didn't have to because my chance came easy, easier than it was for these kids. Tim Cahill helped me. The best Tim ever did was semipro ball in Chicago. But he became mighty proud of me. I was only fifteen when he spotted me working out with the kids at St. Basil's. It was his first year. He later told me that he knew I'd be a big leaguer the first time he saw me with a ball and glove. I wasn't that certain about Stankowsky, but he looked promising to me.

The weather took a turn for the bad on the day that Klingman had scheduled the first game for the schoolboys. It should have been called off. I told that to Klingman.

"Hell, they can play. They're kids. They can take anything."

And Horace thought that the game ought to go on. "We'd beef like hell, playing in weather like this, but these kids are different. They don't want to be sissies. They paid good money for what they're getting and we got to give it to them."

So I got to the ball field before the sun went down. It was a weak sun. The sun looked cold. The sky was gray, battleship gray. The cold was the kind that kept pinching you, and the wind came up, blowing right through your uniform. I set things going, told the boys to warm up, gave them batting practice, explaining to the pitchers that they should throw straight and easy and not take any risks with their arms. I walked around the infield examining it. It was damned hard and uneven, a bitch of a field to play on in such weather. I told this to Stankowsky.

"I don't give a frig in hell what kind of field it is—I'll play."

I knew that much about him already.

"Playing under conditions like this, you sometimes see a lot of injuries. I've seen it happen."

But this didn't register with him. I could tell by the look he gave.

"Most of you kids don't have sliding pads, and we haven't had any instructions on sliding. It'll be risky sliding tonight," I said.

It went in one ear and out the other. On spring training trips we sometimes played on days like this and on fields as bad or worse. Of course there would be bigger stands, but they'd be empty. You'd want the game over with so that you could get back to the hotel or the train, but once the game started, it would take hold of you. You'd forget that it didn't count and didn't go in the records. Somehow, you had an idea that every play you ever made in any kind of game went into the records. It was like there's a Supreme Official Statistician just the same as there is a God and a Guardian Angel watching everyone. Every hit, run, error, sacrifice hit, stolen base, assist, putout, and error went down in a score book and it all added up. So it must be the same with the kids. Maybe playing on the rough diamond and freezing their ears off would be good for them. It would make men of them.

Not many local fans came out. Jackie Bolton drove up in a snazzy sports car, and he looked young enough to be one of the kids. He used to pitch for the Sox, but they traded him to Washington. I never saw him work but know he's a good pitcher. If he had the luck to be with the Yankees or Cleveland, he'd be in the big dough.

Some of the kids looked at him like he was a god. Six or eight of them crowded around him, looked at his Thunderbird, and looked at his clothes. He was wearing a loud-checked flannel shirt.

"You gonna stay out with us, Jackie?" one of the kids asked.

"Yes, for a while. I want to get an early start, getting myself in condition this year."

"You signed your contract or are you holding out, Jackie?"

"I'm signed up."

"I hope they gave you a raise."

If he got much of a raise, I thought, he must be mighty smart or a real fast talker. Mr. Griffith was harder than the Old Roman or Harry Grabiner, his little secretary. Grabiner used to sign you up, and he was tough. He used to say a ballplayer got more money than a ditchdigger.

I watched the Sunnyside boys practice to get a line on them. They had a local boy, a third baseman, who was signed by the Phillies for their Class D club, but I've seen hundreds like him. He was good form but not much else, I guessed. I filed away notes in my mind about him. Matt makes a report on every player he sees, and I have to do that. Years ago they wouldn't do that, but now baseball's run like an up-to-date business. We've got records of hundreds of players in the front offices at Chicago, and I have to file reports, too.

It was starting to get dark, and I still can't get used to night games and lights. Just before the game started, I heard Hazelton say to Stankowsky, "Play ball and show your stuff, and the scouts will find you."

"I guess so."

Our boys batted first. Stankowsky was leadoff man. The Sunnyside pitcher was a big kid, about six-two, and fast but wild as they came. He threw every ball fast but didn't know where it was going.

"Every kid with a fastball is the same," Horace said to me, as the big kid threw four wild fast balls, one in the dirt, one over the catcher's head, and two wide of the plate.

"This kid won't have an arm if he keeps it up," I said.

"What's the matter with his goddamned coach? He's a high school kid and the manager coaches the high school team. He ought to know better than to let the kid throw that way."

"We can't let our kids do it. I've told them already," Matt said.

"Don't worry, Matt, most of our pitchers can't throw. I don't know who told them they're pitchers," Horace said.

There was a base-on error by the shortstop, the kid who was signed by the Phillies, another walk, and then on a wild pitch Stankowsky tore home. There's a hole near home plate. I remember telling the kids about it and warning them when they would slide. Stankowsky's fast, and he came tearing in. The backstop's only ten feet or so away from home plate, and the ball bounced back to the catcher. The lanky pitcher came in to cover home. I saw Stankowsky, knew it was going to happen, and wanted to shout. He started to fall away for a hook slide, checked himself like I said, and hit that hard dirt. It had to happen. I rushed over to him, and he was groaning, but bit his lips to stop showing any sign of his pain. I could see how bad a break he had. There was nothing to do but tell him to lie quiet and get him to a hospital. It made me feel sick, almost hurt myself. About the only thing worse on a ball field is to see a batter lose his reflexes and get beaned.

A couple of fellows carried Stankowsky to Klingman's car and he was driven into the hospital at Belleville.

The game went on. It got colder. The kids were full of pepper. Each was for himself, playing as if for all of his life. And to them, that's the way it was. They weren't a team like mine in Washington Park, the Rocks, back in 1917. We were a team, and only a couple of us really thought that we could ever make the big leagues. Me and Joe Hines wanted to be ballplayers, but we never said much about it. We were shy compared to kids today.

Kids maybe learn team play nowadays, but they usually are each for himself. That was the way the kids were at our school. They were all there because they wanted something and needed help to get it. Like Debling. He was twenty-eight and had been earning about $3.56 an hour as a tool-and-die worker in a factory in Michigan. He quit to go to baseball school, hoping to get a Class D contract.

"He might just as well go back and ask for his job in the factory," Horace said.

"Even if he wasn't too old, he's slow and doesn't have good baseball intelligence," I said. He was at first base in an old white uniform. The kids all brought their own uniforms of course, and with the different suits they looked scrub, very scrub.

So, a ball game in Florida. Every ball game has got to end. This one would. But it was going to take a long time ending.

Charlie Allison came out because he didn't have anything else to do. He just looked lazy, even when he kept moving about, and slapping his arms around himself, or stamping his feet in the cold. "These kids are wasting their time and money doing this," he told me.

"They like it. And damned near every one of them has hopes."

"They can go on hoping for all the goddamned good it will do them. They'll spend more money to play ball than they can ever earn. A few of them will get a Class D contract and be dropped in a month or two, let out in a small town in Georgia, or out in the desert, and then, he'll go home to Mom and tell his buddies he never got a chance."

"No," I said, as a Greek kid, playing in Stankowsky's place, swung at a ball in the dirt. "Run."

That was a third strike. The Greek kid, Popolos, looked at me, deadpan. Then as he started to run, the catcher picked up the ball and tagged him.

"Some of these kids go home crying at the end of their month here, Mickey," Charlie told me.

"I can believe it, Charlie."

"Don't they know they haven't got a chance? Horace said that it's the hope that springs eternal—hope, my ass."

I didn't like what Charlie said. After throwing away his chance, it seemed to me he shouldn't have talked this way.

"They want to make good," I said.

"Everybody wants to make good—I do, you do. Do you know what that is? That's crap. Making good is getting dough. Money. Some of 'em get it. They get the gold. Others get the horseshit, and it's not even golden horseshit. I liked baseball until I made so much easy money out of it. That spoiled me."

"I never got spoiled in my day. I got fifty bucks when I signed my first contract with the White Sox."

"And I got fifty with three zeros added behind it. And these kids couldn't get fifty pennies. There's no justice in the world."

The game was going on, like I said, slow, with errors, mental errors, being committed all over the place. The wind had mean fingers on you. It seemed like we were somewhere in nowhere, out of this world. Nobody much cared what happened, except the kids. I kept the score and wished the game would hurry up. But it was slow.

I heard that portable radio, like I said. The songs made me hope I might feel warmer than I could. I had to keep rubbing my hand because it got numb. I hoped I'd hear songs of the old days, when I was young. And then the news broadcast came on. And then I heard the news. Like I said, it hit me.

There I was out in Florida in Hell-and-Gone. And Buck Weaver had been in Hell-and-Gone on a sidewalk near the apartment where he lived.

Sunnyside had another pitcher in now and he was trying to throw fast, but he had a jerky motion. He was going to ruin whatever arm he had. Kids. They didn't know nothing. But by the time you knew anything, you were past your prime. What was I trying to say to myself? It wasn't clear.

I felt worse than if I had been knocked down with a duster, a fastball that hit me right plunk behind my left ear. That's all.

And the ball game went on on that cold night out there in Hell-and-Gone in Florida.

V

I did not want to go to the camp and be alone in the cabin, hearing the wind come off the lake and go through the trees like a fastball. The wind in the trees would make me nervous and I wouldn't sleep. I used to sleep like a log. I don't always sleep that way anymore. You think of the past, and play games in your mind. I've been playing baseball in bed at night ever since I was seven or eight years old. I used to play the games I hoped to play starring, being a hero, outdoing Ty Cobb, let alone Buck. Now I played over the games I played in, or the games I might have played. For years I've played in the 1920 World Series. I made Wamby's triple play and hit Earl Smith's home run and set the all-time record for base hits in a World Series, fifteen. I never got my name down in the record book once.

But I didn't want to go right back to the cabin. Horace said he could have a beer or two, and he and Charlie, Jackie Bolton, and me, we went to the Elks Club in Belleville. The town is dry, but at the Elks or Legion you can have a beer.

"He was the best," I said. I was talking about Buck.

"So I've heard. He must have been good," Horace said.

"He's only a name to me. I heard his name, that's all," Charlie Allison said.

"He was a ballplayer's player," I said.

"That's what they always say about you, Mickey," Horace said.

"I was pretty fair, but Buck was great. I'd sit on the bench and watch him, just watch him."

"His tough luck was getting caught. Never get caught stealing," Charlie said.

"He didn't get any money, I'm sure of that," I said.

"I just hear about it, the names of the players, and the story that they were banned for life," Jackie said.

"You still hear that Series talked about in Chicago," Horace said.

"Didn't it damn near ruin baseball?" asked Jackie.

"Yeah, I guess it did," I said.

Pat O'Manley came in, fat as ever. We were all glad to see him. Pat is one of the best scouts in the business. He weighs about 275 pounds, and he's well on in his years. He pitched about thirty innings in the other league before my time, but he's one of the best there is in sizing up young ballplayers.

"What are you doing here, Pat? Did Horace or that left-handed monkey wrench tell you they had a prospect in school here?"

"I'm looking for ballplayers, not candidates for psycho wards," Pat said.

"Christ, a lot of mixed-up kids come down here," Horace said.

"I was out to Ritchie Hogan's talking about ballplayers. He's bought into a club in Quebec and he's going to run it. He wanted a line on young players. I told him that he was always blind and never knew a strike from a ball. How can he know a ballplayer?" Pat said.

"He threw me out of the ball game out in Los Angeles. It was the first time I was ever thrown out of a ball game," I said.

"He never got to umpire in the big leagues, did he?" asked Charlie.

"He wasn't that bad," Pat said.

"Did you know Buck Weaver?" Horace asked.

"Donovan should have known him better. I saw him play. I pitched to him once out on the Coast when my arm was dead as an old man's pecker, and he hit a triple off of me."

"He was a good hitter, I hear," Charlie said.

"In those days he couldn't hit his weight. That's what made me know I was done for. He learned himself by becoming a switch-hitter."

"That's true about Buck," I said.

"Was he the greatest third baseman?" asked Jackie.

I was going to say yes, but Pat answered.

"Greatest? Ty Cobb was the greatest ballplayer, and Babe Ruth was the greatest hitter. But everybody has a right to his opinion. Was Speaker greater than DiMaggio? Who knows. But I wish to hell I could find an infielder like Buck Weaver today."

I thought of that kid, Stankowsky. Klingman had told me it was a bad break. It would be x-rayed in the morning. I suddenly realized that he looked a little bit like Buck Weaver. He did. He had the same kind of long jaw and lean face.

"What the hell was the real story about that Series, Mickey? I never could understand the goddamned thing," Horace told me.

"I was on the club," I said. "But I was only a rookie, a busher. I never really knew what the hell the whole story was. I'm not sure all of them fellows did themselves."

"You played in the Pacific Coast League, didn't you, Donovan?" Pat asked.

"About a half a season in 1919. Then the Old Roman recalled me to the bench. That's how I was on the 1919 White Sox," I said.

"I tried to get you for the Redlegs."

That was a ton of surprise to me. I looked at the old fat coach, blank and open-mouthed.

"You fellows never saw Donovan play ball. He was a sweet ballplayer, and I wanted him. In 1919 the Redlegs didn't have much of an infield except for third base and first base. I wanted you, boy, but the Old Roman had his hooks in you. I thought of that lots of times. Your career would have been different. You got lost there on a second-division club after 1920."

I didn't say a word. There was nothing to say. I felt like I took a blow in the solar plexus. Or like I had been beaned by a wild young pitcher like the lanky kid who had started the game that night for the Sunnyside club.

Just then a young AP writer named Sleighton came in and joined us. He got a bottle of beer and sat beside me. I knew what was coming and didn't like him.

"Did you hear, Mickey, that Buck Weaver died today back in your hometown?"

"Yeah, it came over the radio," I said.

"You played with him, didn't you?" He had his pad and a ballpoint pen out.

"I was only a busher."

"You were on the club during that crooked Series, weren't you, Mickey?"

I had to warn myself to hold my temper. "Yeah," I said.

"Tell me, what was the inside story? Was Buck Weaver in on the fix, or wasn't he?"

"I don't know. That's years ago and I was only a busher."

I think the others there understood how I felt. They're ballplayers, and even when you've retired and finished, you're still a ballplayer. Once a ballplayer, always a ballplayer.

"You must remember something, Mickey. The whole country knew about it," the writer said.

"Those men suffered hell," I said. I know they did because I did, and Ray Schalk did. All of us did.

"Some of them are dead, like Buck. I won't talk about it."

"Haven't you something to say about Buck?"

"He was the greatest third baseman I ever saw," I said.

Most writers are a ballplayer's enemy at all times. And for years they have been at me, trying to get some of the lowdown about that whole tragic mistake.

"The man is dead. Let him rest in peace," I said, and I was sore.

"I didn't mean anything, Mickey. I'm merely trying to get a story," Sleighton explained to me.

"I never talk about that Series. It's past. Let the dead past be dead. Those fellows paid a heavy penalty. They were blacklisted for life."

And I thought how one by one they're dropping off. Every time one of them goes or one of the players of your own day, you ask yourself, who's going to be next? I sometimes now look at the obituary page of a newspaper before I turn to the sports page and the comics. I didn't want to talk to that young writer. As a kid, I just wanted to be a White Sox player. Now, I wished that I played with any club but my hometown club. Those men were my heroes. For years I wanted to forget it, to forget them. How could I talk to a writer? I don't know what to say or think about it. I couldn't have talked to the writer even if I had wanted to.

Why can't they ever forget 1919?

I let Pat tell the writer what kind of a ballplayer Buck Weaver was, and I just nodded my head in agreement. Then, I drove to the cabin. Hearing that wind shaking the leaves, I thought how when I was a kid in short pants, I'd sometimes hear an engine whistle at night. It was a sad, lonely sound. So was the sound of the wind in the trees.

I took a long time getting to sleep. I played some of those games over again, and I thought of them and of myself when I was a kid. I took a long time going to sleep and, yes, I was dreaming baseball. I couldn't sleep because of it. I couldn't sleep because I was dreaming baseball, dreaming away the life I already had lived. And I was dreaming, too, of finding a kid, a kid like myself, a kid like Buck, a kid like Stankowsky, who would get up there to Cooperstown the way Ray Schalk did or Eddie Collins, our second baseman, did.

The wind in those trees was lonelier than those engine whistles at night, coming from the trains on the Rock Island tracks over past Wentworth Avenue. Those trains at night used to go past the White Sox ballpark at night.

Everything in my life seemed like it had happened only yesterday. That's the way I fell asleep in the cabin. And I had some queer dreams, but I couldn't remember them. All I could remember in the morning was that they had been queer dreams.

CHAPTER TWO

I

Buck Weaver wasn't my only hero when I was a kid. He didn't come to the White Sox until 1912, and I was then twelve years old. I was a century baby, and by the time Buck got his name in the box scores, I was a dyed-in-the-wool fan. Back in 1906 when I was just a beginner in the first grade at Crucifixion, at 49th and Grand Boulevard, there was all of the excitement over the World Series between the White Sox, "the Hitless Wonders," and the Cubs. I didn't know much about baseball then, but I knew I wanted the White Sox to win, and I got excited.

My old man was a good father, and he was a baseball fan. In 1906 he went all the way out to the West Side, to the old Cubs Park, to see the White Sox, the Hitless Wonders, win one of the World Series games. He wanted to take me, but my mother said I was too young. He went with a couple of his pals, and they celebrated on cans of beer. He came home crocked and happy, talking about the White Sox. That was the first game of the Series, and Nick Altrock beat Three-Fingered Brown 2-1. My old man felt so damn good that I felt good myself. He slipped me a nickel, and that was a lot of candy in those days—a lot by comparison, at least. I was just beginning to learn what the hell baseball was all about.

He explained to me that the Series was four out of seven, but that cut no ice with me. After the second game, I asked the same question, and I whooped and yelled and jumped up and down each time I heard that the White Sox won a game. I picked up the names of the players

23

and went around reciting them like I was reciting poetry. Big Ed Walsh, Pat Dougherty, Nick Altrock, Billy Sullivan, Lee Tannehill.

"I'm going to grow up and be a White Sox and win the World Series," I said.

My old man got a kick out of that. "What position are you going to play, Mick?"

"Shortstop."

"Why do you want to be the shortstop?"

"Because I am short and I can stop the ball short."

He laughed and asked me who played shortstop for the White Sox.

"Lee Tannehill." I don't know how I learned that, but I had. "And when I win the World Series, I'm gonna buy Ma an automobile." There weren't so many automobiles then, in 1906, and the streets were full of horses and wagons. But I'd seen a few automobiles, those old ones, built high, like carriages, the kind you can see in museums now.

I believe in God and am a Catholic, and I believe in luck, too, but I never could decide if it was an accident or how I come to think I'd be a White Sox player and win the World Series and that I would buy my mother an automobile. Part of it came true. And I would have bought Ma an automobile, too, before she died, but she would have none of it. I did drive her to church in my own car, and I think it made her proud.

My old man got a kick out of my enthusiasm for baseball, and I guess that strengthened my resolve to become a ballplayer. With all the talk and excitement about the World Series and the Hitless Wonders, baseball seemed important, like the most important thing in the world. And in those days, I think baseball was more important than it is today. There wasn't as much competition or as many distractions. The movies were only in their infancy, and nickel shows were just beginning to sprout in old barns and stores. I heard about baseball and saw big league ball games before I saw movies. I don't remember seeing any movies until I was eight or nine years old. I was taken to one or two vaudeville shows, though, and I liked the singing. I was in the big leagues before ball games were broadcast on the radio.

There wasn't as much for a man to do then. Pa read two newspapers, played poker now and then with his cronies, had a glass or two of beer in a saloon or maybe a couple of times a year got a little drunk, took us to the park or for a Sunday walk, or visited relatives once in a while.

Baseball is still the biggest sport, but in those days the only sport that came near it was prizefighting, and fights were outlawed at that time. Pa used to talk about seeing fights at Tattersall's, and he liked to talk about Gentleman Jim Corbett, John L. Sullivan, and the original Jack Dempsey, the Nonpareil.

Kids nowadays don't know how exciting it was to be on tenterhooks waiting for the final box score edition of the newspaper to arrive. The earlier editions of the newspaper would print part of the game, and then you'd have to wait for the late or final editions. Sometimes you would be waiting on edge two, three, four hours to find out who won the ball game. The early editions would have the news of part of the game, with the play-by-play account of the first innings and the score on the front pages. At five o'clock you would only know how the games were going for three, maybe four or four and a half innings. You could wait an hour or two before knowing how a 1-0 or 2-1 ball game finally came out. A pitcher could have a no-hit game going for four or five innings, and you felt the suspense as you went home, or played knowing that you couldn't find out any sooner. When you saw a ball game, you had plenty to talk about, filling in what might not have been included in the accounts of the game written in the newspapers.

I used to think how, one day, kids would be waiting around or else going off to play and they would come back to get the final box score extra and they'd read about me. I'd make up the play-by-play account of imaginary games, placing my name in with that of real players in the American League. In all of those daydreams, I never imagined things changed in a new world of tomorrow. Everything would be the same except I would be grown up, a man and a baseball player. I never thought of automobiles taking the place of horses so that you wouldn't see a horse on the street unless you went to New York and went to 59th Street at the entrance to Central Park across from the Plaza Hotel and saw the horses and buggies there that people ride as a novelty. And I didn't have any idea there could be such inventions as radio and television and talking moving pictures or that the streetcars would give way to buses or that you'd fly in airplanes almost like we used to take the streetcar or the El, or that the White Sox park would be remodeled and practically rebuilt or that the lively ball would be introduced and somebody named Babe Ruth would hit sixty home runs to set a world's record.

In those days, I'd read every word of the baseball news and gobble up the play-by-play accounts of the game. By 1908 I could read, and the pennant races were terrific. Ed Walsh won forty games. Think of that record. Forty games. I had my heart in my mouth all that season. The American League pennant was decided on the last day of the season when the Detroit Tigers beat the White Sox. Look at these standings:

Detroit	90	63	.588
Cleveland	90	64	.584
Chicago	88	64	.579

And look at the National League:

Chicago	99	55	.643
New York	98	56	.636
Pittsburgh	98	56	.636

That was the year Merkle didn't touch second and the Cubs won a playoff game. Think of a pennant race like those two, and with no radio or television but only the newspapers to give you the results, except for a few big scoreboards on some of the saloons. And everything was simpler then. You heard men talking and arguing on the streets, and the stars were real heroes. Ty Cobb, Napoleon Lajoie, Big Ed Walsh, Three-Fingered Brown, Tinker-to-Evers-to-Chance, Big Six Christy Mathewson, Muggsy McGraw, Honus Wagner. Every one of them is a baseball immortal and is in the Hall of Fame. They were all playing, and their teams were in a red-hot pennant race, blazing right down to the last out of the last inning of the last game of the season.

I was in the third grade then and had an old maid teacher, instead of a nun, named Miss Rooney. She was a homely sourpuss, homelier than an early movie actress that most people have forgotten or scarcely ever heard of, Flora Finch. She asked me a question in catechism and I got up and answered, "Big Ed Walsh." She blew her top and sent me to the principal's office, Sister Marguerita. She said I was disrespectful of God. It was a catechism class. But Sister Marguerita laughed and told me that she understood boys and said that I must pay attention in class, especially in catechism. "I hope the White Sox win," she said as she dismissed me and sent me back to the classroom.

The kids called me "the Spitball" after that, because Walsh was an artist with the spitter. I didn't like the name, and I beat the hell out of a kid named Jackie Mulligan for calling me Spitball in front of Mary Collins and another girl. Mary is now Mrs. Donovan. She remembers how I fought and said she thought I was a roughneck, but she thinks that that was why she fell in love with me. I was brave and good looking, she told me. But that's her story, not mine.

Sister Marguerita got wind of the news about the fight, and she bawled me out, told me that she was not allowing anybody like Terrible Terry McGovern in Crucifixion school and made me stay after school and write a hundred times as penance *"I must not think I am Terrible Terry McGovern."* That made Terrible Terry McGovern my hero, too. But she sent for Ma, and Ma bawled me out. My sister Ruthie—she's five years older than me—kicked up a row and said I was a disgrace to her, and my old man took me in the bedroom and gave me the razor-strap persuasion. He did it, he said, because I fought without justification. I thought he did it because Ruthie cried and threw a fit. I was sore at her for a long time.

The kids stopped calling me Spitball, and then I wished they'd call me by that nickname, because Big Ed Walsh was my hero. Think of his record that season. He won forty and lost fifteen games. Forty games. He pitched 464 innings, struck out 269 batters and only walked 56.

I prayed for the White Sox to win that last game of the season. And when they didn't, I was as heartbroken as a kid could be.

I grew up on baseball.

II

We lived in a gray stone building on Prairie Avenue, across from the Convent of the Good Shepherds. There were six rooms, and it was always noisy and a little crowded, because besides Ruthie and myself there was Billy, four years younger than me, and Jenny, who was born in 1907. Pa was a plumber, and he made good money. The rent was $50 a month, I believe, and we lived in a pretty good neighborhood, not really a poor one. We all went to Crucifixion, and the tuition was a dollar a

month, and we went to high school. But I paid for Billy and Jenny and
helped Billy out at college. Pa died in 1918 of a heart attack.

We never had any luxuries, but we ate, and Ma saw to it that we
had clean clothes, but she didn't have an easy time of it with me because I was always running and wrestling with kids, and I'd slide and
dive for balls when I played ball. But Pa was kind of looked down on
because he was only a plumber and it was dirty work. He went out on
jobs in overalls and carried his lunch in a lunch box. He was big, about
six feet, and when he wore his black Sunday suit to Mass, he looked
different. He wore a black mustache, and most of the other kids' old
men shaved clean and dressed better than he. He could only afford
to give five dollars for the collections at Christmas and Easter. The
names and the amount each person or family gave in the collections
were printed in the church calendar, and I, and Ruthie more than I,
felt we weren't considered as good as some of the other kids whose old
men could give more. And when Ruthie graduated from Crucifixion,
she couldn't go to Saint Paul's, which was considered the swankiest
Catholic high school for girls, but instead she went to Saint Catherine's,
which wasn't considered as swell a school.

Hell, how childish all of this seems now, but then, it was important,
and we felt socially inferior. I'm not sure we had to, but we did. I got
it from Ruthie. This didn't seem to bother Billy and Jenny so much.
I didn't care too much, or at least I pretended I didn't. But I really
didn't care, except now and then I'd feel it. I was already living and
dreaming baseball.

I played as much as I could, and every kind of game. We used to get
a soft or small indoor ball for a dime in a drugstore or a candy store. It
was about the size of a big league ball, or maybe a little smaller, and
you could play with it without using gloves, and all you needed was an
indoor bat that was cheap. I forget the price of them but think they
cost two bits or a half a dollar. We played overhand swift pitching, and
if we didn't have enough on a side, we'd play pitcher's hands is out.
And we played with a big indoor ball. They used to play real indoor
ball in a gym with one of those indoor balls. The ball was bigger than
a softball and you pitched underhand. There were vacant lots all over
the neighborhood, and some of them were big enough for real baseball
games. On Calumet Avenue it was almost all vacant lot between 51st
and 53rd Street, and there was a vacant lot on the corner of 50th and

Calumet with hard, even dirt, and we played baseball there. We played indoors in the little Crucifixion school yard facing 50th Street by the alley between Calumet and Grand Boulevard. And then there was the big ball field in Washington Park.

I played on a couple of teams when I was in grammar school, and by the time I was fourteen, and still wearing short pants, I sometimes got into games with men over in Washington Park. I played any position but liked shortstop best, and I was a switch-hitter. I practiced every time I could. I'd shag flies or field grounders as long as anybody would hit the ball to me. I tried to study baseball, to play inside baseball, fool the other players. Before I was out of grammar school, they used to talk about me in Washington Park, and sometimes one of the men would remark, "That kid Donovan might be a ballplayer someday."

III

I didn't care for school. On some days, especially in the spring, sitting at a desk was just agony. And I used to hate school during Moving Week. That's what they used to call the first week of May. In those days, so many families moved in May that the kids in the public schools had a week off. We didn't get that week off, and I'd envy the public school kids and think of them playing ball and having fun, with me in a classroom. I ditched school for days during Moving Week when I was in seventh grade but got caught and was almost thrown out of school. That was the last time I got the razor-strap persuasion from my old man.

I didn't really want to go to high school except for the sports. We'd had a uniform team in Washington Park, the Shamrocks, and I worked to earn the five bucks for my uniform. When I got it, my old man bought me my first pair of spiked shoes. You can guess how I felt walking over to Washington Park with my gray uniform trimmed with red and carrying my brand-new pair of spiked shoes. Sure as hell, I was going to be a big leaguer.

But in high school I'd play in a league and sometimes in enclosed parks. I always dreamed of that, playing in an enclosed park. One of the reasons why I picked St. Basil's, out southwest on 63rd Street, was because the school had an enclosed field with a small stand and fences. I made the team in my first year, being the only freshman on it, and I played a fair average, hitting .280. I was put in right field and was leadoff man. I fielded 1.000 and made one shoestring catch. Of course I played my other three years, being the shortstop, and was captain in my last year, when we copped the Catholic League title. They talked about me all over the league, and I even got a couple of write-ups in the newspapers.

I didn't do much in classes, just getting by on the thinnest skin of my nose. One of my buddies, Jim Clancey, helped me. He was crazy for baseball, just like I was, but Jim couldn't hit even a roundhouse outcurve. He was lucky if he could hit a fungo fly. But Jim was smart, the smartest kid in class. I didn't go for smart kids who stuck their noses in a book. I figured that there usually was something wrong with them. But Jim was different, true blue, and to this day he and I are friends. I never could have gotten by but for Jim's help, and he always gave it to me. I supposed trigonometry was good for somebody, and maybe it was good for the Greeks in Socrates's time, but it was worse than Greek to me, and but for Jim I'd still be doing those problems.

I don't think I was dumb. It was just that I wasn't interested. Don't ask me how I knew it, because I don't know, but I just knew that I was going to be a big league player. And I used to tell myself as a private joke, "All I need to learn in school for my career is how to sign my name to a contract and how to read what my salary is."

I grew up, you see, thinking that if you became a baseball player, you would be one of the most famous and important persons in the country. And of course it's so, and you get your share of the limelight, but it's a different kind of thing, and a different kind of feeling than you expect it to be. They cheer and love you and forget you. You have your day and, then, time marches away from you. I've thought about it a lot, and I just can't put it the way I ought to because I'm not that articulate. But the thing I mean is that it's baseball itself that you love, and not the fame or the attention. I always felt that I was fully myself, that it was me, Mickey Donovan, when I was on a ball field, in uniform, wearing my spikes, with a glove on my left hand or a bat in my hands. And because I could do things with a bat and ball and glove, I wanted to be looked up to. I thought I'd be loved the way that I used to love and look up to ballplayers when I was a kid.

Now, it isn't easy for me to remember those days when I was a kid. Kids seem different, and you look at them like they were a different race. You forget your own childhood, or most of it, but it's always there inside of you, only it seems lost.

I don't think I was dumb, because I've read books since. I like to read history books sometimes. Then, I couldn't put my mind to it. Often, I've felt sorry I cheated on my studies and didn't use my time better. My old man was working hard, paying my tuition, and he was proud to know that his son was getting an education. "I'm just a plumber, Mick, but a good one. I want you to do better than that." I wouldn't pay much attention to him. I'd think that I'd be in the big leagues and the whole nation would know who Mickey Donovan was.

But those were good old days at St. Basil's, and even now, thinking of them puts a catch in my throat and I wish I was back there with Jim Clancey and my old classmates and teammates, Joe McCallam, our catcher, who was built like a tub and was always laughing and joking, Art McCann, our pitcher—and a damned good one—and so many of the other boys. I could name them but nobody would know them, except Jim Clancey, who became an alderman and has a big law practice. When I had hard sledding after my retirement, Jim helped me. Some of the boys have passed on, may God have mercy on their souls. Every Sunday at Mass I say a prayer for them.

I often think of Tim Cahill, my old coach at St. Basil's. Tim was solid gold, twenty carat clean through. I think he helped me as much as any person I ever knew, and I have always remembered Tim for how he helped me and what he did for me. He was like a second father to me. Tim was gruff, but, like I've just been trying to say, he had a heart of gold. He loved baseball and never got much out of it—$10, $15, $25, or maybe a little more for playing semipro ball on weekends, and his salary for coaching at St. Basil's. In those days, I don't see how it could have been more than $100 or $200 a month. There wasn't big money floating around like there is now. Hell, my first contract only called for $150, and in 1919–20 I was making $200 a month on the White Sox. Tim, coaching a high school team, couldn't have done better than a big leaguer. He had a political job, too, an inspector of some kind, and this permitted him to be free to coach us in the spring. But he wasn't in it for the dough. He loved baseball and he knew the game.

Tim, of course, seemed to be pretty old to me when I first saw him that day late in March 1915 when I walked onto St. Basil's field, trying to act like I was sure of myself and not nervous or afraid. I was sure of myself as a player, but a kid going among strange kids older than himself has got to be nervous and maybe leery, or at least thinking that he might be leery. And I had been at St. Basil's since the previous September, but I didn't know the older kids well, and I was a stranger daring to say I could beat them out of a regular position on the school team. That's just what I did.

Tim was about forty then. He was a big fellow, broad shouldered with heavy brows, dark hair, and hairy hands. He looked tough, not the kind of a guy to run afoul of. He sounded mean when he gave you orders and acted as if he had no interest in what you did or even bothered to watch you. But that was his way of testing you and finding out what you were like and how much you could take and give.

"If you can't take it and dish it out, you don't belong on no ball field," he used to say. And he could make you feel like you wanted to crawl off in a corner by the way he'd say, "You, Donovan, or Murphy"—Tom Murphy, a kid who played on St. Basil's—"you don't know the difference between tiddlywinks and baseball."

Tim didn't curse much, the way managers and players do in professional baseball, but he talked the same as if he was cursing. Father Donahey, our athletic director, said he wanted us to learn to be gentlemen and not curse, and he kept Tim's cursing under wraps.

For the first few days he didn't seem to notice me much, and I was sore and depressed. I felt I wasn't getting a fair chance, but I kept trying as hard as I could. Mostly I caught flies in the outfield. But when he picked sides and had us play a scrub game, he put me in at second base on one of the teams. I fielded a couple of balls and got a base hit, a Texas leaguer. I used to hit a lot of them, especially when I batted left handed. The next day he had me work out at second base, although Jack Canavan, a senior, was expected to be the regular second baseman. He was a pretty fair high school ballplayer and was elected captain that year. But he was tough, and that day when I was leaving school to walk to the corner of 63rd and Western for a streetcar, he came up to me, and said, "Do you think a goddamn little freshman punk like you is gonna take second base away from me?" He was bigger and stronger than I was and I was afraid he was gonna clout me. "You should be a mascot, you punk," he said.

I didn't say anything.

"Do you hear me, you snot nose?" He was almost on top of me, looking down at me. "I got a good mind to teach you a lesson."

Just then Tim came along, and Canavan didn't do anything. Tim didn't say anything, but the next day he put me in to practice at second base with the kids he planned as regulars, and Jack Canavan must have felt like knocking my teeth out. He and his pals rode me, but they didn't rattle me.

I was given a uniform. That meant I had made the team. I was worried about Canavan. He might poke me around, I feared. But I knew I couldn't give up. And Tim settled matters by shifting me to the outfield. He had been testing me. I was in every game, and the next season I played second, and shortstop in my third and fourth years.

Tim was the first person who really thought of me as a potential big leaguer. Of course kids in my neighborhood, or fellows in Washington Park had said I looked like I'd make it, but this wasn't the same as Tim saying it. Tim saw me in practice and in games, when I was good and when I was bad, for four straight high school seasons, and he watched me developing. I began to get a sense of team play from him. Of course I knew that there should be team play before I went to St. Basil's, but with kids running their own games and teams, you don't really get much team play. It's every kid for himself. And I got the idea of usually playing a shorter infield from Tim. He told me I'd get more outs than I'd make errors and that many of the fields we played on were slow. A deep shortstop gave the batter a better chance to beat out a grounder. I learned lots of little things like that.

I played not only for myself and St. Basil's, but for Tim. If I struck out, made an error, or didn't come through in a pinch, I'd feel that I was letting Tim down.

When we were practicing at the beginning of my junior year, Tim told me he wanted to talk to me. I took my time taking a shower and dressing. Almost all of the kids were gone. When I was dressed and ready to leave, Tim left with me and bought me a soda at the Greek's ice cream parlor near school while he had a Coke.

"Mick, I'm buildin' the team around you," he told me.

I was sixteen. You can guess what that meant to me. I didn't know what to say, I was so thrilled.

"You got to keep the boys fired up. You got to inspire them. Every minute you got to be on your toes."

"I'll do my best, Tim."

"I want more than your best."

"I'll give everything I got."

"I want the boys to begin thinkin', 'With Mickey in there, we can't lose.'"

I couldn't say anything. I could have bawled.

"You got to make a team fight—even if it's fightin' with itself. If kids ain't mad to win, why in the goddamn hell are they on a ball field?"

"Yeah," I said.

"You've been comin' along. Now you're bigger and more experienced. You gotta tear the league apart."

"I'll try," I said. And I had a big season. I hit over .400 and snarled and cursed and yelled myself hoarse.

It was at the end of the season, after we beat St. Stanislaus in Jackson Park 10-1, and I made four hits, that he told me, "Keep playin' this way, Mick, and you'll be in the big leagues." Those words were like a contract. Sometimes, I remember playing high school ball with even more sentiment than I do my big league days.

Everything was ahead of me. The dreams I was dreaming—you'd laugh if I told them all. I didn't think I'd be a fair, steady ballplayer then. I was going to be a star. I was going to hit like Ty Cobb, run bases like him, play shortstop not only like Buck Weaver but like Honus Wagner. Nothing turns out like you dream it's going to be. You're sixteen and you don't know what life is like, and you only imagine how wonderful it's all going to be and the great things you're going to do and how love is going to put you in the clouds and a kiss is going to be like being in heaven and you're going to be famous, a hero with everybody cheering you and admiring you. You don't think of the disappointments of life, only of the successes. And you don't know what people are like and what they'll do to you. You don't imagine they can do anything to you because in your dreams you always beat them and win. Nobody's like what you imagine yourself in your dreams when you're young, a kid, and everything is new and the whole world is your oyster. I can't feel that way now, no more than any man can. You're living in a world without an umpire, or anybody that's better than you. You're everything. You're the hottest stuff that was ever blown across the world, and you're always looking ahead to the day when your dreams come true.

I'd go out to practice with the big leagues in my head, with my future waiting for me, and each day I was gaining on it. I was working for my dreams. I was young, strong, and I felt nothing could stop me.

And in my last year I was good. They talked about me all over the league, and I felt Mickey Donovan was a name plenty of people had already heard about. We won the championship of the Catholic League, and that was a big feather in Tim's cap.

I felt good when we won that last game against Christian Brothers on our own field, 3-2. I was captain. Tim was coach. He was so happy, he could almost have cried. And yet I just wasn't happy. There was Tim, grinning and proud, patting us on the back in the dressing room in the school basement. But Tim never did it himself. He never got beyond semipro ball, not even as far as the Three-I League. There he was, past his prime, and he had failed. He hadn't been good enough to do the one thing he wanted to do. It made me feel half ashamed of myself for my dreams. I expected to be better than him. I felt kind of bad.

After that, I remember him saying to me, just before I graduated, "Mickey, you got a wonderful future. Don't lose it." And the way he said it made me feel he was sad inside, sad because of what he'd never been. Even though I was a big leaguer, I have felt that way many times since I retired.

CHAPTER THREE

I

I don't think I ever thought as much and remembered as much about my kid days, and my long pants, high school days as I've now been doing. I didn't know I remembered all of these things. I often have thought about and remembered my days in the American League and that 1919 Series, but not so much from before I realized my hopes and dreams and found myself wearing a White Sox uniform.

I graduated from St. Basil's in June 1918. I was sorry to leave, to think I wouldn't play ball again for St. Basil's with Tim on the bench or standing nearby to call to me, "Come on, Mick, start things goin' against these semipros." He always used the word "semipro" against another team, or for a player who had goofed something up or who wasn't much good. "You played that ball like a semipro, Mick," he used to tell me if I made an error or played a ball badly.

Getting my diploma at the exercises, I was happy, and my old man and Ma were too. To them I was educated. I was one of the school heroes. I was well liked and everybody was sorry to see me go. By then it was being predicted that I would become a big league ballplayer. I believed what was thought of me and what Tim said about my chances. And I was more happy than sad about it.

But the next morning it hit me when I woke up. I had my breakfast of bacon and eggs and coffee and buns from O'Leary's Bakery on 51st Street. I used to like those sweet buns, especially the ones called butter rolls. I still like sweet rolls or sweet buns, as we sometimes called

them, but they never taste as good any more as they did when I was
a kid, living on Prairie Avenue.

That sunny June morning when I woke up after graduating the night
before, I felt lost. I was seventeen, almost eighteen. I was a man. Now
I was going out in the world. The White Sox had not come knocking
at my door. Fifteen other major league clubs had not come knocking
and rapping either.

That's the way we are and that's the way life is. Things don't turn
out like we expect them. That morning I had just passed a milestone.
I was out of school. Those last months had been agony, except for
the baseball. I used to sit in the classroom dreaming of Mary Collins,
because I was already going with her, as I'll explain presently, of baseball, of classes letting out, of the school year ending, of myself being
signed up by the White Sox and making good and starring right from
the beginning, making three straight hits off Walter Johnson in my
first major league appearance, a single, double, and triple. Somehow, I
didn't have the nerve to dream of myself, a seventeen-year-old punk,
hitting a home run off of Walter Johnson in my first big league ball
game. After all, there was a limit, and I don't know that Ty Cobb, Babe
Ruth, or Shoeless Joe Jackson ever made a full house, single, double,
triple, and home run off Walter Johnson. Hell, I was grandiloquent,
but there was a limit to my grandiloquence.

But remember how we used to blow a paper bag full of air when
we were kids, and then we'd break it for the boom and throw the bag
away? Well, that's about the way my dreams and hopes and plans were
when I sat eating my breakfast.

Everybody gets down in the mouth, but I don't think I was ever as
down in the mouth before, or possibly since. I had been riding along
handsomely. It was like being in a hitting streak. Once I had a twenty-
one-game streak. That was in 1928. And then, I woke up, and it seemed
like I had been pretty much deep, lost, in a dreamland and wearing
rose-colored glasses, and I found myself right back in the world, and
plumped square on my ass.

I didn't only feel low. I felt ashamed of myself, like I'd done something
rotten, played with myself, or been a goofy and disgraceful clown and
muttonhead. I was ashamed of myself not only because I was feeling
so sorry for myself—brooding, moody, letting my thoughts go slobber-

ing inside of me—but more than that, I was afraid that I had no guts. That was the time of the war, the First World War, we call it now. I said I didn't care for studying, but history did sometimes interest me, American history, which we had at Crucifixion, and I thought of wars, of the battles and being a hero. After all, that was what I dreamed and thought of becoming and hoped to be when I'd make the major leagues, a hero. Well, what's a baseball player, even a Ty Cobb as a hero, compared to a soldier? I must have weighed about 160 then and been between five-eight and five-nine, and I was growing strong. I was a man and could have been a soldier, and wanted to become one. I remember that at breakfast that morning after I graduated I thought of running away from home and joining the army, the navy, or the marines. I felt I should and that it was my duty to my country, America, and being a soldier, going to France and fighting, that was romance and adventure. Why, I could even get my name in the history books, because sometimes in the daytime, or when I was in bed at night, and passing off to sleep, I'd imagined myself a soldier, a dough boy, or Sammy boy, or a devil dog marine, capturing the Kaiser single-handed.

There had been movies, and I read the war news sometimes, and I wanted to get in. I walked around singing "Over There" and other war songs of the time, and even to this day I like "Over There" and could sit and listen to it again and again. It makes me wish I had been a soldier and fought in France, in Château-Thierry or in Belleau Wood.

It was all romantic and unreal to me, just the same as big league baseball. And I thought of the mud, the blood, the cooties, going over the top with my bayonet fixed, jabbing into the Germans—the Huns is what we always called them then—capturing fifty, sixty, a hundred of the Heinies and crawling out across No Man's Land at night, with star shells going up, and then going on in the darkness in and out of shell holes, being as quiet as I was able to, until I came close to the machine gun nest I had volunteered to wipe out. And then, I'd either imagine myself throwing a hand grenade in to them or taking them by surprise with fixed bayonet. I was better than any hand grenade thrower in the whole American Army, the AEF. I had an imagination. I had it bad, I guess.

But I didn't want to die, or be wounded so I wouldn't be able to come back home after the war to become a big league star. I didn't want to be shot blind or have my face blown off or lose an arm or a leg or get my balls shot off. But that worried me. That made me afraid I was a coward. I remembered reading about Nathan Hale in my history book. I'm not sure I remember the exact words, but it ran something like "I regret that I have but one life to give for my country."

I sometimes thought of myself like Nathan Hale and Patrick Henry and Paul Revere and Hobson—wasn't that the name of the fellow who carried the message to Garcia? Nathan Hale, he was a bigger hero than Ty Cobb, Hit-'Em-Where-They-Ain't Willie Keeler, or any of the greatest baseball players. And even if I did, I could go to heaven, a martyr on the battlefield. I'm not too religious, nor was I in those days. But what man wants to burn in hell?

But to give up baseball—why, that was like giving up my right arm. And I would have given up baseball by losing my right arm. That was one reason why I was sunken below the cellar that morning after graduation.

Ma was smart. She knew if I had some worry on my mind, and many a time she could guess what it was. Of course then that used to embarrass me. Now I feel different. I remember her coming back into the kitchen from the bedrooms where she had been making the beds. I had finished my breakfast and I was sitting at the kitchen table.

"Now Mickey," she says to me, "with your education, you should be getting the kind of work with a future."

I didn't say anything. I knew what Ma meant because she'd talked this way before.

"You should take a few days of rest, like a vacation."

"I was thinking of going to the park and playing ball," I said.

I thought that it wouldn't be such a bad summer if I could play ball in Washington Park all summer. If I could have done that, I figured I'd really make progress. I knew that I was beginning to develop as a player, and I didn't at all like the idea of having to work at anything else. We had a pretty fair team that we'd organized in Washington Park, the Rocks, which I'll mention in a minute or two, and with daylight saving, I could go out after supper and play. I wanted to get in every minute I could. I was a kid and, out of school, I was desperately anxious. But I didn't know exactly what to do about it. I was too shy to go to the White Sox and ask them for a tryout, and I thought of writing them a letter about myself and signing a false name, suggesting that they look me over, but I didn't do it. I also hoped I might get into semipro ball. In those days, semipro baseball was thriving, and there were a number of first-class semipro teams. They had a good league. The players were paid and played in closed parks. But I was kind of shy about that, too. I didn't want to be turned down or laughed at. I guess I didn't want to grow up and be a man.

But I was talking about that morning after my graduation, and about my mother.

"Now, Mick, you got to be thinking more about your future than about baseball," Ma said.

I sat there and I guess I sort of sulked.

"Your father thinks you should be settling down and giving thought to your future," she said also.

"I know what I'm goin' to do," I said.

"Your father's not so young anymore. He's been working all of these years and sacrificing for you children, and now he'd like to see you make something of yourself."

"I'll take care of myself."

"I'm only telling you for your own good," she said.

I guess I got sore and shouldn't have lost my head. I told my mother to mind her own business, and I just caught myself in time or I would have cursed and said "your own goddamned business." When I left, I slammed the door.

That day I damned near went downtown. I almost went. But back in October 1917, my mother had guessed that I wanted to enlist and had gotten me to give her my word that I would not do anything like that without talking about it first with my old man and her.

I was sore when I left home and walked over on 51st Street to the Washington Park ballpark, but my temper quickly cooled. I felt pretty rotten. After all, my old man and my mother were only thinking of my own good and my future. I guess I must have been confused and afraid. But when I got over to Washington Park and started playing ball, I forgot it all—I forgot everything. That always happened to me. Once I got out on a ball diamond, nothing else was important. It was like the rest of the world didn't count or even exist.

That's the way I always was. Something happened to me when I got out there on a ball field.

II

Those days of playing ball in Washington Park—of shagging flies, play-ing scrub games with easy pitching, playing any kind of game—those were some of my happiest days. It was out there on that big field in Washington Park that I developed myself and made myself ready for the White Sox so that I was really a big leaguer from the start, even if I never became the great star I dreamed of becoming.

It was a big field running almost from South Park Avenue to Cot-tage Grove and from 51st to 55th or Garfield Boulevard. In those days, there were eleven diamonds running around the rim of the big field, from near 51st Street and swinging east and then south toward 55th. The big center of the park and the west side were not marked off in diamonds with sand baselines, but there was plenty of space, and fellows could mark out diamonds and play a game. You had to have a permit on Saturdays and Sundays for the eleven regular marked-out diamonds during the best months, but there was always space for everybody—room for kids, for fellows who liked to fool around, knock out flies or just have a scrub game. And many more young fellows and men used to play then than now, or at least that's my impression. From the first possible weekends in March, before all the snow was melted, until well into October and even early November, if the weather stayed good, you could find fellows and kids out there, knocking out and catching flies if there weren't enough for a game. And a hell of a lot of them were nice guys.

I began going out there when I was seven or eight and kept right on until I became a White Sox. Once in a while after that I'd drop in, and I was always intending to do that, more than I ever did. I remember how in those years when I was growing up, I'd dream and imagine how, when I became a White Sox star, I'd sometimes come back to see the boys and the fellows and knock out some flies to them, chat, and how they'd all be glad to see me and as proud of me for making the grade as if they had done it themselves. Of course many of them were proud of me, but it was not exactly like I dreamed it and imagined it would be. I was naive and dumb, or as Buck Weaver used to say about himself when he broke in as a rookie, "I was a goof."

I guess I believed more in hero worship than I should have. What I mean is that while people, especially kids, need heroes and need to be hero worshipers, they all aren't just waiting for you to become their hero, and if you do, they just don't think of your success and your deeds as more important than their own lives and problems. Like once I went out to Washington Park on a Sunday morning, maybe in 1923 or 1924, and I saw some of the fellows I used to know, and I heard Art McCallum, who played third base on our team, the Rocks, saying to some fellow I didn't know, "That's Mickey Donovan of the White Sox."

"So what friggin' good does that do for me?" the stranger asked.

I was kind of hurt, but the incident made me realize what I've been trying to explain here. Becoming a ballplayer didn't mean as much to a hell of a lot of people as I imagined it would. They didn't care as much as I used to imagine.

But I used to love it, going out to the Washington Park ball field. All winter I'd wait for spring and the new season. In 1918, there was daylight saving time, and I used to go out after supper. We'd have a game with easy pitching or the Rocks would practice, and sometimes when it got too dark, we'd sit around and talk about baseball and girls, the war, everything. You didn't get to know most of the fellows too well. You only knew them in Washington Park. But a couple were my good friends, especially Joe Hines.

I haven't seen Joe in years. I guess he must be in business or doing all right. His old man was well off, some kind of a businessman. Joe was a big kid, and he had a fine pair of hands. I thought he was better than me, and maybe he had a better chance of making the big leagues than me, especially because he had a lot of power and could pull the ball into left field. He always played first base, and he wasn't a bad fielder—that is, in high school or Washington Park ball. At sixteen or seventeen he was fully developed, about 180 pounds of bone and muscle, with big arms, and he dreamed of the big leagues, even though he didn't say much about it. He was quiet, kind of shy. He and I were the two best on the Rocks. He went to Crucifixion and graduated with me. He went on to Loyola on the North Side and played first base and batted cleanup for their team, and he'd always be out in Washington Park, just like me, ready for anything from a game of catch to a full-fledged ball game.

We'd walk part of the way home together. Joe lived on 49th Street, east of Grand Boulevard. Sometimes we'd go to a movie and then have a soda at Dunne's ice cream parlor on 51st Street, near the El Station, or at Schraeder's at 47th and Grand Boulevard, where you could get such good ice cream, maybe the best in Chicago.

Joe and I felt very close, like real friends, but we never really talked personally. Most of the time, we'd talk about baseball.

"You're getting better all the time, Mickey," he used to tell me.

"I don't know about that, Joe."

"Yeah, I do. I can tell. I've seen you play now since we both were in short pants. Your arm is stronger and you're hitting the ball harder. You're getting a lot of them straight in a line, especially batting left-handed."

That was all music to my ears, especially coming from Joe. And I'd talk about him and his playing.

"No, something's wrong. It must be my stance."

"You're meeting the ball, Joe. I made it a special point to watch you close last Sunday. You were swinging clean and straight. But you seem too anxious."

"I know—I like to slug the ball and I swing too hard, too anxious."

"When you meet the ball square, you get more drive and power to it, and you hit those liners to left field that way. They're damned hard to judge."

We could talk for hours like that. I used to like to dream that Joe and I would both go along together, maybe getting signed up by the same minor league, and that we'd go away together, room and play together, and come up to the White Sox, with Joe playing first and myself at short.

Joe must have had the same kind of hopes. He used to say, "I hope we go on playing together, even if you do burn my hand with your arm."

I had a good arm.

I knew what Joe meant—that we'd go to the big leagues together. Joe, like me, was thinking of joining the colors, and I thought of us doing it together and being in the same outfit. We would have, except for what happened. Joe joined the navy, but the war was over before he ever got to see any active service. One Sunday in late August, I met Joe at nine o'clock Mass. I was with the White Sox, and he was a gob in a navy uniform. I envied him more than he could have envied me.

There were lots of guys who came to the park. Flinty always hung around, but he couldn't play worth a damn. He was a little fellow, maybe five-five, broad, built like a barrel, and tough. He was older than us, maybe thirty-five or so, and he had some kind of a political job that didn't tax him any or take up much of his time. He was a kind of race track sporty character, but strictly small time. I didn't realize it then. He talked big and tough, and he'd been around some. He'd even ridden the rods. He used to tell us all how to play, and it was Flinty who organized the Rocks, arranged the games, got us permits and handled all the details. At first I didn't like him because he seemed like a loudmouth, but I got to like him. He was amusing. He always took credit for me making the big leagues, but about all he did was hit me vicious grounders for infield practice. He'd damned near knock us down, and every time we missed a ball, he'd be on us. I can still hear him: "Donovan, you goddamn butter-fingered Irish bastard, go play shortstop for the bloomer girls."

He wasn't married and lived at home. He used to go to a whorehouse once a week, and he'd hang around the pool room on 51st Street or the park, chewing on a big cigar, more than smoking it, rolling the butt in his mouth, taking it out to curse and tell you something. He was always right, to hear him talk, and he claimed that he was once a featherweight fighter and could have beaten Abe Attell if they'd fought.

"Flinty, you're a lot of shit," Art McCallum used to say.

"Why you skinny young sonofabitch," Flinty would say, going for Art. Art would dodge him, laughing, and we'd all laugh. "I got a good mind to drop you punks and let you try and run your own goddamned ball club."

"Don't, please don't," Art would say.

Flinty would look at him, starting to relent. "I'm glad you have some sense."

"Don't—we need you as chief cook and bottle washer," Art would then say.

"You foul little Irish ——" and Flinty would use all of the words. Then, a minute later, he'd seem to forget that he'd been so sore he could have brained Art and would talk to him as if nothing had happened.

He took managing seriously and had a real McGraw complex. I'm sure he liked to think of himself as a kind of Muggsy McGraw of Washington Park. He always talked of McGraw, and in 1917 he said the New York Giants were going to win the Series over the White Sox only because McGraw was their manager. Sometimes I'd kid him and call him "Mr. McGraw," but he didn't take this as kidding. He lapped it up. If I'd call him McGraw, he'd be pretty sure to say, "I wish all you dumb punks was like Donovan. Then this would be a ball club." He was always talking about strategy, and he nearly lost us a couple of games during the time I played with the Rocks, which was from April to July 1918.

We had gray uniforms with "Rocks" written across the shirt at a slant. They were good-looking uniforms, and I was proud of mine. We played every Sunday and sometimes on Saturday, and we all chipped in to make a pot. The pitcher got five bucks if we lost, ten if we won. The rest of the money was kept by Flinty in a pot, to be divided among us at the end of the season. I never did see any of that money, and Joe told me none of them did, although there was a couple hundred dollars in the pot.

Flinty disappeared and wasn't heard from for years. In 1928 I saw him on Broadway, looking seedy but talking big. His hair was getting gray, and he was shabby. He told me he was making plenty bootlegging, but still he hit me for five bucks. I guess he's dead now.

All of the fellows who came out to Washington Park weren't dreaming of the big leagues, of course. Some of them just liked to play, and they found their speed. There were older men who liked the exercise and enjoyed the association. Playing ball was a kind of challenge, something different from their work, and something to enjoy. It was better than the saloons, I guess, and it didn't cost much—the price of a glove, maybe, but that lasted for years, and a bat or chipping in now and then for a ball. It was good relaxation for a poor man. And some of the guys were from small towns or farms, and they were lonely guys, living in furnished rooms or boardinghouses. They didn't know many people, and some of them weren't loaded with dough, either, so they found companionship in Washington Park. Then there were oddballs and screwballs like Cash-and-Carry Hoskins. Cash-and-Carry didn't have all of his marbles. He was about thirty or so, and he lived in a room in Forestville. He made his living delivering packages and messages, and he must have made maybe $10 a week. He couldn't play ball worth a damn and swung a bat like a girl. When he tried to catch a fly ball, I was always afraid he would get hit on the dome or in the puss. He'd get into scrub games with easy pitching, but he kept his averages, and what he batted was mighty important to him.

"I'm hitting .455 this year," he might say.

Everybody liked him and felt sorry for him, and we pretended to take him seriously, never laughing at him or playing tricks on Cash-and-Carry.

"You are, that's damn good, Cash."

"Oh, last year, I hit .563. I haven't found my eye yet."

We used to let him make hits for his batting average, because it was just about the only thing he had to feel proud about. He ran like a girl and walked on the balls of his feet. He wore an old, spotted, gray serge suit and a short, peaked blue cap. He looked a little funny or queer—that is, not quite all there. But he was harmless and always friendly. What happened to him? But what happened to many people?

I'll bet every now and then some fan or old ballplayer will be sitting down and thinking about the past, and maybe he'll start wondering, and asking himself, "I wonder what happened to Mickey Donovan?"

That's the way life is. Then there was Rex McNulty. Rex was washed up at Denver in the Western Association, which was as high as he ever got in organized baseball. Rex was about thirty-five. He looked like a ballplayer. Of course, when I say that, I mean he did to me. He was the first professional ballplayer I knew, except for Tim, who had only been a semipro, but we even looked up to a semipro and a minor leaguer. Rex was a southpaw. Once in a while he'd pitch a game, and he looked good. Just standing out there on the mound, but he never threw hard. Still he mixed them up on you and was hard for us to hit, and I began to get the idea that there's a hell of a lot of difference between a guy who's a pitcher with experience and savvy and somebody who goes out there and throws the ball. Sometimes Rex would throw one so slow that you could just about read the trademark on the ball, and you'd be all set to hit it, thinking you were going to send the ball sailing for a mile, but you hit a measly grounder or pop-up. He never would let you get set or give you what you wanted.

Rex came out because he loved baseball. He played semipro and worked hustling freight. He was a disappointed man, with his dream behind him. He wasn't bitter, but he had failed, and you knew it. "Baseball's goddamn tough," he used to say. "You got it or you don't, and you got to be born with it."

I'd sometimes get depressed, and think that maybe I was only dreaming myself up to a bust, so that in the end I'd only become another Tim Cahill or Rex McNulty. He was a big guy and he had a kind of walk, taking short steps, which made you notice him. He never got too chummy but always held himself a little aloof and kept a distance from everyone. Still, he wasn't unfriendly. He'd ask you questions about how you were feeling and about your playing, and you had the feeling that he saw through you and knew all of the answers to anything about baseball. Once in a while, he'd try and pep things up and would talk you into shaking your ass more. He wouldn't talk much about his experiences in professional baseball, but he liked to discuss plays and fine points of the game, the squeeze play, the defense against the double steal with runners on first and third, the many kinds of situations that can arise in baseball.

I wanted Rex to notice how I played. If he thought I was good that would have meant that my hopes had more basis in my ability and my growing confidence was, perhaps, not misplaced. And Rex gave me a feeling of being closer to professional baseball. He had been a minor leaguer. He was friendly to me and, well, I liked it. But Rex was pathetic. I could feel that then. Now, of course, I understand it. But you have to have been a ballplayer yourself to understand it fully. You have to live with your future behind you, and not be recognized or important anymore, to know the feelings of being on the other side and for good. And when a player does get a start, but spends his career in the minor leagues, then, he can be eaten with feelings of failure. And that's what happened to Rex. It's happened to hundreds and thousands. They didn't learn how to do anything else, and after their hopes and dreams, what then? What kind of a living can they make? Most of them take to drink, even old time big leaguers.

I was young. I just felt that there was something sad, too bad about Rex in the old Washington Park days. I was most interested in myself. I felt sorry for most of the fellows. I was going to make it, and then, I thought that all of the young guys wanted to be in the big leagues and the older men were unhappy because they had not made it. It was the only thing in the world, except for the war and being a hero.

And like I said, that caused me problems. After the 1917 season, the Cubs bought Grover Cleveland Alexander and Bill Kellifer. I don't need to tell you what kind of pitcher Big Pete was, not if you're a baseball fan. How many were there like him? Look at the record. I hit against him in the city series. He'd fox you. He was drafted, and there was a lot about it in the sports pages. Maybe his career would be ruined.

It seemed like a tragedy to me. I felt it more because I thought of myself. Alexander had already become great. He'd be remembered even if he didn't come back. But me, I might be killed and never be remembered.

Why had there been a war? Of course I still want to know, but I don't know much about politics and deep subjects.

Well, I was seventeen, and that's part of my story. There's more to it—Mary.

III

I was in love. I'd been in love with her since way back in grammar school. I was kind of shy, or maybe a little afraid of girls. I think we kids were a little different from kids today. Those days were more simple. We looked up to girls, except our older sisters. They were superior. And we thought we'd be considered a sissy if we paid too much attention to girls. We were kind of afraid to say much to them. We didn't know what to say. And especially the girl of your heart, you pretended not to be interested in her.

She was a pretty kid. I still remember her with her black hair and dark eyes, her smile, the way she would laugh and tease and run, the green coat she wore in winter, her hair ribbons—I remember so much about her. I kind of worshiped her. I did worship her. She was one of the prettiest girls in the class, and popular with everybody. And like I said, her father, old Jack Collins, was pretty well-heeled. Back about 1916 or thereabouts he owned an automobile, a Pierce-Arrow. It wasn't just because of that, of the Collins family having dough, that I cast my eyes on Mary. I don't know why it was. She was the girl I wanted to love me. Hell, this seems sentimental and kid stuff now, but it wasn't then. You hate to admit having feelings and dreams because they seem to be sissy, not manly. But of course you have them. And I did for Mary. But during grammar school, I didn't make much headway. There were a couple of parties, birthday and surprise parties, and we played kissing games. I guess I kissed her a few times. But I always thought that she would be the one, the girl, and that I would win her by becoming a great baseball player, making her proud of me. As a kid, I always hoped she'd see me play. That was especially why I liked to play in the vacant lot at 50th and Calumet Avenue. But Mary wasn't much interested in baseball then, no more than any of the other girls were. She became a fan later, after we got married. Maybe the word "fan" is a little too strong, but she got to understand baseball and like it, and sometimes she'd come to see me play.

A couple of times or so when I was a kid, she passed by on the street when I was playing. Of course, I got excited and hollered, but she passed on. I remember once when I was in eighth grade, she spoke to me on 50th Street.

"You like to play ball all of the time, don't you?"

"I like to play," I said.

"You don't think of girls or much of anything else, do you, Mickey?" She was giving me an opening, but I was then too dumb to take it. But no, more than dumb, I was shy.

I didn't really know what to say, what to talk about to a girl like Mary. I didn't dance then, and, as a matter of fact, I didn't learn how to dance until I was in my fourth year of high school and was going with Mary. She taught me.

"What's so interesting about baseball?"

I don't remember how I answered that question. But I do remember that she looked pretty, beautiful to me that day, and I felt awkward. I was tongue-tied and almost stuttering. She had on a print dress, white and red, and white stockings and wore a red ribbon in her hair, which she wore long, down her back, and her eyes were sparkling, and she was smiling as she talked. And me, I was like a lug, only not in what I felt. I wanted to be a hero for her, rescue her like the heroes in movies, like Eddie Polo in the Saturday-afternoon serial, and I wanted to star and shine and scintillate in baseball with her watching, and I felt that if I could do great things for her, then she'd know what I really was, and she'd love me. That's romance. We feel that way only once in our life, and we don't know that we aren't going on always feeling that way. And we're kind of ashamed of it, thinking how we'd be laughed at if our feelings were known and exposed. Hell, I would have laughed at some of the other kids in my class, Beans Dennison or Tommy Clancy or the other boys. I haven't seen any of them in years now.

It's different today. Kids learn more and are told more. They smarten up quicker. Of course they got TV, which is a wonderful thing for them. Nobody ever told us much of anything, and even though Chicago is a big city, it was like a small town. You knew most of the people, or who they were, and your folks stayed home most of the time, and Sunday after Mass, people stood in front of church talking for a little while. The stores were different, nothing like the supermarkets, and Ma liked to gab with Mr. Morris, or stop and pass the time of day with a neighbor woman, and it was sort of intimate and neighborly. Many of the people had lived in the neighborhood a long time, since you were young, and you felt and everybody felt that they'd go on living in the neighborhood, and you would too, for a long time. It isn't that life is so totally different now but that, as I look back, it was more simple then. People weren't so much interested in the outside world, and they didn't do as much. Ma never belonged to a bridge club or any other clubs like Mary does, and Mary's mother was the same, except she belonged to the women's club in the parish, and she used to fix the flowers on the altar sometimes. Maybe I'm being nostalgic and making it simple, or maybe it is that I was a kid then, and everything is different when you were a kid from the way things are later on. It was all friendly, too, and I believed how I was going to grow up to be so famous and I'd have Mary.

But that day in eighth grade I didn't have much to say to her. I was no dashing short-pants Romeo. But I went home on air.

I was slow. I was so slow I could have missed out. I went to high school, like I said, and saw her once in a while at church or on the street but I never got up the courage to ask her for a date. But on Christmas Day in 1917, my fourth year in high school, I met her in front of church after Mass. By then, she was beautiful, a young woman, not a kid, and she had a muff and was wearing a fur coat. She was going to see her aunt who lived at 62nd and South Park, and I walked with her. Suddenly, it was easier to talk to her. She, like me, was going to graduate from high school the next June, and she told me she wanted to get a job. After graduating, she was going to go to a secretarial school to learn typing and shorthand. She didn't think her parents particularly liked the idea, especially her father, but she wanted to work.

"I don't want to sit home and twiddle my thumbs being just a home-body," she said.

We were walking on Grand Boulevard toward 51st Street. There was some snow along the sides of the sidewalk, as I remember, and it was kind of chilly, a gray morning. Her cheeks were red and her face was round, not fat but full, and with her red cheeks and red lips, she was mighty pretty. I remember, I was thinking that now was my chance and I was in luck. She was real friendly and real nice, and she had smiled when she saw me in front of church. Why, her smile and that little walk was like a Christmas for me.

"What do you think, Mickey, of a girl working?"

"I guess there's nothing wrong with it—my sister, Ruth, works."

"The world's changing. Maybe when my mother was my age, it was different, but this is 1917, almost 1918, it's the twentieth century," she said. It seems funny and quaint to think of a girl talking like that now, but that's how much times have changed and the world has gone around. "My father asked what do I want to be—a suffragette?"

"Suffragette?" I said, sort of laughing. A suffragette, that was somebody like an anarchist or an IWW, which used to be called an I Won't Worker.

"What are you going to do, Mickey, when you graduate?"

I held back from saying I was going to become a ballplayer, so I said I didn't know.

"I hope you're not going to go running away to join the army and go and get yourself killed."

That sort of made me think she liked me and was mighty encouraging.

"Maybe I will—we got to beat the Huns."

"I wouldn't like you to go and get wounded or killed, Mickey. I'm afraid my brother Tommy is going to enlist."

Her brother Tommy was twenty-one. I didn't like him at the time, but I didn't have any good reasons for this. He was older than me and liked to run around with girls and was something of a sport, and me, I wasn't as grown up as I liked to think I was. But if Tommy could go, I could. I knew I had to go.

"It's going to be the duty of all of us men to defend our country," I said, looking at Mary, and wanting her to know I meant defending her as well as my mother and my sister. We had heard tell and read in the newspapers of the Germans raping women in Belgium.

"But Mickey, you aren't a man yet," she told me.

That took a lot of starch out of me.

"I'm old enough to fight," I said.

"You aren't. Oh, Mickey, you mustn't do something foolish and go and get yourself killed." She talked like she meant it, and of course she did. She had liked me all those years as much as I did her.

I remember that it was a problem for me, too, if I should or shouldn't take her arm crossing 51st Street. This is something to laugh at, I guess, when you look back on it, the problems of first love, the way you hold back from letting on to your feelings and stew about the littlest things. What'll she think or do if you take her arm or kiss her? I went through it all. And I didn't know how I got the courage to do it, but I did it, I took her arm and she gave me a smile, and God, what that did to me then. I wanted to sing. I wanted to sing "My Wild Irish Rose" and think of Mary as My Rose.

Before I left her in front of the building where her aunt lived, I had a date to take her skating at the Washington Park lagoon the next Sunday.

I went home for my breakfast, because I had gone to Communion as I always did, and still do on Christmas morning, with my head full of dreams, spinning like a top with dreams. I had seen couples, arm in arm, and sitting holding hands in the movie shows, skating together, and I had reached the age where I wanted all of that. I wanted a girl. I wanted a girl as mine and I wanted everybody who knew me to see me going out with her, taking her arm, knowing that she was my girl. I wanted a girl to shine before and to inspire me. I wanted to be a hero for a girl. It was like being a knight. I wanted a girl to hold and kiss and hug. I wanted more, too, but I couldn't think of Mary giving it without thinking of myself as a heel because she was a good girl. But I wanted to be in love and I fell head over heels right then and there. I'd dreamed of this, of Mary and myself. And my dreams were coming true. If my dreams about Mary came true, so would my dreams about baseball.

When she said goodbye, she looked right up at me, looked right in my eyes with her face shining, full of softness. I could have kissed her then. Walking off, I had to do something, anything. I stood, packing snowballs and throwing them at the trees and the bare branches of the bushes across the street. Now, that memory makes me know that it was a white Christmas that year.

We went skating. There are days you never forget as long as you live, days when something happens to you and living is like poetry, or being in the clouds. It's more than a thrill or a kick. A poet could describe what I mean. I can't. But everybody or nearly everybody must have had these days, and anybody who didn't, well, I feel damned sorry for him.

That Sunday, as I remember it, was just right. The sun was out in the morning but there was a sting in the wind, enough to make your cheeks red and to give you a good circulation. And of course, I'd been waiting for Sunday and my date to go skating with Mary. I'd imagined every moment of it over and over just as I lived my big league career in my dreams before I even set a spiked shoe on the field at the White Sox Park. I tried to think of jokes and witty things I'd say to impress Mary, but I guess I've never been so good at that. I could think quick as lightning in a ball game, but I never could think fast like that with my tongue. And I had my dreams, driving Morris's grocery wagon and delivering groceries, which I did that week. I got $5. I kept imagining how I'd tell Mary about my desires to be a ballplayer. She'd understand. I thought then that love meant that you should share every thought you had, tell everything, all that you think and dream and the feelings you have. Of course I know better now. But it's always a question as to what you should tell.

A man loves his wife, and I love Mary to this day. But it's all so different from what you imagine it's going to be when you are young and romantic for the first time. We make fun of being romantic, of a man dreaming wonderful damned-fool things, of a kid dreaming about romance and love, dreaming about baseball as all romance and heroes, but we need to do this and we only pretend that we don't. We put on another face to the world. But what would the world be if we weren't like this, and what man would ever get married if he didn't have these dreams of romance? Hell, of course it all isn't true, but neither is Santa Claus. What would Christmas be without Santa Claus?

I counted the hours. Then, on Sunday I counted the minutes. We walked through the park with the snow in it. I never realized how quiet the world is in the snow. It makes you feel quiet inside. I've felt that way sometimes when I've been hunting. The sun came and went, and the sun does something to the snow, makes it glitter and shine, gives it a brightness and it dazzles. And the world is different, covered with snow. The trees were bare and black and brown, and the wind was hitting them, but it wasn't a tough wind. Off on the left, the ballpark was covered with snow and I thought that it looked a little dreary. I can never pass a place where there are ball diamonds without feeling something, if it's winter or if there isn't a ball game on. I imagine I hear the shouts of a ball game. It's so real it seems like I really do hear shouts. I think that's called having hallucinations, but I don't have any of them. Hallucinations are like the DTs, only you have them without having had any booze.

"There's the ball field," I said to Mary.

We were kind of restrained.

"Yes, I suppose you wish it were summer and you were playing ball instead of going skating with a girl." Mary always used perfect grammar. She reads books, some of them high-brow books.

But I didn't know what to say. It was true and not true. I wanted to be playing ball with her watching me.

"No, I like ice skating, too," I said, dumbly, instead of telling her that I was glad to be with her, more glad to be with her than I would be doing anything else or being anywhere else in the world. Even to this day, Mary sometimes says to me, "Mickey, you're as romantic as an umbrella. But I love you."

It isn't so, or at least it wasn't so. It was only that I wasn't quick on the uptake, except on the ball field. I didn't have a line. I was too over-whelmed to talk much. Actually being with her, taking her on a skating date, walking with her in the park was different from daydreaming about Mary. I had all of the feelings of daydreaming but it was real and true, not what I was just imagining. It was like it was not really hap-pening to me, like I was watching this happening when it was actually happening. Maybe this isn't clear, but as I have said, I'm not articulate about these things, and it's too late for me now even to try to be what I'm not. Anyone who has fallen in love in what's now called the teenage years will know what I'm talking about and what I mean.

So, we walked to the boathouse. That's a pretty long walk, well over a mile, I guess. We walked slow, and we didn't keep talking, but there was something between us that we both felt. It was like the two of us were alone together. Of course we were, walking in the park, but we could have been alone in the world, and we were.

Not having my tongue, and because this was new to me, a new situ-ation, I wasn't sure of myself. I was anxious to get to the lagoon where I could show her what a skater I was, and I was a pretty fair skater. What I couldn't do talking, I could accomplish by skating. Still and all, we walked slow, sometimes looking down at the path and at the snow, and sometimes looking off or straight ahead, but not looking at each other much.

"Remember, sometimes we'd go skating at the duck pond," she said. She meant the Washington Park duck pond at the South Park side of the park and around 53rd Street. I remembered. That was where I learned to skate. But it was too small now and too full of little kids who got in your way, so that if you skated fast you ran the risk of knocking the little kids down and hurting them.

"It used to be fun. Skating at the duck pond," she said.

"Yeah, it was."

"You didn't care much for girls then."

"Not exactly, I mean, it wasn't not exactly that I didn't care but . . ."

"But what, Mickey?"

"They couldn't skate."

"I still can't skate much."

"Yes, you can."

"How do you know I can, Mickey?"

"I can teach you if you don't."

"And pick me up when I fall down."

"Yeah. But we all take our spills."

That's the way we talked. A couple of times I felt like a goof and wished we were already there at the lagoon, skating. She would admire my skating, I was sure. But Mary was friendly, and she smiled at me, and took my arm, so I was doing all right.

And then, skating. I always enjoyed skating, and it wasn't until a couple of years ago that I gave it up for good. I'd go skating at least a couple of times a year during the winter, but age caught up with me and my knees went bad so I had to give it up. But back in those days when I was young, skating was one of the compensations of winter, and I liked it, gliding along in stride, feeling myself move in rhythm, taking long strides, swaying, going along the ice at the Washington Park lagoon with my hands behind my back, looking ahead and just feeling good at the way I would skate and feel myself moving. I did show off a little that Sunday afternoon with Mary and liked it when she said I was a good skater. She was a fair skater. And we skated together holding hands and with our arms crossed. She looked like the prettiest girl in the park, too. The wind and the cold put such a fine color in her cheeks, and she was gay and laughed when she took a spill.

We decided to skate all of the way around the lagoon. That was a pretty fair distance, too, I thought, for Mary, but she was the one who suggested it. By that time I'd have done anything she wanted because I was that gone on her. We got away from the crowd and skated under the stone bridge at the south end of the lagoon and then turned. We were alone, and the trees were all bare, the park was covered with snow. You could see your breath, and it was all pretty. It's prettier when you are young and have a girl. We skated, not saying much for a while, and then we went by a big and bent old oak on the edge of the ice to rest a minute.

Mary was looking up at me, the way she had in front of the building where her aunt lived, and she seemed prettier than anyone had ever been in the world. I didn't think or anything. I put my arms around her and kissed her. She let me, and I'd never been kissed like that before. I kissed her and felt wonderful, more important than I'd ever felt before. It was all such a surprise to me, I didn't know what to say. Neither of us said much of anything skating under the wooden bridge in Washington Park and back to the boathouse. We changed skates and walked home through the park. It was getting dark. The trees were black. The snow was spread over the park. It looked cold. But we didn't feel the cold and I kept kissing her again and again. She was my girl. She's been my girl ever since.

IV

I came to decide that I must enlist. Ruthie's fiancé, Tom Cameron, had gone. Some of my cousins had gone. Mary's brother Tommy was at Fort Sheridan. I read the war news every day then. American soldiers were at the front, and there were American casualties. The newspapers printed letters home from the soldiers, and one of Tom Cameron's to Ruthie was printed in the paper. She was proud of Tom, and a lot of her friends phoned her. It was exciting and made me want to go. I would imagine myself in France, writing a letter to Mary from the trenches and putting it down just like that, casually: "Tomorrow, we're going over the top." And I'd imagine the letter being printed in one of the Chicago papers and read by everybody I knew. Sometimes I'd think of the letter being printed after I had been killed, but other times I wouldn't think of myself being killed. And I'd imagine a buddy of mine, maybe Joe Hines, writing to Mary and telling her how I was

a hero, capturing a gang of Germans in a machine gun nest and how I
was too modest to write and tell what I did.

I was always imagining myself single-handedly capturing Germans
in machine gun nests or always wiping them out. It was machine gun
nests anyway that I was always dreaming of taking or destroying.

Baseball wasn't the same in 1918 as it was in 1917, and as the season
went along, many fans began to lose some of their interest. As it later
came out as a result of 1919, the Old Roman lost a lot of money in 1918.
The Cubs, even though they lost Alexander, were up there in the pennant fight, and as is known, they won the pennant but lost the World
Series to a pitcher named Babe Ruth, along with some other Red Sox
players. Some of the sports writers were beginning to describe the
war as the only game worth winning, and players were leaving the
big league clubs regularly to go into the services. A couple of the Sox,
including Shoeless Joe Jackson, went to work in the shipyards so as not
to be drafted, I guess, and the Old Roman was sore at them, blasting
them in public or the newspapers.

The White Sox were a second-division team that season, and while
I and many fans were interested in them, it wasn't the same as 1917,
and not only because the Sox were a pennant contender. A spirit was
gripping the country, I guess, because it sure was felt in Chicago. If
a man didn't go and fight, he was considered to be a slacker by many
people. In June, I was eighteen. That made me old enough to go, and
plenty of eighteen-year-old kids went. Some were under eighteen, but
they ran off, joined the colors, and even became heroes.

I was getting passed by. And I came to think I had to go. It was my
duty. I remember the billboard pictures of Uncle Sam pointing a finger,
and there was the message that the call of Uncle Sam means "you." It
meant me.

I thought, too, like most people. Nobody could lick us. Old Glory had
never hit the dust. That was the way we Americans were. And that
was the kind of person and an American I wanted to be. Everything
I wanted to be as a big league ballplayer, I wanted to be as a soldier.

And like I said, Ma had guessed that I wanted to go. She was so dead
set against me going that I even felt ashamed. I had promised her not
to enlist without telling her. She wasn't un-American or unpatriotic.
She wasn't for the Germans. It was that she was my mother. But she

bothered me and made me sore, made me glum and gloomy. I would sometimes get all mixed up.

Pa, he didn't say so much. And in 1918, Pa used to say less and less. He didn't seem as interested, and now I know why. I didn't notice any change in Pa, not much, but Ma did. She noticed everything. My Ma was smarter than many who went to college, smarter in the practical things. She used to tell Ruthie or me that Pa wasn't looking too well. "Your father doesn't look himself."

I can remember her saying that just as though I was hearing it now, and I can remember Ma, just like she was standing in front of me, alive, a small woman, plump, and a round and kind of fat face, and strong arms with short hands that she never took care of, her blue eyes so full of life and twinkling, and Ma wearing maybe a black dress with a gingham apron on, telling us, Ruthie and me and the younger kids, "Your father doesn't look himself."

I guess Pa lost a little weight, and he would be tired when he came home from work. He didn't have as good an appetite and sometimes complained of pains in his stomach but always said that this was nothing much. "It's just a little belly ache."

"Father, can't you say 'stomachache'?" Ruthie would sometimes ask. She was always worried about the manners of all of us and criticized us plenty about our manners. "Don't try to teach an old dog new tricks," Pa sometimes said to Ruthie.

Pa wanted me to become an apprentice and learn his trade, and I didn't want to. It wasn't really because it meant that I'd be a working man instead of a salesman or a businessman, but maybe it was that, at least a little, after I began going with Mary, but I don't know what it really was. I wanted to be a ballplayer, like I said, and I guess I was sure I was going to be one, sure underneath and in my heart. Somehow or other, I didn't want to follow in Pa's footsteps. That was it. Many kids are like that. And hell, what kid knows what he really wants to be or is capable of becoming? Nowadays, the kids get vocational counseling and all kinds of help and I guess that's better, everything considered.

All during my last year in high school, Pa kept at me, telling me that it would give me a good living, like it had him, but I was bullheaded and one track. I didn't want to think of any kind of work but playing baseball, and I didn't think of that as work at all. Yes, I was dumb and goofy about the future, and I can see how my old man was right. Of course I did become a ballplayer, but suppose I hadn't had what it takes?

"If you've got the stuff to be a big league ballplayer, Mick, that's well and good. But what are you gonna do if you ain't?" He used to ask me questions like that, and I didn't like to answer them. I didn't like to discuss them. I have got to admit it if I want to be honest and say that as I grew up, and in my father's last years, we didn't come to open fights, but we weren't near to being close. And this hurt my old man. It's made me feel bad ever since. So he'd ask me what I'd do if I didn't have the stuff in me, and I'd palm off some answer.

"Suppose I have. I got to find out first."

"You can learn a trade first and then try to be a ballplayer. Hell, I'd be proud of you if you became a big league ballplayer. Hell, they make good money, better than I make."

Some of them on the White Sox didn't, not when I started.

"Tim Cahill thinks I can become a ballplayer," I'd say.

"But does he tell you not to learn a trade so you'll have something to fall back on?"

I couldn't answer my old man. I wanted to be different and not follow in his footsteps. And Ma, loving Pa like she did, was sometimes on my side because she wanted me to become something more than Pa. My going to work in a good suit of clothes and not carrying my lunch like my old man carried his was only a sign of what she wanted. She wanted me to become an important man, more than I could be, the way she saw it. I did become important. A big league ballplayer's an important man.

I held out because I was afraid I was going to give in and do what Pa wanted, and I guess that even though I did act stubborn and bullheaded, I knew my father was right and only talking what made good sense. All of this came to a head after my graduation.

Pa wasn't a well man. He lost weight and didn't eat as well. He got tired and he had pains in the stomach. He was short of breath. He seemed to know what was coming. He talked to me, kind of gentle, and he was trying to tell me because he must have guessed that he didn't have more time left.

"I've seen a lot of change, and I remember young fellows when I was your age, Mick. Billy Sweeney, he was a nice kid," Pa said one

night, and then he began shaking his head. And he told me the story
of how Billy Sweeney ended up poor and broke, dying and not leaving
anything for his wife and children. Hell, I was too young and thought-
less, maybe, but I didn't want to hear it. And I didn't want to go out
with Pa as an apprentice every day. I was sure I'd take care of myself
and that things would work out all right for me and for all of us.

V

It was just right after my graduation and on a Friday night. It was
June 1918. I went to Mary's house for dinner that night, for the first
time. I had of course met her parents when I called for her to take her
to a movie or for a walk, but I'd only exchanged a few polite words.
I was nervous. I didn't know how they'd take to me and I was afraid
that they'd think that I wasn't good enough for their daughter. I felt
guilty too, because, after all, Mary and I were in love, and one night in
the hallway before either of us knew what had happened, well, you can
guess. I don't want to go into details about such matters, and Mary is
my wife. I don't love her the less. But I was guilty. I was afraid that
maybe I'd ruined their daughter, and that her father or mother might
sense it, or guess it, or catch on.

I let this worry me, and I sometimes imagined myself facing her
parents with them knowing, and my saying that I loved Mary and
would marry her. I was a little afraid. With fellows your own age you
talk one way about girls, although I never did about Mary. But alone,
you don't think the same at seventeen. I didn't, and there was nothing
unusual or exceptional about me other than the fact that I was a better
ballplayer than anyone else in my neighborhood or at St. Basil's High
School in my time. I was bothered and I couldn't trust myself alone
with Mary, and she loved me.

Since we were secretly engaged, that was another worry, because
how was I going to support her. And as I have mentioned, Mary's father
was pretty well off. They had a nice home, much nicer than ours. I felt
a little ashamed of our home after I saw Mary's a few times. I couldn't
take Mary home to live with us, or at least I thought I couldn't, and
how was I going to make enough money to support her? Two days
after my graduation, I got a job driving a horse and wagon at $100 a
month, but that was not enough for us to get married on, not a girl

like Mary. Of course, we didn't have to get married right away, and we didn't plan on doing that. We even talked it over and decided we had to stop making love the way we did when we had a chance, and we went to confession. I went to Father Thomas, a new young priest in the parish, because he was easier in confession than the other priests, but that was a sweating experience. I was ashamed and didn't want to have to confess and admit it, especially because it was a girl like Mary, and I was afraid that even Father Thomas would be rough on me, and I didn't know what he'd think of me even if he didn't recognize my voice in the darkness of the confessional box. And I was afraid that I'd be told not to see Mary or go with her, and she felt the same as I did. Worse, I am sure, because this was harder for her to admit and confess. But we did it.

And later we both felt wonderful, as wonderful as I thought you could feel. I was carrying a heavy load on my mind, something a man wouldn't feel, not the same way. A man might be unfaithful to his wife and feel rotten, even like he's had experience and he's come to know what human nature's like. But a kid of seventeen, and I was a kid even though I liked to think I was a man, doesn't know anything. He's not experienced. I wasn't. Some of the boys around school or the neighborhood or Washington Park used to say that any girl can be made, but I did feel bad. But I walked out of church like a new person. I always had that feeling after going to confession, and I still do. But I never had it quite as much, quite the same way. I could have walked on air. I saw my way out of what was bothering me and I wouldn't be lowering Mary, who was going to be my wife, Mrs. Mickey Donovan. And she felt good, smiling, happy. She squeezed my hand.

"Mickey, dear, I love you. I'll always love you," she told me, and she squeezed my hand, again.

It was a spring night in June. Now I think back on that night, so many years ago when we were both eighteen and the world was ahead of us. We were absorbed, and there was something fine about our love. I had the finest feeling I have ever had in my life. There was something big in loving Mary and, yes, pure. I had an idea that I understood how my mother and father must have felt, and what love and marriage were. But how am I going to tell you how happy I was and how it felt to be so happy? I don't know that somebody much more articulate than me and better educated could do it.

I felt like I was important, mighty important, the most important guy in the world. I felt that way because Mary loved me, and because I loved her in the right way. And I felt that I was the luckiest guy in the world. And the night was grand, the kind of night on which a young fellow is lonesome as hell if he is alone and doesn't have a girl. It was just one of those nights that make you moody and moony. The sky is big, twenty times as big as the world, twenty times twenty times as big as the world, and you almost could feel that what's inside of you is as big and as important as the sky. And the moon was out, and just to look at it made you think of your girl, made me think of Mary. It was balmy, warm, and the air did something to you, woke up all the feelings I'm trying to suggest.

We walked the two blocks from Crucifixion Church to Schraeder's at 47th and Grand Boulevard for ice cream sodas, past the good houses owned by people who were pretty well off, and thought how we'd one day live in one of those houses, and the whole idea of being married, living alone with Mary, the two of us, became the thing I wanted most in the world. I thought I was grown up and knew what love was, and thought that we'd always be on the high key just as we were then, walking to Schraeder's.

"I feel good, Mickey."

"So do I."

"Do you love me?"

"Yes."

"Really?"

"Yes, honey, I love you. I'm crazy about you. I want to get married right away."

"I wish we could."

And I thought that if only I was a big league ballplayer, we could be married, because a big leaguer earned good dough.

I was a damned-proud guy, walking into Schraeder's with Mary. She was one of the best-looking girls in the neighborhood. I saw Joe Hines and said "Hello," and others I knew.

We were half-kids and half–grown up, but of all the nights of my life, that was one of the best.

In front of the building on Calument Avenue, Mary looked at me. I was awkward.

"It's not a sin if you kiss me good night, Mickey."

I kissed her and I didn't walk home on a cement sidewalk. I walked home on air.

And then, a couple of nights later I had dinner at her house. I didn't at all feel sure of myself. I knew from the way Mary talked of her father that he thought the world of her, and that made me uneasy, uneasy the way not even Walter Johnson ever did. I wasn't on the ball field where I felt at home. I was uneasy and worried for fear that I'd be awkward, or wouldn't talk right or sit right. I was on show, and being tested, and it was all well and good to tell myself that I could meet any test, but I was still worse than plate shy.

Mary's father was a wonderful man, a fine man, and he and I became good friends. He was a big man, about five-eleven, plump, with a paunch, and he was soft although he'd been hard and strong and a pretty good sandlot ballplayer when he was young. He was already gray-haired, and this was becoming. It gave him a sense of dignity and importance. I was in awe of him and a little afraid, the way I would have been of a senator, or of the mayor, or the way I was the first time I saw the Old Roman face to face. All of this was mixed up with me and Mary and that made me feel more shy than I think I ever felt in my life, before or since.

We sat in the big parlor with the shiny furniture and the baby grand piano and a fine, rich, expensive rug, and I was tongue-tied. My tongue was in knots. What did he think of me and Mary? Did he think of me kissing his daughter, and would he trust me? I had all kinds of fears and questions like that in my mind.

He told me he was glad I was coming to dinner so that he and his wife could get to know me better since Mary had taken such a shine to me. I guess I just grinned and blushed.

"You graduated, didn't you, Mickey?"

"Yes, sir."

"Well, now what kind of plans do you have? What are you interested in, what kind of work would you like to do, Mickey?"

"Well, I don't know if I can be what I want to be."

"What's that, Mickey?"

"A baseball player," I said, shyly and almost guiltily.

"That's not easy. You've got to be a crackerjack to get into the big leagues, and if you don't you become a minor league ballplayer. There's no percentage in that. And then what can a fellow do if he's not gotten himself set or trained in some other line? I don't think that if I was a young fellow I'd put all my eggs in a basket like that."

I wasn't ready to hear talk like this from Mr. Collins any more than from my old man. I was too much of a kid. I could see myself being a big league ballplayer, or a soldier, but how could I have thought of myself being important in some other line? I could not even imagine myself being a success in business, working my way up to the top like Horatio Alger. I read some of the Horatio Alger books when I was a kid.

And there I was, wanting to marry Mary and have a good home with her. I wasn't consistent.

"No, Mick, if you want my advice, learn something, work at something with a future in it. Your father is a plumber. You could be apprenticed and learn from him. Then you'd have a trade."

"I don't know that I could be a plumber," I told Mr. Collins, meaning that I didn't know if I wanted to be one.

"You couldn't be a plumber, you say?" he asked, looking at me with surprise.

I didn't know what to say, but I knew I'd pulled a bull.

"You mean you don't want to, don't you, Mickey?"

"Maybe. I've thought all along how I wanted to become a ballplayer, and now, I just graduated, and all of a sudden I'm graduated and now I got to try and get a chance to show what I might be able to do playing baseball."

"Being good out in Washington Park is one thing, and being good in the major leagues is something else, Mick. And here you are with a high school education. That's more than I had. I never finished high school."

I just wished Mary would join us in the parlor, and she did soon. I felt rescued. Soon we went to supper. There was a big, thick steak, and that was my meal. But I was worried about my table manners. I did spill some gravy on the white linen tablecloth and that bothered me because they all saw it. They didn't say anything to me, but I was certain that they were thinking plenty and what they were thinking was that I wasn't suitable for Mary. I'd already gotten the job, driving a horse and wagon. I was a young teamster, really, and when that came out I could tell by the expression on Mr. Collins's face and the way he looked at Mary that he didn't think I was the kind of fellow for her. She had told them I was working, but she hadn't said what I was doing.

"Mickey's just working for the summer because he'll be out in the air and it will make him stronger for baseball," Mary said.

That hurt me. I interpreted what she said as meaning that she was apologizing for me.

Mr. Collins said how he couldn't understand why any young fellow with as much as a high school education would want a job driving a team of horses. You didn't even have to go to grammar school to do that, let alone high school, he said. And he talked about the opportunity there was in America and how things were going to be better than they had ever been in America, once we licked the Germans.

His speaking of the war seemed to make Mrs. Collins sad because her oldest son, Tommy, was already a soldier, and Mary had told me he was going to be sent to France any day.

Mary's mother was a wonderful woman. She was just about as wonderful as my own mother, and now of course I think of her like she was my second mother. She was a wonderful cook, and that night we had a real good supper, just like we did every other time that I ate her cooking. She was tall and thin and still looked young then, not like most of the mothers of the kids and the girls I'd gone to school with. She dressed in the fashion of the day and used lipstick and powder. Ma didn't. I remember Ruthie used to try to get her to and Ma never would. Mrs. Collins was always real nice to me, and that night when I ate supper in the Collins home for the first time, she wanted me to eat a big second helping, which I did, and when Mr. Collins kept talking, she told him once to let me eat.

But I guess this will give you an idea of that dinner, except for Mary's kid brother Harry, who was then about fifteen. He tripped Mary up about baseball and then talked about it. She didn't know anything about baseball, but she had gone all of the way to St. Basil's once to see me play, and another time she'd gone from St. Paul's to Jackson Park and watched us beat St. Stanislaus on a cold day.

"You don't like baseball, you like Mickey, Sis," he said.

I know I must have turned red as a beet, and I wished I could have given him a crack on the nose or bent his arm until he yelled. And I could have sunk through the floor.

"Mind your own business," Mary told him, and it was a giveaway.

Mr. Collins and Mary's mother both told him not to talk that way, but Mr. Collins kept giving me and Mary queer looks, and Harry had really spilled some beans on us. Mary hadn't told them about our having become secretly engaged or the rest of the story either, but thanks to Harry, they knew we were in love.

After we ate, Mr. Collins talked about how a man couldn't support a wife on a teamster's salary and made it plain that while he had nothing against me, he didn't like it to have his daughter dating me if I was only going to be a teamster.

I left in a low mood, even though Mary did give my hand a squeeze, which told me she loved me. And it was another of those wonderful nights. I didn't want to go home. I didn't know what I wanted to do. I wanted Mary with me in the moonlight. Whenever I remember those days and think of Mary and me, and our first days of love and moonlight, I think of that night. I looked at that vacant lot on 50th and Calumet, and there was a mist over it, like silver with the moonlight gleaming, and the vacant lot looked like some place in a dream.

I thought how I wasn't a kid any more, and I felt sorry as hell for myself. I was afraid that Mary's parents would break us up, and I didn't see how I could live or do anything if Mary didn't love me. But her father and mother would never consent to our getting married, I told myself. And they'd turn her mind and she'd look down on me because her parents didn't think that I was good enough for her, and I thought too that they'd think that the Donovans were below the Collins.

"It's all off," I told myself. "She'll think I'm not good enough for her."

I went over to the park. It was like being hurt, seeing other couples, seeing a fellow kissing his girl on a park bench. I heard a couple on the grass, too, the girl moaning and I looked at the sky. I saw the sky full of stars as if I'd never seen the sky and the stars before. Stars, stars—like there were thousands of them. And there was a mist over the park, mist and moonlight. It was beautiful. I wanted love. I wanted Mary to be my wife and to be walking in Washington Park as if it were someplace else, a park or garden of a king where no other couples could go.

By the time I reached the park I was convinced that I'd lost Mary and that it was all over and there wasn't any use of my hoping or even dreaming. It was then that I decided I'd go to war. I'd go downtown the next day and enlist with the first recruiting sergeant I saw. The first booth—army, navy, or marines—was the one where I'd sign up. But I wanted to go into the marines and be sent to France to fight as soon as possible. I'd be killed and be awarded the Congressional Medal of Honor after my death. I'd go to war and die a hero. I walked in the moonlight, killing Germans and dying, giving my life to save that of Mary's older brother, Tommy.

I went to the ball field and stood near Diamond No. 1. In back of me and a little on the left was a field house. I was all alone. I heard the crickets. I wanted to have Mary in my arms and kiss her. I'd never be the big league star I had dreamed of becoming.

There was the big ball field. The diamond was before me. I'd play on it on the coming Sunday afternoon. We had a permit for Diamond No. 1. I thought of the baseball career I'd never have. I imagined myself breaking into the big leagues as a White Sox, leading off and facing Walter Johnson. I stepped up to home base on Diamond No. 1 and put my hands together like I was gripping a bat. I saw myself in a White Sox uniform at the White Sox park on a Sunday with the stands packed. There was Walter Johnson on the mound. I imagined him winding up, pitching. I swung and imagined the roar of the crowd as I connected, lining the ball to right field. I ran down to first base.

I came back to home plate and imagined myself up a second time with the crowd going wild. The bases were full. I went through all of the motions of waiting, swinging my bat, and bang. This time I hit an imaginary double to right center, and I tore down to first, rounded it, and ran toward second base, when I slipped and fell on the wet grass. I got up slowly, feeling like a punctured balloon.

I walked home slowly, and when I got on 51st Street I saw that I had gotten dirt and grass stains on my Sunday suit. You can guess how I felt—like a fool, a goof.

And when I got home, and started sneaking into my room so that they wouldn't see how I had stained my clothes, I heard Ma sobbing and Ruthie crying. It seemed I knew immediately what had happened, before I found out.

Pa had died of a heart attack. Ma and Ruthie and my kid brother, Billy, had gotten him—that is, his corpse—onto the bed in his and my mother's room.

I felt sick, clean through. Sick and hurt. And that's the night I think I became a man. They all looked to me, and I tried to calm them down and prayed with them for the repose of my father's soul. We all knelt at the side of the bed and prayed, while two holy candles burned on the dresser. Pa lay, stiff, and I couldn't fully believe he was dead. In one night, too, he seemed to age so much. Looking at him on the bed, he looked like an old man.

I wanted to cry myself. I wouldn't let myself cry.

CHAPTER FOUR

I

It was about a month after my father's death that I got a telephone
call from the White Sox asking me to go to the ballpark the next morning and try out. The call was made by Harry Grabiner himself, the
secretary of the club. At first I didn't believe the evidence of my ears,
but I said I'd be there at ten o'clock sharp, and then, after I hung up
the receiver, I thought someone was playing a practical joke on me. I
tried to figure out what guy I knew who would play a joke on me, but
I couldn't make up my mind, unless it was Flinty. Flinty would pull
such a trick on me, I decided, but I wasn't sure.

I got myself in a stew about that telephone call, trying to figure it
out, or to dope out who might have pulled this kind of a gag on me, and
also trying to figure out a way I could find out the truth. Who should I
telephone and talk to? I didn't know. I didn't want to let anyone in on
the joke, if it was a joke, because I determined that the laugh wouldn't
be on me. Not the last laugh. I thought of not going to the ballpark,
but then, I'd decide it was true, and that if I didn't go I'd be refusing
to open the door to opportunity, and as everybody used to say in those
days, opportunity knocks only once. It was a quandary, all right. One
minute I was sore at everybody and nobody, and then at Flinty. The
next, I was dreaming of myself as a White Sox, imagining myself sock-
ing the first ball pitched to me in batting practice and parking it out
in the right field bleachers. I went to the telephone to call Joe Hines
and ask his advice but hung up while his number was being rung. I

thought about talking to Mary and her father, but I had stopped seeing her because I had developed the foolish notion that her family thought I wasn't good enough for her. It was false pride. And Mary wouldn't have given me any advice, because she didn't know anything about it. Her father, maybe he could give me advice, I thought. But I wouldn't swallow my foolish pride.

Finally, when I thought I'd go nuts with stewing about that telephone call, I thought of Tim Cahill, and I was lucky to catch him at home. He told me that it was no joke and said he had recommended me to the White Sox. By all means, I should report for the tryout. Then, I was on air. I was in the clouds. I wasn't anywhere near the earth.

And that tryout looked like a way out for me. Pa left some insurance, and Ma was going to get something for his business, but there were five of us, five mouths to feed. Ruthie and I were working, but we were afraid that we'd have to move, take an apartment with lower rent and maybe move to a neighborhood that wasn't as good as the one we lived in.

I was the man of the house, and the main responsibility fell on my shoulders. I said I hadn't been telephoning and seeing Mary, but it wasn't because of how I felt that night I went to supper at Mary's and came home to find out that my father had dropped dead in the dining room after playing some games of Canfield like he did on so many nights. With Pa gone, and two younger kids, a big burden was falling on me, and I felt I had no right to think of getting married for a long time to come. Ruthie was engaged to Tom Cameron and they were going to be married when he came home from the war. At this time, he was in the trenches in France, fighting. The Germans were attacking and I'd been afraid they'd capture Paris and win the war, but they were stopped. Ruthie prayed and worried, and sometimes I'd catch her crying. "After my father—Oh Mother, it just can't happen. Tom can't be killed." I heard her in tears, talking like that to my mother.

I was disappointed that I couldn't join the army or the marines, but it was out of the question with my father just having passed away. It had been an unhappy and miserable few weeks for me. And then, like out of nowhere, there came that telephone call and I was told to report to the White Sox ballpark the next morning for a tryout. I was eighteen then.

It was the biggest break of my life. It was the silver lining in the dark clouds. It was my chance. I'd make good, and then, I could see Mary again. And, if baseball wasn't stopped because of the war, why, I had my chance to be in.

I fell asleep that night, daydreaming about how great I'd be in my tryout and how I'd get a contract and break into the big leagues like a sensation. I imagined hitting a triple off Walter Johnson on my first official American League time at bat.

II

I was up the next morning at seven o'clock, fidgety, and I paced the apartment like a caged lion, I guess. You might have thought I was going to play that day in my first World Series ball game. But then, it was mighty important to me. Looking back on it now, I can see that it was one of the most important days of my life. It was my dream, my life.

After I had breakfast, I didn't know what to do with myself. On other mornings, I'd have been leaving for work. I never did like waiting around, and that's the one thing about the life of a baseball player that I really didn't like. It always was hell, the waiting around. And the waiting on that first morning of my tryout, it was eating me.

I had a second cup of coffee and looked through the open door. It was a sunny morning in July, early morning with that feeling of freshness. God, just thinking of it now makes me wish I had it all over again, and that I was back again in life on that morning in July of 1918. Of course, if I had it all over again, some things could have turned out different and better.

Often now, when I wake up on summer mornings, my mind goes back to when I was young, a boy or a young fellow, a teenager, except we never used the word then, and somehow I can't think of myself as having been what you call "a teenager." But like I said, waking up on those summer mornings, those mornings of June, July, and August and thinking of the day ahead of you, of playing baseball and having that dream of your future so bright and shining in your own mind. And seeing that it was sunny outside and it was going to be another of those good days, and maybe laying in bed and closing my eyes and imagining. What wouldn't I give to have those days back. We never get our second chance.

And that was one of the reasons, I guess, that I was nervous and fit to be tied on that morning of my tryout. I thought, you don't get a second chance. And deep down I was confident. Only I wanted to be in a uniform and out there on the White Sox field, showing my stuff. I remember, too, seeing the sky, clear and blue, a light sky, and thinking that in France there was shot and shell, with fellows like me dying to stop the Germans. I felt like a slacker for a minute even though I knew that I wasn't one. I'd have gone but for my father dying.

"What time do you have to be leaving, Mickey?" Ma asked me.

"Oh Ma, I got lots of time. I don't have to be there at the ballpark until ten o'clock."

"Ten o'clock. By that time, many a man has almost half of a day's work done."

"I know, Ma. But baseball is different," I told her, as I drank my coffee.

"A pity they won't pay you for losing a day's work," Ma said.

I tried to explain to her that I was getting my big chance and that the White Sox didn't owe me nothing, but I wasn't very successful. I felt that the Sox were doing me a favor.

"I don't understand them, keeping a boy from work, to play for them, and them giving him not a cent," she said.

I tried to explain to my mother what it was but she didn't understand and didn't know what it was all about.

Ruthie did but she didn't think anything about it. She didn't take my baseball playing seriously or imagine that I would ever become a professional ballplayer. When she came into the kitchen, she said, "Let him go to his baseball, Ma."

"Who's stopping him? I'm only saying those men shouldn't take him from his work and not pay him."

"If I make good, they'll pay me, Ma, better than I'm getting now."

"They better."

My kid brother, Billy, thought that I was a hero and wanted me to take him with me to the tryout but I told him I couldn't. I didn't think they'd let him in, but I could have taken him with no trouble, only I didn't know it.

It was a long wait before I took the streetcar, going on 51st Street to Wentworth Avenue and then north on Wentworth to 35th. I often took this route to the White Sox ballpark, before that morning, on occasions when I would go to see a ball game, and afterward when I became a player. For years I've wanted to ride that same route and remember how I used to feel and dream. Of course, the streetcars are gone now and there are trolley buses in their stead.

III

I was more shy than most of the kids today, and I was half-afraid I wouldn't be let into the ballpark or the clubhouse that morning. Of course I was. But walking into the clubhouse was in itself something wonderful. I thought I'd have a wonderful feeling too, something I'd never felt before. But I was only confused and felt that I didn't belong. Maybe the players would laugh at me and give me the business.

I almost knocked at the door of the clubhouse, which is under the grandstand on the third base side of the ballpark. Nobody paid attention to me, and I stood there for a moment, feeling like a goof who didn't belong.

A clubhouse is like a dressing room in a barracks, a toilet and a shower, but for the uninitiated kid it's the next thing to heaven, and he thinks, like I did on that morning, that if he only could get inside it, something would happen to him.

Some of the players were dressed, and others were dressing. They didn't pay attention to me. I didn't know it at the time, but kids like me came often to try out and work out at morning practice. We were so many punks and bushers to them. But seeing the players up close in the clubhouse, it was a sight too good to be true. Some of them had been my heroes, and I admired all of them. I'd been a White Sox fan all during my boyhood, like I said, and I knew the records of the players the year they joined the White Sox. Buck Weaver was sitting on the bench before his locker, naked, talking, with every second, third, or fourth word a curse.

"They're goddamn right to think of every friggin' cent they can get," he was saying.

I didn't know what he was talking about but I learned later. At that time, there already was talk of ending the season ahead of schedule. People old enough will remember that the government issued a work or fight order for all men not engaged in industry and in occupations considered essential for the war effort. And Washington then didn't classify baseball as essential like President Roosevelt did in the last war. It wasn't definite that there'd even be a World Series either. The Cubs were in the pennant fight in the National League and looked better than ever to win, and the Cub players were all reported to be talking all of the time about how much money they could get in the Series. A couple of writers were on their necks for talking like this and thinking of money rather than the war and the war effort. Buck was defending the Cub players. That's the first thing I heard him talk about except to say hello to a fan in front of the clubhouse. Like many other kids, I used to stand in front of the clubhouse and watch the players come out of it and leave after a game.

"Maybe there won't be no more goddamn baseball," Chick Gandil said. He was a big, handsome guy, but he looked mean, and I didn't like him even then, the first time I saw him close up in the clubhouse.

I stood a moment, tongue-tied, afraid to say anything, and wanting to turn on my tail and get the hell out of the clubhouse, lickety-split. I noticed Spike Cannon and knew who he was, of course. He was the clubhouse boy. He's still there in charge of the White Sox clubhouse. Then he was about twenty-two, twenty-three. I knew who he was because one day a few summers before he'd come out to the Washington Park ball field on an off-day when no game was scheduled. He was wearing a White Sox shirt and he acted like he owned Washington Park. He let six or seven of us kids stand around and admire the White Sox shirt he was wearing and, of course, the wearer, too. But he seemed kind of snotty to me, and when some of the kids asked him questions, he told us to go fly our kite. Seeing him, my heart kind of fell. He talked gruffly to rookies and kids showing up for a tryout. He asked me what I wanted and my heart was in my mouth a second time.

"Is this the White Sox clubhouse?" I asked.

"Looks like it, doesn't it?" Spike said, very curtly.

"Spike, give the busher a uniform," Swede Risberg said.

"I was told to come down here for a tryout. My name's Mickey, Michael Donovan, and I come from Washington Park," I said, still flustered.

"We don't care where anybody comes from. What we want to know is can he help us win some goddamned ball games," Ray Schalk said.

"Who told you to come down here?" Spike asked, sort of asserting his authority. He was always proud of it and jealous of it.

"Mr. Grabiner. He telephoned me last night. My high school coach, Tim . . ."

"You say your name's Donovan?"

"Yes. Yes, sir," I said.

"Yes, come on."

He turned. I stood for a moment, and then, feeling like I was doing something almost daring, I followed him across the clubhouse. It seemed like those few feet were a block. He gave me a dirty old White Sox suit which he pulled out of a locker.

"This ought to fit you."

I took the suit and stood holding it, like a goof. Then Clarence Rowland came over to me. He was dressed. Somehow, when he walked toward me, I felt more at my ease.

"Hello, boy. You're Donovan, aren't you?"

"Yes, sir."

"Yes, I was expecting you."

That made me feel more calm. I felt that the players were all looking at me, but most of them weren't paying any attention to me.

"How old are you, boy?" Rowland asked.

"Eighteen, sir."

"And where did you play?"

I told him about St. Basil's and that I played with a team in Washington Park, the Rocks.

He shook his head as if he knew all about my playing.

"You're an infielder, aren't you?"

"Yes, sir."

"What position do you play?"

"I play any position, but usually I play shortstop."

I saw Swede Risberg give me a glance, and then he shrugged his shoulders.

"Well, put your uniform on and we'll see what you can do." Then he turned and told the players to get on the field.

"Okay, Professor," Risberg said.

That was the first time I heard him called "Prof" by the players. Most of them didn't like him or think that he knew much about baseball. Of course, I liked him. He was my first manager, and I was sorry when I read in the newspaper at the end of the 1918 season that he wouldn't be back for the 1919 season. He was real nice to me, Rowland was. Now he's an old man and still in baseball. I'm always glad to see him.

But to get on with my story.

The players started piling out of the clubhouse. I undressed and put on my uniform. A tall fellow in uniform came over to me, held out his hand and said, "My name's Stanton, Bill Stanton."

I shook hands with him and told him my name, and he said he was getting a tryout, just like me. His father knew the Old Roman and wanted him to try out. He didn't think he was good enough to make the big leagues, but his old man wanted it. And even if he did get signed up, he'd be going as soon as they pulled out the draft numbers. He was twenty-one and he'd be throwing hand grenades at the Germans and Kaiser Bill, not baseballs. Baseball was going to fold up anyway, and nobody knew anything about the future of the game.

I was afraid of that because of what I'd been reading in the newspapers, but I didn't say anything. But I just couldn't think of baseball not continuing.

By that time I had the uniform on. I felt as if I had never worn a baseball suit before, and I wanted to earn the right to wear that uniform every day. I wanted to be proud of that uniform.

IV

I mentioned Bill Stanton. There's a story I ought to add. When Bill and I walked into the dugout, a busher named Tex Morgan was standing there. He was a big, dumb busher who'd been with the club for about ten days. He'd pinch hit once and struck out. Tex walked up to Bill and asked, in a southern drawl, what position he played. Bill said he was trying out for the outfield and that he usually played center field.

"You all ain't taking my job away from me," Tex said, and he blew a gob of tobacco juice in Bill's face.

Bill just took out a handkerchief and wiped his face. I couldn't have done that. I'd have torn into the dumb busher. Bill was right. He explained that if he was to have gotten into a fight the minute he put his foot in the dugout, what chance would he have had, especially since

Tex had been considered a good prospect, even though he turned out to be a lemon.

I looked pretty good in my tryout. I was determined. I hit the ball well when I took batting practice and made some good hits, one or two of them doubles. But once I batted against Eddie Cicotte, and he threw the ball past me so fast I couldn't see him. I hadn't any idea he was so fast, and then, he must have been thirty-three or thirty-four. But determined as I was, when I watched the White Sox infield, I was depressed. Being on the field and seeing them was different from watching way out in the right or left field bleachers. I think the team was then in fourth place and sinking into second division, but they had their 1917 world championship infield, Chick Gandil, Eddie Collins, Swede Risberg, and Buck Weaver, and that's as great an infield as I ever saw.

I asked myself, "What the hell am I doin' here?"

Eddie Collins and Buck Weaver were great ballplayers, and Swede Risberg and Chick Gandil were almost up to them. The way they handled the ball and played their position was beautiful to watch. And Buck Weaver was the greatest third baseman of them all, the greatest of them all that I saw. My God, did he have baseball intelligence! He was all baseball intelligence. He knew where to play every pitch, and he could do everything right. He could pick up a bunt or slow roller without bending down for the ball and make his throw. You didn't bunt on him, not often. He had a standing bet of five dollars with Ty Cobb that he'd throw him out every time Cobb tried to bunt on him. I never saw Cobb beat him. I don't think I ever saw Cobb even try to beat out a bunt when Buck was playing third base.

That week of my tryout, I worked at shortstop and also at second and third base. I did pretty good in every position. You could put me anywhere except pitching or catching and I could play the position, and I think I could have caught, too. I didn't like catching or I would have tried it. It was then that I first noticed some funny things. Chick Gandil and Eddie Collins didn't speak off the field, and they scarcely did on the field either. I noticed that Gandil's throwing seemed peculiar in practice. He didn't throw much to Eddie Collins, and when he'd throw the ball home to Ray Schalk, he'd throw it high or wide or in the dirt, and Ray would curse him, but it didn't do any good. Gandil was a big fellow and tough as they come. He and Risberg were both real tough. Well, a couple of times when I was in the infield, I ran from shortstop or second base for him to throw the ball to me, but he didn't. Twice he turned and made the motion to throw, but then he flung the ball to Ray.

"Throw the ball to the kid," Ray yelled once.

"Shut up, you German runt," Gandil yelled, flinging the ball at him.

"You goddamned big hunk," Ray said.

Of course, ballplayers don't talk a language for the parlor. They use *words*, all the words that you don't like used in front of your wife. But when I tell you about what the players might have said at one time or another, you can imagine what the words are and there isn't any use in my repeating them much. I never liked these words. I don't know why except I guess it was because of Ma and because my old man didn't curse much, except for a "hell" or a "damn" or something like that.

And anyway, I thought that Ray and Gandil were going to set to it, but they didn't.

"Hey, for Christ's sake, if you guys want to fight, join the navy," Buck Weaver yelled at them.

Rowland couldn't stop them and didn't say much.

This came as a surprise to me. The ballplayers weren't much what I expected them to be. I don't know exactly what I expected them to be like, but it was something different from what I found. They were my idols, my heroes. It wasn't quite the same as it is nowadays concerning ballplayers. Today, you hear it said all of the time that the ballplayer is the hero and the inspiration of the kids, and that the player has got to live up to the hopes of the kids. There wasn't much talk or publicity of that kind when I was a kid or when I broke into the big leagues. You didn't read or hear much of the private lives of the players, and there wasn't gossip in the newspapers like there is now. You just thought a player was somebody different, not like anyone you know, not like your old man or the fathers of the kids you knew. Without thinking of the idea at all, you imagined that they lived in a world all of their own. Hell, you thought of them almost like they were gods. To be a ballplayer was almost like going to heaven. You didn't think or imagine much of what heaven was like, either, but you wanted to go there, because you could always be happy, or you'd burn in hell. A baseball player's life was in another world to me.

I thought of players different from other people, people I knew. To

me, they were baseball players in uniform, out there on the field playing baseball, which was the most important thing in the world to me.
They were playing historic ball games. I was seeing them as my father
had seen the Hitless Wonders. I would watch them come out of the
clubhouse and down the clubhouse steps in their street clothes after a
ball game, but I thought of them first of all as ballplayers in uniform.
It was naive on my part, but when I first saw them in the clubhouse,
half-dressed or naked, it was kind of a shock to me. It was almost as if
I was discovering that they were human beings like all of us instead of
idols, almost gods. Kids maybe are different today, not shy as I was. I
was too shy ever to think of asking a player for an autograph. I'd have
been afraid to. When I was a kid, I never saw another kid go up to a
player and try to get an autograph. We kids didn't dare speak to the
players. I don't think young ballplayers coming up to the big leagues
are quite the same today.

It was kind of a shock to me to hear the players cursing and snarling
at each other; and some of them seemed quite cynical about baseball.
They liked to play. Buck Weaver loved to play ball. But it was their
living. And me, I was a pop-eyed kid. But nobody got my goat. Gandil
sometimes threw them in the dirt, or over my head, but I tried for
everything. I gave everything I had, and practicing on the White Sox
ball field, I was impressed. In a way, I couldn't believe that it was true,
or that I wasn't dreaming it all. But I went after the ball, I threw, and
I dug in at the plate when I was told to hit and I hit it.

That week flew by me. I didn't know what kind of impression I was
making, or what any of the players thought of me as a prospect. Some
of them hardly talked to me, or if they did they addressed me as "you"
or "busher."

Buck was real nice. "Hello, kid," he'd say every morning after my
first one, and he'd smile. Buck smiled a lot. He asked me how I was
or said something. That made me feel good because he had been my
idol, more than any other player, even Eddie Collins. Nearly all of the
players liked him, and players on other teams did, too. They kidded a
lot with him, and he kidded, and he was very much like a guy I might
have known and played ball with out in Washington Park.

He didn't like Eddie Collins, and a lot of the players didn't. Eddie was
getting $15,000, and I don't know what Buck got that season, $6,000 or

$7,000. The next year, that was 1919, he got $7,500, but that was on a new three-year contract. But Eddie was different, smart, intelligent, a college graduate, and there weren't so many college graduates in baseball then. Eddie was the only one on our club, I think. He was a great ballplayer, just about the smartest I ever saw. He knew it and had a lot of confidence. He was kind of morose, and some of the players had no use for him. Buck used to say he was only out for himself, but he was a great team player. If he saw a young player was good, he'd help him and tell him things. After a couple of days, he spoke to me, and called me "Donovan." I didn't know it then but I later found out that he told Rowland I was a real good prospect. But he didn't say much to me except a hello or something like that during my tryout week.

The White Sox weren't going anywhere that season, and it didn't seem to make much difference. The players were worried about their status, and the draft. The papers said that married men and those with dependents weren't going to be drafted, but nobody seemed to know what was happening or what was going to happen. You didn't know how long the season would last and if the World Series would even be played. There was talk and rumors in the newspapers that the schedule might be revised so that travel could be cut down and that eastern teams would only play with eastern teams, and the same for the four western clubs in the league. The ballplayers didn't know from day to day what would happen and they didn't know what to do.

The country was patriotic, and there was lots of talk about slackers, and sometimes a man was looked at mighty queer on the street if he wasn't in uniform. There was bloody fighting in Europe and our own soldiers were in it, acquitting themselves with glory. You didn't feel right, walking around in civvies, that is, civilian clothes. I know I didn't. The players talked about all these things in the clubhouse. And they had to drill, too. I was in two drills that week, and I couldn't stay in step. We marched with bats over our shoulders, and then there was practice. The circumstances of those days put queer thoughts in my head. I could only break in, I reasoned, if some of the veterans enlisted or were drafted. It made me feel a little lousy. I couldn't wish for one of the veterans to go off to war and be killed so that I could get my chance, but I wanted to break in. I knew I was young and could be shipped to the minors for seasoning, and then come back when the veterans had aged, but I wanted to stay in the majors, and I tried like hell.

Bill Stanton tried too, but he expected to be going into the army. He thought I was good and might develop into a big leaguer, if baseball didn't fold up for keeps. Rowland told me that I ought to play all the baseball I could. But I wasn't told anything else about myself, and at the end of my last practice session on Friday of that week, I was alternating on hope and gloom, just awful gloom. I did the same things I had done on the other mornings, and every minute or two I wondered if Rowland would call me and tell me the news. But he didn't, and the practice session ended. We tramped back to the clubhouse, and I was still hoping.

"Well, another week gone," I said to Bill Stanton. I was talking with him, hoping that he might be able to tell me something, when I knew that he was like me. He knew nothing.

"Yeah, Mickey. Another week, and we had our chance. Well, at least, we can both say that we had a tryout with the White Sox. That might impress some loogin here or there around some of the parks in this burg."

"Yeah, but that cuts no friggin' ice," I said.

I fell into the habit quickly of talking like the players. Of course, the fact that I had my tryout did impress fellows in Washington Park and kids around the neighborhood. Almost any young guy who wanted one could have gotten a tryout then if he really wanted one and asked for it, but most fellows didn't know that and it wasn't too many who tried on their own behalf. You sort of thought or imagined that if you just showed up, said you were good and wanted a tryout, why you'd get booted out of the ballpark. You didn't expect any welcome mats or red carpets, and while you knew that ball clubs needed and wanted new young fellows who had the goods, you somehow felt they got them and that you might not be welcomed or taken seriously if you showed up without having been asked or recommended. I had no very clear idea as to how I was going to break into baseball. It was going to happen somehow or other, I hoped and dreamed.

Nowadays, there are scouts everywhere, all over the country, and there isn't any kid who goes without scouts from a number of clubs taking a look at him if he shows any ability whatsoever. And a kid gets coaching and is taught. The attitude is entirely different. It doesn't mean much for a kid to say he's been looked at or that he tried out with a big league club. All of the clubs hold clinics for prospects and some of them, like the Washington club, run a baseball school. If a kid is persistent and thinks he's got the ability, he can get himself looked at easy. And today a kid gets off much easier when he joins a big league club than in the old days.

I walked into the club expecting to see Harry Grabiner there waiting for me, or else for Spike Cannon to have a message telling me I was to go to Grabiner's office to sign my contract. There was no reason on earth why they should have signed me. After all, they had Chick Gandil at first, Eddie Collins at second, Risberg at shortstop, and Buck at third base. Then there was Fred McMullen, who would have been a regular on most of the other major league clubs. He'd been the regular third baseman in the 1917 series, with Buck at short. The White Sox had need for me like they had holes in the head, and I knew it. But when you're a kid and you've got a dream in your head, you think of that dream and of it coming true.

For me, every second in the clubhouse was precious. I felt that if I wasn't told that I was being signed up, then my ambition to be a player was hopeless. I looked at the players, envying them, wanting so much, so damned much, to be one of them, even a sub. They walked into the clubhouse, belonging there, sure of their jobs. It was like me walking into our home on Prairie Avenue.

I remember Buck getting a cigar from Spike and lighting it. He sat before his locker puffing on that cigar, blowing out smoke, and saying, "Next season, I'll be a mother's ———, if I don't hit way over .300."

"Next season, you'll have your ass full of mud somewhere in France, Buck," Chick Gandil said.

"I'll let him take care of the Kaiser," Buck said, nodding his head at Ray Schalk, who was standing on his left foot and pulling off his uniform.

"No goddamn draft board will take him. They'll tell him he's a minor," Chick Gandil said of Ray.

"Maybe his draft board won't take him, but John McGraw or Hughie Jennings would take him faster than the Peach could steal a base," Buck said.

"Goddamn right they'd take me. Goddamn right they'd take me to catch on their ball clubs," Ray said.

"If John McGraw takes you, Ray, put in a word for me with him," Buck said.

"He's a goddamn hard man to work for," Chick Gandil said.

"Maybe he's hard on the ball field but his club ain't so friggin' hard on the day the ballplayer gets his paycheck," Buck said.

"You bastards talking about paychecks when we got a war to win," Fred McMullen said, kidding.

"Won't win no war if the soldiers fight like this club plays ball," Ray said.

Ray walked into the shower.

"Look at that thin ass," Gandil said.

I loved it all. I didn't want to take the uniform off. I might never put one on again, I mean a White Sox uniform. That's the way I was thinking.

"You Yanks, you all talkin' about war. If Uncle Sam wants soldiers to win this war, he knows where to get 'em in Texas," Tex Morgan said.

None of the players spoke. They thought he was a fresh busher.

I had sat there listening. I took a long time taking my shoes off, and then I knocked the dirt out of the spikes. I dropped one shoe on the floor. I let the other shoe hit the floor. Out of the corner of my eye, I watched Rowland. He had been speaking with Eddie Collins. Then he talked with Eddie Cicotte. Then, he undressed and went into the showers. I knew I wasn't going to be signed up. But I dallied waiting to hear what I knew I wasn't going to hear. It seemed kind of cruel to get so far and then to have to go back to playing on the Rocks. By the middle of the week, I had stopped thinking of the last day, Friday, and it had seemed that I'd go on all the rest of the summer, and unlikely that I'd even be signed and play.

I took my suit off like a mope. Bill was beside me.

"Seein' the ball game again today?"

"Yeah," I said.

Bill and I had seen all of the games free that week. We were let back in free at the players' gate after going out and having something to eat.

"Well, don't mope so long. I'm hungry," Bill said, getting up to take his shower.

I finished undressing and took my shower, thinking it was maybe my last one.

When Bill and I left, Rowland said, "Donovan, you want to keep playing all the ball you can. Play semipro ball instead of playing sandlot out in Washington Park."

That took some of the lead out of me. I couldn't ask him to recommend me but I wanted to. I didn't have to. He did, but other things happened before I played semipro ball.

V

That Sunday following my tryout I played with the Rocks. We played a rough, tough team. I think the name was the Owls. Flinty had told us the Owls, or whatever their name was, were real tough and good, too, and we'd have to play our asses off to win. There was something like $20 or $25 on the game. We played on Diamond No. 3. That was near Cottage Grove on 51st Street at the north end of Washington Park.

It was kind of gratifying to be looked at the way I was and to overhear a couple of men I didn't know saying, "That kid's named Donovan. The White Sox gave him a tryout."

I'd practiced one night with the Rocks that week and they had asked me lots of questions about the Sox players, especially Joe Hines. They were all proud of me. Some of them, but not Joe, were envious. That was something I learned. Everybody isn't glad if you make good and become somebody. You get patted and slapped on the back, but some of them want to see you strike out with the bases full.

The Owls, or whatever the name of that team was, were a hard bunch. And they gave me the razz from the minute the game started. Some of their gang or their followers had come along to see the game and to do their duty in case a fight broke out. They were on my tail, too. They called me plenty. When I came to bat, some of them yelled, "White . . . . Sox. White . . . . Sox. White . . . . Sox. Shit!" They thought that was funny. And they yelled and cursed me to thunder when I struck out my first time at bat, missing a fast ball at my knees.

Some of the Rocks thought I had a swelled head, too. But their pitcher, a little fellow with a lot of speed, didn't fool me anymore. I got two straight hits. The game was tied up, something like 5-5 or 6-6, in the sixth or seventh inning when a fight started. It turned into a near riot and the cops had to save us. The Owls had too many followers. I didn't get hurt. One big guy swung on me and missed. Flinty was in the center of the scrap, pummeling like a little champion. The fight was broken up and we stayed in the fieldhouse while the park cops protected us. The umpire ran away with the money.

That was my last game with the Rocks. I was hired to play semipro ball, shortstop for the Morgan Aces. I played years later with them and Buck Weaver was at short then. I played second. But back in 1918, I didn't get to play with the Morgan Aces. I had a whole series of boils, and they were mighty painful. Two of them were lanced by the doctor. In August, when I was ready to play after the damned boils, there was another telephone call from the White Sox front office. I was asked to go down to the club offices at the ballpark the next morning at ten o'clock and to bring a parent or guardian so that my contract could be signed legally.

By then, the Sox were really wrecked by the war. Besides the players they had lost early in the season, Eddie Collins had gone into the marines. Risberg and McMullen left to join the colors. Their infield was shot except for Chick Gandil and Buck Weaver. For a couple of games, they had Eddie Murphy in the infield. Eddie was called "Honest Eddie," and he was one hell of an offensive ballplayer. If he could have fielded a ball, our club in 1919 and 1920 would have been stronger than it was. And talk about pinch hitters today all you want, but there's been few if any I ever heard of who were tougher than Eddie in the clutch. In 1919 he hit .486 and .339 in 1920. He was only used as a pinch hitter. In my time I don't recall hearing the word "clutch hitter." It came later.

I don't need to tell you how I felt after that telephone call. I'm sure you can well imagine it. I remember I went out and walked and walked, just thinking of it. I kept telling myself, "Tomorrow, I'll be a White Sox ballplayer."

I wanted to telephone Mary to give her the news, and even to this day I regret that I didn't. I had worked myself all the way around to the notion that I wasn't wanted at the Collins home because I didn't have dough or prospects. And I used to think and daydream of getting even by suddenly becoming a star, making the Collins family realize what they had missed for Mary, all when it was too late. But I couldn't stick to that story. So I would imagine a reconciliation after I became the star. The truth is that I was ashamed and stubborn.

It was a summer evening and just after there had been a terrific heat spell. I remember being uncomfortable in the heat with bandages on my legs because of the boils that were draining. I walked around the neighborhood. I couldn't believe it, and I believed it. All of those streets—51st, 50th, Prairie Avenue, Calumet, South Park, Grand Boulevard. These, too, were the same, and it's now South Parkway, Michigan, 48th. These streets. That was a wonderful neighborhood, and I have never lived on any other one about which I feel quite the same. And the people on it were mighty damned fine and decent people, too. I have always missed that neighborhood. And so has Mary. The colored drove everybody out of it. Now all of the grown-up folks of those days must be dead. Almost all of them, at least. And those of us who were kids in that old neighborhood and grew up in it are now gray haired. I sit and think of this. It happens over and over again, new generations come, old ones go, and their time comes. And the new generations are like all of us have been when we were young. They don't think of the older ones and many of the things the older ones think about and remember. My old man, he must have thought and worried about many things that I don't know anything about. Sitting there in our dining room, playing Canfield, he was growing old and I was full of myself only.

It was that night in August. I remember I stopped in at Crucifixion and said a few prayers and lit a holy candle for Pa. I liked to think then, and I still like to think, that he helped me, may his soul rest in peace. Yes, I said a few prayers in thanks for my old man. I'd try to make good for him, I decided, as well as for Mary and because—well, I knew that I had to make good. That's the way I was built. And my old man could look down and be a bit proud of me because I'd be able to look out for everyone he loved, his family.

I came out of the church and thought of Mary and I wanted to be with her terribly. I walked. I had an ice cream soda at Schraeder's and saw a couple of fellows I knew. I was itching to tell them the news but I didn't. It was more than shyness. I relished the idea of the dramatic surprise when people might read about it in the newspapers or see my name in a box score. I thought of that. I'd get my name in a box score. And once I did no one could erase it. It meant that I had gotten up to the big leagues, and I was in the official records.

Of course I was hoping to get right into the lineup, and I expected I would before the season was over, but I didn't know I would right off the bat. I had been laid up with boils, like I said, but I was sure I could go into the ball game and show my stuff. I remember that I hadn't gone to Washington Park that night because I had decided to play on the safe side one more night. I was to have been on the Morgan Aces on the next Saturday. It was a Thursday night.

I walked all around on the streets I had walked on and that were familiar to me ever since I'd been a kid. Growing up I had gone all around that neighborhood dreaming and thinking that when I grew up to be a man, I'd be a big leaguer. And there I was, eighteen, Mickey Donovan, White Sox. I thought how lucky I was, getting my start so young. I could play twenty-five years and I'd only be forty-three.

It was getting dark. There was daylight saving time then, I remember. It was because of the war that daylight saving time was first started. And it was getting dark. Where there were front porches, people were sitting on them, talking and letting the day go away, like Pa and my mother sat on the back porch sometimes on summer nights. People were walking and I knew many of them and they'd say "hello" and I'd say "hello." I told myself that they didn't know that they might be reading about me in the newspapers in a day or two. Strangers passing me on the sidewalk didn't know that they had just walked by Mickey Donovan on the night before he began his meteoric and sensational and scintillating and brilliant baseball career.

That night seems only like yesterday to me. Only like yesterday. And it's a long time ago. A long time ago in any man's life. A mighty long time ago in the life of a baseball player or an ex–baseball player. I was just a kid, and you could fill volumes with what I didn't know then. It isn't that I know so much now, but I have had experience. I think now how I told myself on that night that I was lucky. I was luckier than I could have realized then. Most people don't have too much in their lives. Their friends and family know them, and their business associates or those they work with. But the world never hears about them or knows that they lived or died. We're all sort of alike, and want people to know about us, and remember us, and we want to have some kind of fame or celebrity. That's why people need heroes and why they love baseball and will always love it unless the game is killed by greed. I had, well, a little bit of fame and celebrity. I'm not in the Hall of Fame like Eddie Collins, Ray Schalk, and many men I played with and against, Ty Cobb, Babe Ruth, Tris Speaker, Walter Johnson, Lou Gehrig, and others. But I had my chance and my day. And ever since that night I've been talking about, that August night, practically, I've always had something I could tell myself. I could always say to myself this: "I'm Mickey Donovan."

Maybe that's not so much, but it can't be taken away from me, and I'm in the records. I got into the box score of this life or the box score of my time, and the figures in that box score—well, with the mistakes or errors I might have made, yes, well, it's the best I could do.

And so I walked around, and it got dark, and I thought, and at times I was kind of stunned or numbed with the news, and I thought how, unless baseball was killed by the war, I just had the most wonderful future and that almost every kid in America of my age or younger would have envied me if they knew me. Everything I thought I had been living for was going to come to me. Of course, I had not then made good. But I really didn't have doubts but that I would.

That night, like you could guess, is one that has always stood out in my memory. But I did, too, think of the war. I thought how I wasn't fighting and felt I should be. I wasn't a slacker. I was put on the spot at eighteen of being a man with a family. I thought of the American dough boys and devil dogs fighting the Germans, of some of them being killed, robbed of having any of the kind of chances I was getting, and I was getting them ahead of schedule because of the war. And I hoped and hoped and hoped that the war wouldn't kill baseball. But I really knew it wouldn't and that America would win. And I really knew that I'd make the big leagues.

I guess I must have walked around an hour, an hour and a half, two hours. I went home and hit the hay and fell asleep dreaming of myself making four straight hits in a World Series game, winning the series and becoming a World Series hero.

VI

Ma was in mourning. She dressed up in a black silk dress and black hat and wore a black veil to go with me to see Harry Grabiner at the offices at the White Sox ballpark. It was an exciting morning. Ma was proud of me, even though she knew nothing about baseball, as I have already indicated. If they telephoned for me and asked for her to come along, then it was something important. My kid brother and sister looked up to me as a hero. Before rushing out to catch the El train for work, and afraid as usual that she'd be late again, Ruthie said I simply must wear my Sunday suit, look neat and make a good impression. I wanted to go down to the ballpark in my shirtsleeves or wearing my sweater, but Ma would have none of that, and said that either I dressed up and did what she wanted or she was sitting right where she was on a straight-backed chair in the kitchen.

"You're only eighteen, Mickey, a minor," she said joking, but I knew Ma, and behind her joke she meant it. So I got dressed up.

I didn't like it, having to have my mother go with me, and no kid would. I loved my mother but I didn't want to have it thought that I was tied to her apron strings. I could go out and get jobs myself, but she had to go with me to sign my contract. Of course it stuck in my craw.

I carried my glove, spiked shoes, and jockstrap in a big paper grocery bag. Ma always saved bags. Walking to 51st Street to get the streetcar, Ma said, "What a pity your father didn't live to go with you today, instead of me!"

It would have been different if I was going with my father. And I missed him. I could see that my mother did. Sometimes, she would sit alone in her room and cry.

We took the same route, 51st to Wentworth, Wentworth to 35th Street. I felt a little foolish, I guess. Harry Grabiner was there and had a contract ready. Harry was a little, sharp man, and I don't think he liked ballplayers too well. He was a tough man to talk to when you were holding out or arguing for a raise, but of course in the Old Roman's day, Harry was carrying out the Roman's orders. I thought I was going to meet the Old Roman instead of Harry, but I didn't. We went upstairs to Harry's office under the grandstand and were brought to him, sitting at a big desk. On the wall were some pictures that caught my eye, one of Ed Walsh, another of Fielder Jones, manager of the Hitless Wonders, and a third of the Old Roman in his playing days. All three of them were, of course, retired, and I thought of how you would be remembered if you became a great player, and I wanted to be remembered. I thought that someday I wanted a picture of myself to be hung on the wall in the White Sox offices. And I wished I could have been alone to see Harry Grabiner and sign my first contract.

Harry explained that the club wanted to sign me for the remainder of the season. I had looked promising in my tryout. If I did well in the few weeks left of the 1918 season, of course, I would be offered a contract for 1919. He told my mother that this was a great opportunity for me, and he handed her the contracts. He asked her to sign them for me and showed her where to put her name. My salary was to be at the rate of $150 a month with a monthly bonus of $50 for giving the club an option on the renewal of my contract the next season. I was a little disappointed, or rather surprised, because I had been under the impression that the salary of a ballplayer was a little more than that. But I'd have signed for $1 a year. Because of the war, the 1918 season was curtailed and ended on Labor Day. So I only had a couple of days more than a half-month, and with the bonus I got somewhere between $140 or $150 as a White Sox in 1918.

It was a Friday morning when my contract was signed, and on the next Sunday evening the White Sox were scheduled to go to New York on an eastern trip. My mother seemed like she was going to balk at that, and I could have fallen or sunk right through the floor. She spoke about my never having traveled alone before, and was concerned that I not miss Mass. But Harry Grabiner didn't talk to my mother the way he might have to a ballplayer trying to get a raise. He told her that it was an honor for a young man like myself to travel as a member of the White Sox, and said that the men on the team were heroes to the boys and men of America and that they would be a good example for me and that they were almost all married men with families. And he spoke of the Old Roman, what a fine and noble man he was, the friend of important men. My mother was impressed, all right. Harry asked about my clothes, if I had a suitcase, and would I have everything I needed for the trip on Sunday night. He gave my mother and me some advice about traveling, suggested that I had better get an extra suit if possible and said that if I went in the morning to the Hub downtown in the Loop to get it, he would telephone the store and ask them to be sure to have it ready in case alterations were needed. I wouldn't have thought of such things and might have gone like a true yokel on my first trip if Harry Grabiner hadn't reminded my mother and me.

Anyway the contract was signed, and Harry had the $50 bonus and a $25 advance on my salary given to me so that I'd have enough to buy what was necessary for the trip. Ma, of course, took the money. I gave her my salary checks until I was married. My old man always brought his earnings home to my mother, and I had been doing the same while driving the wagon.

I missed the military drill with bats that morning but did get on the field for part of the practice. Spike Cannon gave me my suit, but it was a dirty one. Harry Grabiner was saving money on laundry bills that season, but I didn't care. I liked playing in a dirty white suit. Buck Weaver usually had the dirtiest suit on the ball field, and I sort of liked the idea of emulating him. Batting practice was ending when I reported to Rowland. He had me take a few swings. Eddie Cicotte was on the mound, pitching batting practice. I remember stepping up to the plate, digging in, and then, with a grin, he threw. He might have been pitching in a World Series instead of to a rookie in practice. He threw a fastball by me that I saw, but maybe I saw it in a dream. I cut a lot of air with my bat. He curved on me, and all I did hit was about three ground balls, one-two and you're out. If Eddie had pitched that way in 1919 in the Series, I wouldn't be trying to tell my story and my entire baseball career might have been much different. Eddie himself and nearly everybody in the club would have had a different life. I guess he pitched hard to me to test me and put me in my place.

Clarence Rowland told me to take second base for infield practice. Buck Weaver was at short. I was raggedy and didn't look good.

"Take it easy kid—relax yourself," Buck yelled over to me.

I was relaxed enough but I had to handle the ball and get my soundings after not playing for a couple of weeks because of my boils. I knew enough not to make any excuses or give alibis for my bum showing in that infield practice. I never liked alibiing. I settled down a little before we finished practicing. But I was open-mouthed by Buck. What a beautiful ballplayer he was. The exhibition he gave that morning was almost enough to walk off of the field and never come back.

"How in hell can I ever play with these fellows?" I asked myself on the field. But I spit in my glove and told myself that I had to.

When I played a few semipro games with Buck on the Morgan Aces, I talked with him and told him how I felt during that first practice. He laughed and told me how he felt much the same when he saw his first big league game. That was about 1908 or 1909. He saw Charlie Dooin's Phillies. "I'm a goof, I'm a goof. I can't play with these fellows," Buck told me.

I walked off the field that sunny August morning thinking that I might be in the lineup that afternoon, playing second base in Eddie Collins's position. Me, Mickey Donovan, an eighteen-year-old kid trying to fill the shoes of the greatest second baseman who ever lived. And I'd be playing alongside Buck Weaver.

It was like the world was all miracles.

And then, as I trotted off the field when Rowland called the end, I suddenly realized that we were playing the Detroit Tigers. If I played, I'd be playing against Ty Cobb.

VII

I remember that I had a sandwich and a cup of tea in a restaurant on Wentworth Avenue on my first day as a member of the White Sox. As I was walking on 35th by the big park, I saw Ray Schalk and a couple of the players go into a wooden frame house across on the other side of 35th. They were going to have lunch with Ma Kelly. I only met her later, and she was a wonderful woman, wonderful to ballplayers. That was the first time I noticed her place.

I was shy about going back to the clubhouse ahead of time, but I had no place to go and there was nothing to do. I walked on Wentworth Avenue and then, hearing some kids shouting, I drifted into Armour Square Park. A playground tournament was being held. There were a hundred kids in short pants, maybe more. A few men in sweatshirts or shirtsleeves were with them, and one was umpiring a game in progress. These men were playground directors from public parks and playgrounds on the Southside. I guess playground ball isn't played any more. They play softball instead. And the mayor has hired Rogers Hornsby to teach the kids how to play the game right. Like I've already mentioned, there was nothing like that in my time. Around my neighborhood, there wasn't a public playground during my short-pants days, so I didn't play any playground ball except a couple of times when I was more or less of a ringer and helped Fuller Park win the Southside championship. Playground ball was played with a big indoor ball and you didn't wear a glove. There were ten on a team, with two shortstops. One played the regular shortstop position between second and third base and the other played up close to the batter to get twisting balls hit on the ground near home plate. No bunting was allowed. It was optional with the batter to run to first base or third on a batted ball. The pitcher threw underhanded.

Well, I stood watching the kids for maybe a half-hour. Hell, I was only a few years older than some of them. Four years before, I'd played in the same kind of tournament and had yelled and screamed like they were doing. And there I was, signed up as a big leaguer and expecting to make my debut that afternoon. In the morning or final box score edition of the evening newspapers there might be a story about the Sox signing me up. If I played in the game that afternoon, some of the kids on the playground might see my name in the box score. If they were like what I was, they'd be interested and curious about my name. And maybe I'd become the favorite of some of the kids, and they'd look at the box score every morning or night to see how I'd done, feeling happy if I hit and fielded good and disappointed if I had a bad day.

That's how Buck became my favorite. I saw his name in a box score back in 1912, his first season. He was a rookie and his name caught my eye, or my fancy. I'd followed him ever since and don't think that in all of those years I missed seeing and reading one White Sox box score. Buck, he didn't know that anymore than I'd know it if I became the favorite player of some kid or other. You don't play for the kids, but you like to think that some of them or some of the grown-up fans are rooting especially for you.

The kids were playing, making a hell of a lot of noise, and so I watched, thinking along the line of what I've said here. The kids were pretty good, and I stood there with my hands stuck in my pockets and my cap pushed back on my head, dreamily watching. I sort of wished I was one of them in short pants and playing in the tournament. Just those five days of my tryout and the morning practice I'd participated in after Ma signed me up, well, that was enough for me to catch on that big league ball isn't at all like games you play just for the fun of it. It was a living, a trade, just as plumbing was my old man's trade. It isn't done anymore, but when I broke in, many of the players traded hits so that they could boost their batting averages and maybe get a raise the next season. I'd heard talk of trading hits in the Sox clubhouse, mention of some players in other clubs who tried to do this and even were like beggars, asking for hits instead of pennies. Most of the time, hits were traded when the outcome of a game or a pennant race wasn't at stake. So I guess it might be more exact to call it mutual aid instead of crookedness. I never traded hits because I always wanted my hits to be earned, but many times when nothing was at stake, I let a player I liked get a hit.

But the kids I watched, they were just having fun. They were just playing ball. It didn't matter much if they made hits or errors, except to the kids themselves. Of course, and like I said, I dreamed of making the big leagues, but I'd always played ball like those kids were. But in the big leagues, a ball game had to be for keeps because everyone in it was making his living that way. All of this thinking, of course, really meant that I was growing up. I was becoming a man. And also I was beginning to get what I call the big league feeling. It's a feeling that sets you apart from other people. You feel different. You're a ballplayer, or you're in baseball in some other capacity. You're in the inside, and everybody else is on the outside. I don't know if I am clear, but what I'm trying to say is that your life is in baseball, and everything else, even your wife, revolves around baseball. Everybody has heard it said that birds of a feather flock together, and this was one of my mother's favorite sayings. People in baseball are birds of a feather.

I was just beginning to feel all this when I watched the kids playing in Armour Square. But I wished I was with the kids and not the White Sox. It was just a passing feeling of course, but I remembered it all of these years. It was a beginning of a new life, with new associations. After I was in baseball a year or so, I drifted away from old friends, not because I got a swelled head or anything like that, but because we didn't have anything much that was common between us. There was baseball, but the game was different to me than to them. I was living it. Maybe it's like Latin. You can translate Latin into English although I was punk at doing it, but there is a difference.

I watched the kids. This was something for me only to remember and never to live again, my days as a kid, my days growing up, all my days before Ma put her John Hancock on my first White Sox contract.

Then I left the playground. "Now I'll go to make the name and fame of Mickey Donovan," I told myself as I walked back fast to the ballpark and clubhouse. I wanted to run. And somehow or other, it wasn't in me to think that I wouldn't make the grade.

VIII

Like I said, I was impressed to be playing in the American League, alongside Buck Weaver and against Ty Cobb. I was at second base. I just felt something, being on the ball field with him, seeing him, getting into position when Old Joe Benz, our pitcher, wound up and pitched to Ty. I remember he made a scratch hit to third base, and, standing on the bag, he called over to Buck and laughed.

I think it was Veach who was up next, or maybe it was Harry Heilmann. I thought, now Donovan would find out what he was made of. Cobb might steal. I was nervous.

I remember hearing Cobb talk once about baseball. It was at a banquet or dinner, and he was giving reminiscences and explaining how he played. "You always want to split the other fellow's thinking," he said.

That hits the nail.

"Hey, busher. I'm coming down," Cobb yelled at me.

"Come on down, you bastard," I said under my breath and as I gritted my teeth.

Cobb could always fox you and beat you one way or another and, like he said, split your thinking. He could demoralize a whole ball club. But he could also get you fighting mad and rouse up all the competitive spirit that was in you. You had to fight him back, I figured.

"I'll take this one, kid," Buck yelled over to me.

That disappointed me, but I think it relaxed me, too. Cobb came down on the first pitch. Buck took Ray's throw and tagged Ty out.

We won that game but I don't remember the score. I got a hit my first time up and scored the first run of the ball game and didn't make any errors.

"You brought Old Joe good luck," Benz told me after the game.

I think that was the last game Joe won. He had been better than a fair pitcher in his day, but he had been at his peak when the Sox weren't very strong. In 1917 he already looked over the hill, and in 1918 he wouldn't have been a regular starting pitcher but for the war. He threw a spitter and he was a strong thrower in his day. He was a big fellow, a country boy who talked with a drawl, and I never heard him speak of himself in any other way than as "Old Joe." That game meant a lot to him because back on July 4th that season, Ty played first base in one of the doubleheader games at the White Sox ballpark. Old Joe got a one-base hit to right field. I guess he was so surprised that he didn't know where he was.

"Old Joe is so used to being called out at first base he thought he was out when he made a base hit," Ray said, kidding Old Joe about this particular play.

"There ain't no goddamned friggin' rule in this friggin' game that tells you you got to be out at first base, you krauthead," Buck yelled at him in the clubhouse.

This happened during the week I was trying out. Old Joe got sore at Buck.

The point of all this is that Ty Cobb pulled the hidden ball trick on Old Joe. He took a ribbing for his bonehead play the rest of the season and also the next year in spring training. By beating Ty and the Detroit club in my first big league game, Old Joe felt that he'd gotten some revenge.

And in 1918 he was a worried pitcher who had lost most of his stuff. He hadn't saved any money and he was afraid of having to take a cut in his salary for 1919 after he took one for 1918. Of course nobody knew then if there would or would not be a 1919 season, but there's never been a law against hoping, and Old Joe was hoping. Now he's really old and he's failing. The last time I saw him, he looked like a man not long for this world. Old Joe said that I was better than finding a four-leaf clover. That's how I got my nickname, Clover Donovan.

It was a big thing for me to read the play-by-play account of that ball game and to read my own name in the paper. There was a little story about my being signed by the Sox. Mary cut that clipping out of a newspaper and saved it. It was the first one she pasted in the first scrapbooks of newspaper clippings about me that she kept.

I was having supper at home one night and I was only a kid of eighteen, a few months out of high school. I was driving a horse and wagon but had just begun to think I had better get some kind of better work and that maybe I ought to think about going to school nights and learning something like bookkeeping and accounting. And after my siege of boils, I was ready to make my debut in the semipro ranks. And by the time I was eating supper the next night, I had become a member of the Chicago White Sox, and I had played in my first big league ball game. The suddenness of this made it hard for me to believe I wasn't dreaming, and that any minute I was going to wake up and find out that it all just wasn't so.

There was plenty of excitement about my good fortune, and I liked it, naturally. The telephone rang four, five times. Joe Hines called me up. I remember him telling me over the phone, "Well, Mick, I'll be a son-of-a-gun. I still don't know if I ought to believe it or not."

Flinty gave me a call, and Tim and Mr. Collins also rang me. And mother and Ruthie talked about what I needed for the eastern trip. Ruthie and she agreed that they should go downtown with me in the morning and pick out the suit for me, some shirts, and whatever else I needed, like a suitcase.

I must have been dizzy and out of this world, even though I can't remember clearly just how I did feel. It's exciting for every kid when he breaks in. That's one of the biggest moments of every ballplayer's life, the first time he puts on a big league uniform, the first game he plays, the first time he sees his name in a box score. The way it all happened to me was so sudden that it could have happened in a story or a movie, not to a person in real life.

All of this was the beginning of my education. I was so green that I didn't know I was green. When I made that first eastern trip with the club, I might have been sold the Brooklyn Bridge and the Woolworth Building if anyone took the trouble to try and sell them to me. I saw Mary the night before. I decided right off after I had been signed up and put in the lineup that I would go to confession and receive Communion that Sunday as an offering of thanks, and also for the repose of my father's soul and to ask the Lord to help me succeed. I've never been what you call pious and I have been enough of a sinner in my life, but I always have, in special moments, turned back to my religion. And I think it helps. It can't hurt. After Mr. Collins talked to me, I spoke with Mary and she went to confession, too. That's not the way to court a girl, I know, but before our marriage, we did go to church together many times. Mr. Collins was kind of surprised to see a prospective son-in-law courting his daughter by calling for her to walk a couple of blocks to church. But it made me feel good, and even though Mary teases me about it to this day, she liked it.

I can't remember things clearly and in sequence about that first eastern trip with the ball club. I had never eaten in a diner, slept on a train, or stayed in a hotel, and I was greener than the last greenhorn just off the boat. I was afraid that I'd spill soup and be laughed at because of my table manners, and I didn't know what to order on the train and in hotels. All my life, I had heard the engine whistles, and sometimes I would hear them at night in bed. They would sound melancholy then, and I would think of trains in the night, racing along taking people to places I had never seen. And there I was on a train. I had an upper in the Pullman car and I could sleep hardly a wink. And New York sort of surprised me. I don't know what I expected it to be like, but whatever that was, New York was different. I was afraid to go far from the Ansonia Hotel where we stayed. I sat on the benches on Broadway near 72nd Street and gaped. I heard a lot of people talking in foreign accents and I asked myself if I was in America or a foreign country.

I had one terrific day in New York, making four hits, two singles, a double, and triple to win the ball game, and for a few days, it looked like we could end up in fourth place. I imagined myself being the player responsible for a first division drive during the last weeks of the season. You got to laugh at this, at me, Mickey Donovan, inspiring Buck Weaver, Eddie Cicotte, and the rest of the veterans. But that big day in the Polo Grounds went to my head. Hell, I was hitting big league pitching better than I had done against kids in the Catholic High School League or the pitchers I faced in games out in Washington Park. In Boston, I didn't get a hit off Babe Ruth and Mays, and then I turned my ankle beating out a bunt off of Sam Jones.

We finished sixth and I batted .303. After Labor Day, I played semipro ball with the Morgan Aces. Nobody knew what was going to happen to baseball in 1919, but the ballplayers all really believed that they would be back next year. By the time the abbreviated 1918 season ended, the Germans were getting pushed back in France, and the newspapers made things more uncertain than they were. As for myself, I was a ballplayer. I knew that in 1919 I would be playing ball some place, with some ball club. If the war didn't end, organized baseball didn't resume, then I'd be playing with the semipros around Chicago. The semipros were fast and thriving in those days. In September 1918, a lot of big leaguers played semipro ball in Chicago, and it was the same in New York and some other big cities. I played against Buck and batted against Old Joe Benz in September 1918.

That season ended in Detroit, and I made two errors and struck out twice in the last game of the season. I was depressed as hell in the clubhouse, but Clarence Rowland talked to me, told me to stay in condition during the winter because he said baseball would come back big and that I had a promising future. And on the train returning to Chicago, Clarence talked to me some more. He suggested I play semipro for the rest of the season, and that I keep in condition all winter, eat plenty of meat, not dissipate the way many young kids did and give all I had to making good in baseball. That was a real help. I wouldn't have known what to do and might have made mistakes.

A lot had happened to me in just a couple of months after my gradu-ation from St. Basil's, and I was carrying a load of responsibilities. I was going with Mary and we told her family that we were engaged. And I was like the head of the family at home. Ma sold out my father's business, and we were able to go on living like we had been, but I had to think about the future. I had only made a promising beginning in the big leagues.

I was beginning to learn all those things that you only learn by experience. You had to earn money to live. Everything in your home was bought with money, even the bars of soap and newspapers, and somebody had to earn that dough. Ballplayers were fighting for their livelihood and, like other people, they thought and talked a lot about making a living. I was growing up and discovering those things that you only discover by growing up. I wanted things that cost dough. A nice home with Mary, a nice home for Ma, and a class education for my brother and sister, and clothes, too. I even started to become interested in being well dressed.

I was on the bottom rung of the ladder. I knew the climb was hard. But I wanted to go up the ladder. The war gave me one good break and put me on that ladder. I was beginning to understand things like these. What Clarence had said to me in Detroit and on the train coming back to Chicago gave me some confidence, too. It gave me the idea that the White Sox were going to sign me up again. This was why I stuck to my job of driving the wagon. I'd be able to have an outdoor life in Chicago, I calculated, and I'd be in tip-top shape to make my big battle to stay in the majors. Because I knew that despite their 1918 showing, the White Sox were one hell of a bunch of ballplayers.

So there I was, eighteen going on nineteen. I had the most valuable things a man can have, health and youth and the ability to do what he wanted to in life. There must have been thousands like me all over America. Strong, healthy kids wanting the moon. I didn't think of other kids, but only of myself. I was Mickey Donovan, Clover Donovan, and the entire world was like a ballpark with a big diamond on which I was going to perform. Many sat in the stands. Few played. I was one of those who wanted to play. I was learning things, but my eyes were full of stars.

CHAPTER FIVE

I

In September 1919, when we went to Cincinnati, Ohio, on the White Sox special train, I had already gotten a lot of the stars out of my eyes. I had behind me spring training with the White Sox, a half-season in the Pacific Coast League, and a half-season on the bench while the White Sox won the pennant. I was going good with San Francisco, hitting .315, and certain that I was a big league ballplayer. I got over wishing only to be with the White Sox. Naturally, I would have preferred to play on the Chicago ball club in my hometown, but I didn't have any chance to win myself a regular position on the Sox. In 1919, they were just about the greatest ball club that ever tore up a diamond. In spring training, I could see that much. The newspapermen wrote me up and there were stories out of Texas that I might win a regular berth on the club, especially since I was so versatile and could play so many positions. But writers need copy, and the stories about me were copy.

There was no weakness in the infield, and Fred McMullen had to sit on the bench. I looked good in Texas and I fought for a place on the club. Touring with the Yannigans, or second team, I had been put in the outfield, and I thought that maybe I had a better chance to break in as an outfielder. Shano Collins and Nemo Liebold alternated in right field. They were both damned good ballplayers, veterans, but they weren't great players. But there was no reason for the Little Skipper, Kid Gleason, to give me the call over them or over Eddie Murphy. It was better to send me to San Francisco where I had a chance to play every day. I might have gotten the call over Harvey McClellan, a good field, no-hit substitute infielder, but it was better to send me out for seasoning and experience. In July, McClellan got a broken wrist when he was hit by a line drive in batting practice, and I was recalled as infield insurance. The Old Roman and the Little Skipper wanted the pennant like all hell and they kept me on the bench even though I wasn't needed and could have been playing regular with the Seals.

So there I was, the youngest eligible player on the roster of the two clubs set to play for the championship of the world. I was getting a cut of the World Series, and I knew that I was ready for the big leagues.

I was used to big league travel, and I could order my steak and have soup on a train or in a hotel without being anxious about my manners. I had watched the veterans and imitated them, especially Eddie Collins in little things. It was a thrill to be nineteen, a White Sox, and on a team that could become the world's champion in a week to ten days. But I was just crazy to get into a ball game. After playing every day, I was forced to sit on a bench and watch. Of course, I learned plenty, but I would have learned that anyway, and I was more nervous than a colt. I was sitting on my can in the reflected glory of a great ball club. When I was recalled, my salary was cut from $200 a month to $150 plus the $50 bonus per month for the option on renewal of my contract. But I was getting a bonus in San Francisco, too.

"Listen, Donovan, you'd be driving a team of horses if we hadn't picked you up," Harry Grabiner told me when I squawked about the salary cut. And he told me that I would make it up by my cut in the World Series share.

"We're putting you in a world's championship ball club," Harry said, slapping his desk and fixing his eyes on me like they were needles. "You're in the same ball club as some of the greatest ballplayers of all time." He named them. Most of them were sore as hell and squawking about their salaries, too. "You're just a kid, eighteen years old," he told me. I was nineteen, but didn't correct him. I never did have much luck disputing with Harry on any kind of figures or arithmetic.

Of course in one way Harry was right. The gates of opportunity were open to me, and I had a future. Even if I was only sitting on the bench, I was with a club that looked like it was going to sit on top of the baseball heap for some years to come. That would mean World Series checks added to my salary. I thought I was worth more than $150 per month, but I had to take what I could get.

It was an experience being on that ball club. I had gotten an idea of this in 1918 and more of it during the 1919 spring training season. Like I said, Eddie Collins and Gandil didn't even say hello to each other on the street. Most of the club had no use for Gandil. I missed the fight he had on the ball field with Tris Speaker but heard about it. Many of the White Sox and Cleveland players locked arms to keep the umpires away, and they were hoping that Spoke would clean up Gandil before the fight was broken up. Shoeless Joe Jackson and Happy Felsch would pull Ray Schalk away from the plate on outfield throws just to make Ray look bad. Feuding and fighting, the ball club was the class of the league, and from July on, I sat on the bench watching them do it.

They'd run in from the field in the sixth or seventh inning, and Buck or one of them would say, "Come on, let's win this friggin' ball game." And they'd win it. Fighting and dissension couldn't stop that team. It should have won five straight ball games from Cincinnati.

I didn't mention it, but one of my surprises in 1918 was to hear talk about crookedness and sloughing games. Just about the time that I was signed up in 1918, there was the story about Hal Chase, who was about as beautiful a first baseman as I ever saw. One day there was a story in the newspapers that Christy Mathewson, managing Cincinnati, had suspended Chase for indifferent play.

"You can't prove anything. How can you prove that a player has thrown a ball game?" Eddie Cicotte said in the clubhouse, discussing the news.

"They don't have to prove anything on him," Chick Gandil said.

"He'd steal sticks of gum from any one of them girls at a cigar counter in a hotel while he was trying to romance her," Ray Schalk said.

"What the hell is it all about?" Buck Weaver asked.

Somebody showed him a newspaper and he read the little story which told that Mathewson, manager of the Cincinnati Reds, had suspended Chase. As I remember, Chase denied that he had ever thrown any games and asked for a hearing.

"It don't say that he done anything so far as I can see," Buck said.

"Maybe he didn't. He wouldn't be the first," Chick Gandil said.

"All I say is that he's a great ballplayer, greatest first baseman I ever saw," Ray Schalk said.

"We got him because Frank Chance didn't want any part of him. He's no good for any ball club or baseball," Shano Collins said.

"I remember I lost a couple of games I should have won when he was on this club," Joe Benz said.

"That's a hell of a thing to say against a ballplayer if there ain't no goddamn proof," Buck said.

They talked about it a few times more but in the same way. Chase was signed up by McGraw to play with the New York Giants the next year, that was 1919, and that seemed to me to indicate that there wasn't anything to the charges of Mathewson's except rumors, but you kept hearing stories about ball games being thrown. Out in the Pacific Coast League there was a lot of talk, and there were stories about Chick Gandil. There were stories about Tom Seaton, the National League pitcher who had played in the Pacific Coast League, and Babe Barton, the first baseman the White Sox traded to New York along with Rollie Seider in 1913 when Chase came to Chicago. And there was a Boston pitcher, whose name I won't mention, who was held in suspicion, but I don't think anything about him ever was printed in the newspaper.

You heard all kinds of stories about crookedness and gamblers. I knew some players who associated openly with gamblers and Gandil had suspicious looking friends in every city of the American League circuit. There was a big hue and cry about crookedness and crooked ballplayers after the news of the 1919 World Series was spread all over the newspapers, and a lot of people acted surprised, but the fact of the matter is that you heard talk of gamblers and games not being on the level. This was a real shock to me when I first broke into baseball. But it's the kind of shock you can have reading about what other people's kids do. Your own kids are different. You don't for one minute imagine that your children are doing the things that shocked you when you heard about them.

We left for Cincinnati about nine o'clock on a Sunday night, the last Sunday in September, and the day of the last game of the season. We lost that game, but it didn't matter with the pennant clinched. I played and made a couple of hits, which gave me a .300 batting average, with three hits out of ten. I felt good about that, and even though there wasn't much chance of my seeing any action, you could never tell. Anything can happen in baseball, and thinking now about that 1919 Series, I guess I ought to add that it usually does happen.

The excitement of the World Series caught me up. There wasn't a war on as there had been in 1917, and I wasn't a high school kid leaving home at five in the morning to stand in the bleacher line as I'd done in 1917. I didn't really have to do it. I could have left home later in the morning and still have gotten a decent seat. I wanted to go early so as to be able to say that I'd been one of the first to get in line. A World Series was historic and I wanted to do what the traditional fan had always done. And then, only two years later, I was an eligible player. I was on the inside of the great historic contest.

And that year, especially, it seemed to be the most important thing that was happening in the country. The attention of millions was on the two ball teams. In those days, like everybody knows, there wasn't radio or television, and crowds would stand in front of scoreboards outside of a newspaper building to see the play-by-play account of the game represented for them. Groups of men would stand on corners, talking and arguing about the games and the prospects of victory of one or the other team. There weren't as many things to do and baseball was a big thing in a man's life as well as for the kids. I remember how I'd talk about a World Series, and look forward to it. In 1917, with the White Sox playing, it seemed that the outcome of the Series would mean something to me in my own personal life and that if the White Sox lost, I would be losing something myself. It was like my own fate was at stake in the Series. Of course, this was absolutely true in my case, since I was in the ball club, but I knew that that was the way many fans felt, and not only those who had bet on the outcome.

I remember when we came back from our last eastern trip after clinching the pennant in Boston, there was a crowd at the La Salle Station to welcome us. We were almost mobbed. They had a band out, and men blew horns and shouted like they do at the ballpark. That sort of thing makes a player feel good. It gives him the feeling that he's appreciated. I was recognized by some of the fans at the La Salle Street Station and heard my name mentioned and called out. Of course I came in for reflected glory, since I was only a rookie substitute infielder and I hadn't been needed even for one game the club won. I loved it all just the same and considered myself to be just about the luckiest young fellow in America. I knew that many people must envy me and wish they were in my shoes.

In my neighborhood on the South Side there was a difference. I was always pretty popular, and people seemed to like me, but my being on the White Sox made a big difference. Older men, some of them among the most well-heeled in the neighborhood or the parish, treated me like an equal when they saw me on the street or outside of church when Sunday Mass was over. People I didn't know said "hello" to me and a few of them stopped me on the street to chat. With Pa dying, I became the head of the family, but I was still more or less of a kid in the neighborhood. But I was regarded like a man not a kid when the club won in 1919. And I wouldn't be telling the truth if I said that I didn't like it. I thought of the future when I would be a regular, the star of pennant-winning clubs, and the glory would be mine.

Getting on the White Sox Special, I'd thought of this. The station was jammed with our well-wishers who had come to give us a big morale-boosting sendoff. It was a mob, and the ballplayers had to crush their way to the trains, with fans grabbing them, shaking and pumping their hands, patting them on the back, blowing tobacco and alcohol breaths in their faces, and in general acting like an enthusiastic crowd of fans usually acts. Some of the players didn't like it, or at least claimed they didn't. It seems to me that a ballplayer has got to like it even though it's inconvenient and a hell of a nuisance, because it's fame. And fame is one of the things a player courts and wants.

I got to the station just as Eddie Collins got out of a cab and I followed him through the mob. Eddie would go through a crowd, parting them with his hands, telling them to get out of his way. He was good and he knew it. He knew he was so good that he didn't need any demonstration like the sendoff before the start of the 1919 World Series to make him feel good. Maybe he had more than confidence and was conceited. Lots of ballplayers thought so and didn't like him. I came to like and respect him as one of the princes of the game, and I felt real bad when I read about his death in the newspapers. Following him through the crowd at the La Salle Street Station on that September Sunday night, I thought of how I wanted to reach his peak. I didn't envy him. I wanted to be like him and to get to where he was.

Eddie parted people with one hand. He was carrying a suitcase with the other. "Come on, get the hell out of the way," he said to one man. "Make room, quit blocking me."

Buck was different. He was surrounded on the platform, smiling and laughing, and men in the crowd around him were calling his name, telling Buck that they were with him and rooting for the Sox, that sort of stuff.

All of the players got an ovation and some of them were cheered to the rafters. Eddie Cicotte waved at the crowd from the platform. I couldn't have done that if I was intending to do what Eddie and some of the other players were planning to do. Chick Gandil spoke of the crowd as suckers.

"My God, look at that crowd. We got to bring them back the bacon. That's what they want," Ray Schalk said.

The Old Roman was cheered and it seemed to tickle him.

The players were cheered, and some of their names were called. I remember some of the fans calling for Eddie Cicotte, but he was sitting in the club car, quiet, smoking a cigarette. He often would pull practical jokes and kid, but he was quiet, and I guessed it was because he was pitching the opening game. I was excited inside so that I felt like I had butterflies in my stomach, and I thought that the veterans must be, even if some of them didn't show it. Some of them, Risberg, Gandil, Buck, and McMullen sat down to a poker game while the train was still standing at the station.

Finally it pulled out. I sat with Lefty Sullivan. Lefty was a rookie and one hell of a nice guy. He and I had roomed together and he was a lot of help to me, because even though he was a rookie, he was a little older than me and more savvy. He had just been married about three months before the Series to a girl who lived out around 58th and Michigan, and he had set up housekeeping, and he was happy as a lark to be collecting a World Series share in his first season in the big leagues. Lefty had lots of stuff, enough to have been a hell of a good big league pitcher, but he couldn't pick up a bunt and throw it to first base. Either he fumbled the ball, tripped over it, rolled it around in the grass, or else if he did pick it up, he'd fling it to right field or into the stands. He'd started only one game in August against Walter Johnson. The first three men up, and Lefty threw the ball away three straight times, once hurling it all of the way out to the right field bleacher fence. It was the funniest and darndest thing, but he just couldn't field bunts.

In spring training he looked so good the sportswriters had more to say about him than Dick Kerr, who won two games in the Series. But Dick could field as well as pitch, and so Lefty pitched batting practice all year but he talked about how next season, 1920, he'd learn how to field bunts and throw a man out at first base. I was sure he would and was hoping we'd both be with the club again the next season and be rooming together. Lefty was a lot of help to me. He was somebody to talk to and see a movie show with or go for a walk with, because the veterans didn't pay much attention to me and never asked me to go any place with them. The road trip would have been mighty lonesome without Lefty.

We sat together, the two of us not for a minute thinking that anything was wrong, and while neither of us expected to get to play in the Series, we were thrilled, as you can imagine, and we expected to be members of the champions of the world.

The train was gay going to Cincinnati on that Sunday night. Except for Buck and Eddie Cicotte, the other players involved in that business didn't act any different than if they had nothing on their mind. Joe Jackson sat quiet, but he was a quiet fellow anyway and never did a lot of talking, and some of the newspapermen started a harmony quartet and everybody listened to them, and it was nice. They sang old-time songs and songs of the times. I remember them singing "*K-K-Katy, Beautiful K-K-Katy,*" and I liked that.

Eddie Collins sat talking with the Skipper. The Skipper was the most wonderful man for ballplayers, and he was laughing and smiling. It was a joy to see him. He was a squat, solidly built little fellow, but tough and hard as nails, a ballplayer clear through, an old Baltimore Oriole. I don't think I ever again saw him so happy. He used to call us all "my boys," and on the train he kept speaking of "my boys" and of how they were the best team he ever saw, the best team in baseball. He'd playfully hit you in fun and almost break your ribs because he was still strong as a bull, and he walked through the car making as if to poke one or another of the players, and they'd duck or dodge and laugh and curse him, and he'd tell them he was only giving them an idea of what he'd give 'em if they didn't win two ball games for him in Cincinnati. And everybody yelled they were going to win.

"We'll win you them goddamn friggin' ball games, Skip," Buck yelled, but then I saw a worried look on Buck's face, but I didn't think nothing of it except that I supposed Buck was a little nervous before the World Series.

And two, three, four times I caught that same look on Buck's face. Now as I recall it, it seemed unusual, but I didn't make nothing at all of it. Buck was always smiling and happy and I should have put two and two together then and there when I saw that he wasn't anything like the life of the party. Of course if I had, I couldn't have stopped anything because even if I had guessed, nobody would believe me.

I noticed little things, and I can still remember them. For instance, when we were in New York on our last eastern trip, I was standing by the cigar counter talking to the blonde girl at the counter. Well, I sort of knew her well. I went out with her, to a show, and she suggested I go home with her and I did, but that's years ago now, only I can't help thinking and remembering her. That happens to every man, and he still can love his wife. Her name was Annette, and I often wondered what happened to her because she was gone the next spring when we made our first trip to New York. Well, it was the morning after I had been out with her. I wrote to Mary. It was a hard thing to do and I felt like a heel, but I felt I had to write her and tell her I loved her. I did. I was a kid and with the White Sox and I thought I was going to end up that year a member of the champions of the world.

So I was talking to Annette. A man comes in, a big fellow, kind of fat, and he speaks with a drawl and speaks with her and gives her a fifty cent tip. She introduces me to him. It was Bill Burns. I recognized his name as that of a former pitcher and was glad to meet him and to know that he recognized who I was. Annette had pointed out Burns and Chase to me the night before where I had gone with her, and that had been a thrill. I saw Burns walk away with another fellow, and I only found out over a year later that the other fellow was Maharg, who confessed to a reporter in Philadelphia and that's what broke things open a year later in 1920. They met Eddie Cicotte in the lobby.

I've thought of that scene for years and even dreamed of it. I was standing by the cigar counter, just looking, watching Burns, wearing a ten-gallon hat, and the other man walk across the lobby. Eddie Cicotte was wearing a blue suit and a bow tie, and he shook hands with them and smiled. They walked back to the elevator near the cigar counter and stood for a moment, got in the elevator, and went upstairs to Eddie's room for the first meeting.

I remember that scene like I saw it in a movie or a bad dream, and a couple of times, I did dream of this scene and of myself knowing what it meant and what it was all about but not saying anything or doing anything to stop it. There were a couple of times when I was not dreaming but awake and I happened to remember this scene and I had the same feeling, the feeling that I knew about it and didn't open my mouth. Of course I couldn't have known about it no more than the other players who weren't in on it knew anything about that first meeting when it was agreed to slough the World Series. Even now, I am almost half-convinced that I saw them meeting, and that I knew what they were meeting for and I didn't do a thing to stop it.

I think that it was that same afternoon that I heard Buck saying to a couple of the other players, "You're crazy. It's crazy, I tell you, it's crazy."

And I think it was in Boston when we clinched the pennant that I walked in on Gandil, Risberg, and one or two others in the clubhouse. They were talking and they shut up when they saw me. I heard Mc-Mullen say, "The busher."

Everybody on the club could have just stumbled in on the whole deal but nobody did.

In Boston, when we clinched the pennant, there was some fellow, a gambler, I heard saying, "They'll lose the Series."

It's the things you never notice that mean the most and are most important.

But on the train ride to Cincinnati, I was thrilled and excited and anxious to see the club go out and claw up the Cincinnati club, and I was certain they were going to do it just as they had every club in our own league. And most of the baseball fans of the nation thought the same. When we went to Cincinnati on Sunday night, we were 5-1 favorites. 5-1 favorites.

II

We got into Cincinnati in the morning. It was warm and sunny, fine weather. It was Monday, September 30th. There was still time for something to happen. We went to the Sinton Hotel. There were quite a few men in the lobby, talking loudly. I could see some of them were gamblers. A few were waving money. I heard the odds had shifted to

4-1. That seemed funny, and I thought there must be some damned-fool hometown fans who were diehards and just wanted to lose some of their dough being loyal to the home club.

It was like a holiday in Cincinnati, and the town was all worked up and whipped up, more than Chicago was. Chicago fans were excited but the city was even then so big that you didn't feel the excitement everywhere you went, and the town didn't stop as it did in Cincinnati. I guess it was the first pennant they ever won and the first decent ball club they must have had since 1869 or 1870 when they had the Cincinnati Red Stockings. They were hungry for victory and nobody could have talked rational to them about their team even if they wanted to. This ball club would have been lucky to finish third or even in the first division in our league, and rabid as the fans were, they were worried and afraid because the White Sox reputation had preceded them to Cincinnati and most of the experts, of course, had picked the Sox to win.

Fans who had seen the Sox play or read the sports pages, knew that we had a great ball club, but there are few fans that can grasp the fine points of ballplaying, and it took baseball men, experts and other ballplayers, to know how great our ball club was. But baseball men knew, and they all expected that the White Sox would slaughter the Reds the way Dempsey crowned Jess Willard that same year.

Our club didn't even play together and won ball games with no harmony or team spirit. As we walked into the hotel, Buck was telling Risberg how he had no use for Eddie Collins and that was the way it always was. I haven't described much of it to you because with some of them dead, and the rest of them old and to the four winds, I don't think that it is much of interest to describe how there was wrangling and cursing in the clubhouse. Of course there would be a let-up and sometimes they'd talk and seem to make up, but not for long.

Anyway, we got into Cincinnati in the morning, a Monday morning, and I saw Burns and that friend of his I had seen in New York, Maharg, in the lobby when we entered the hotel. Gandil and Eddie Cicotte spoke to them a minute before they and all of us went to our rooms on the eighth floor. Maybe the two of them, Gandil and Eddie, spoke to Burns about the meeting they had. The meeting must have been held that morning and not very long after we reached the hotel because we had a practice session that morning. The players wanted their money, and Eddie Cicotte had said that he must be paid his dough in advance or else he wouldn't go through with the deal. And it was under a pillow in his room that Eddie Cicotte found $10,000 in thousand-dollar bills.

Some of the players went straight into the dining room for breakfast and others, like myself, went to our rooms first. I'd been in enough hotel rooms by then to be used to hotels. It wasn't like my first hotel the season before in New York. Then, I'd been almost afraid, and not sure about anything I did. But everything like that was gone, rubbed away from me by the time of the 1919 World Series. I felt like I was a big leaguer and knew how to act what I was.

I went to eat, and the dining room off the lobby was pretty crowded. There were quite a few in the lobby, too, although it was morning. By evening that lobby was going to be like a crowded railroad station, Grand Central or the Pennsylvania in New York.

You could feel the excitement about the World Series there in the hotel lobby and dining room, with so many people talking, so many characters and important personages, and disreputable ones. People stood around staring and looking at one another, and from the look on their faces, you might have thought that they were in the know about everything going on in the world. They had a cold-eyed stare. And old friends were meeting and shaking hands. Besides gamblers and Cincinnati people, and our hotel was lousy with them, there were many baseball men, players and old-timers, and there were even a few old men who had played baseball in the nineteenth century, and they had at least one old man who had been with the Cincinnati Red Stockings of 1869, and he was in the lobby, shaking hands and talking.

I had some breakfast with Lefty and we went outside in the lobby and stood talking for a few minutes and looking. The crowd was getting bigger, and gamblers waved money, trying to make bets. I couldn't understand it. How come so many of them were betting on Cincinnati? I know it's always attractive to get good odds when you have a chance and can hope to have luck enough to collect, getting a hundred dollars for every twenty you lay out, but it seemed to me that there was no chance for the Cincinnati club to win. I should have guessed that something was up because one look at the guys in the lobby was enough to make it clear that smart money, not dumb money, was being bet.

I was more excited by the ballplayers, stars of the day and old-timers, who were in Cincinnati. Tris Speaker was there, and Tinker and Evers, who were helping the Reds by giving them some coaching, and

Grover Cleveland Alexander, who pitched to the Cincinnati team in
batting practice on that Monday afternoon, the day before the World
Series and the day we got to Cincinnati. This was exciting to me and
I got a kick out of it and thought how lucky I was and what a privilege
and an opportunity it was to be a big leaguer, to be in all of this. But it
made sitting on the bench harder. That made me feel unimportant. I
had my expectations though, expectations of the future when I would
be a veteran and a star, playing in a World Series, and my name would
be on the lips of people the way our stars' were: Eddie Collins, Buck,
Joe Jackson and the names of the Cincinnati players, Roush, Heinie
Groh, Daubert, Sallee, and the others.

Lefty and I, we stood there in the lobby and looked around. Lefty
was chewing on a cigar, but I hadn't yet started smoking. Even though
I was on the White Sox, I felt like a little bit of an outsider, a stranger.
The lobby was getting fuller and the talk was loud and noisy. Many
were seeing old friends and shaking hands, laughing, talking the way
men do when they meet friends and acquaintances at an affair like a
World Series. How are you, and I'm glad to see you, and you're looking
good—things like that are said, over and over again, and that's what
I heard said around me. That and the talk of the betting. Bets were
being made, and the bettors would pick someone in the lobby to hold
the stakes. I just couldn't understand why so many people would bet
on Cincinnati and on the morning of the day before the Series started.
I saw a couple of bets made for $500 or $1,000, too.

"Goddamn it, I know it's in the bag," I heard a fellow saying near me.

I couldn't understand that. It never occurred to me even to think
that there might be a "fix," but this was perfectly obvious there in the
hotel lobby on that Tuesday morning.

"I don't understand how these guys can be such damned fools as to
bet their dough this way on the Reds," I said to Lefty.

He didn't say anything. I think his suspicions were already aroused.

"How the hell can Cincinnati beat a ball club like the White Sox?
Have you seen them play this year, the White Sox?" a fellow was saying behind me.

"Sure I seen 'em play."

"And you'll still bet on Cincinnati?"

"Wait until you see them play tomorrow," the fellow said, kind of
mysteriously.

"This is a funny place," I said to Lefty.

"Yeah, but we're in the other league now. Maybe this is just the way it is over here in the other league," Lefty said.

We didn't stay long, because we had practice and had to report to the ballpark. We got the field in the morning. The Reds then had it for practice in the afternoon.

The ball club looked good in practice, full of pep, and the hitters had their eye on the ball. There was a lot of talk about the ballpark. It was a pretty one, smaller than ours, and the infield was in perfect condition, better than our own, which was a little bit bumpy and hard. The infield in the Cincinnati park seemed perfect. And the fences looked like easy targets. I almost hit a couple into the right field bleachers. The players weren't nervous and they all seemed confident, sure of winning.

That's what puzzled me. According to the stories, and confessions, there had been a meeting in one of the rooms—I think it was Cicotte's, or else it was Gandil's—just before we had gone to the ballpark for our workout. So, the idea of fixing the Series was all set, and we were like a bunch of innocents blissfully ignorant of the whole business. This was one of the things that hurt. The players who made the deal with the gamblers were fooling us just as much as they were the baseball fans or the Old Roman. They were double-crossing their own teammates, the guys, the men they had lived with and traveled with, played poker with, the men in baseball who should have been closest to them.

I am not thinking of myself here as much as I am of others who were on the club roster, because I was still so new to the club and I was still something of just a busher. And in those days, a busher was like an orphan, almost a worm. But those players had been playing with the rest of the members of the ball club and, in a fashion, living with them. They had played together a number of seasons and they were all reaching the heights of their baseball career together. Hell, they belonged on a great ball club, maybe the greatest ball club ever to grace a diamond in the history of modern baseball. And my God, what more can a ballplayer hope for? Why, they were at the very top of the baseball heap.

Shoeless Joe Jackson was the greatest natural hitter of his time, maybe of all time. Happy Felsch was next to Tris Speaker as a fielding outfielder in center, and some even argued that he was as good as Spoke. Spoke was passing his prime and Happy was just coming into his own. Men like Connie Mack and Ty Cobb said that Buck Weaver was the greatest of all third basemen. He was popular with the fans and players, and he was also a baseball player's player. Buck had no education, and like many of us he was just an ordinary guy. Except for baseball and his ability to play the game, nobody would ever have heard of Buck, and he would have lived and died a working man, maybe driving a truck or working on an assembly line in a factory. But he'd been seen by Charlie Dooin, manager of the Philadelphia Phillies, while playing with a semipro club in Pennsylvania, and Dooin saw his potential. So Buck, too, had reached the top.

And Risberg at short and Gandil our first baseman were both underrated ballplayers. As for playing ability, they were the kind of men any manager would want on his ball club, big, tough, durable, with lots of ability. I think I already mentioned that anybody who never saw Chick Gandil play first base can get an idea of how good he was by watching Gil Hodges, the Brooklyn Dodger first baseman, play his position. Gandil made our ball club, and then, he broke it. The Sox would have won back in 1916, except for one weakness, first base. Gandil was bought from Cleveland and the Sox won in 1917.

It was ironic, too, because the Old Roman could have gotten Hal Chase back when the Federal League folded. Chase had jumped to the Federal from the White Sox. But the Old Roman didn't want any part of Chase, great a ballplayer as he was. Chase led the National League in 1916, playing with Cincinnati, and he hit .339. He would have given us the pennant and the world's championship that season if Rowland would have had him at first base, and if he would have played straight. He was passed up, and when the Old Roman saw a chance to get Gandil from Cleveland because Tris Speaker wanted to be shed of him, Gandil was purchased.

Here was the irony of fate in baseball, if there ever was such a thing. But even though Gandil was not popular with ballplayers, all of them knew that you couldn't take his ability from him. There was only a couple of first basemen in the game then, like Sisler and Chase, who had anything on Gandil. He could take throws any place and he'd pull the ball out of the dirt just as graceful as any man I ever saw. He was big, too, which is always an advantage. He was about a .270 hitter but a dangerous man in the pinches.

And Risberg had had only three years' experience in the league in 1919. He came up from the Pacific Coast League. He permitted Rowland to use Buck at third, where he was better than at short, and still not have a weakness in the infield. Buck played shortstop in the 1917 series with McMullen at third. McMullen was a damned good and steady ballplayer, too, but the club was really better with Risberg in there because that big Swede had such an arm. He could play deeper than almost any other man in the league and still make the throws in time, and he was good, coming in on slow rollers. There were men like Peckinpaugh, Scott, and Chapman in the league, and Risberg did not get all the public recognition that was his due, but ballplayers knew how good he was. And he was another man who hit better when the hits counted than he did normally.

And then, the two pitchers who were blacklisted because of 1919 were the best in the league in 1919. Eddie Cicotte won twenty-nine games that season, and we played only a 140 schedule. Think of that, twenty-nine games won in a 140-game schedule. Eddie was just about as smart as a man could be on the pitching mound. He had perfect baseball instincts and was as good a fielding pitcher as was to be found. He was thirty-three or thirty-four in 1919 but he still had a fast ball when he wanted to use it. He had more pitches than any man I ever saw out there. Eddie was called the shine ball specialist, but he didn't need to doctor up the ball to be effective. He threw a spitter and had a knuckle ball and a good curve. His control was near-perfect, almost as good as Alexander's, and in 1919 Alexander and Walter Johnson were no better than him. And Lefty Williams was the best southpaw in the league. Eddie Collins said he would have become the greatest southpaw in the history of the game. He was another control artist and he had a good curve ball, and I think I'd even take him in his prime over the southpaw the Sox got now, Billy Pierce. Pierce is one hell of a pitcher, so you can see how high I rate Williams.

Five of the regulars, Jackson, Felsch, Buck, Collins, and Ray, were great ballplayers, and our two top pitchers were great, too. You don't often see a ball club with seven great ballplayers on it.

My God, I think now how if somebody only knew and said something back there on that morning of September 30, 1919, that that ball club of ours would be one of the great legends of the game and the whole

history of the game and the American League would have been different. Chicago would have been a club battling the Yankees in the Babe
Ruth era of the 1920s. In 1920 we had it on them.

I rode out to the ballpark for the practice session in the same taxicab
with Buck and Ray.

"Well, kid, this is your first World Series," Buck said.

"Yes, it is," I said.

"We ought to go out and beat the piss out of the other club so that
the Skipper will let you get your name in a World Series box score,"
Buck said.

"We don't want no overconfidence," Ray said.

"Overconfidence, hell," Buck said. "Hell, we can beat any friggin' ball
club in the other league just as easy as we done in our own goddamn
league."

"I won't dispute you, Buck, but I want to see it happen. I want five
straight games," Ray said.

How could Buck talk like this? Because he knew about that "fix."
That's why he was blacklisted. He had "guilty knowledge," the Old Judge
said in refusing Buck's applications for reinstatement. I watched those
games like a hawk, sitting on the bench. Buck played beautiful ball, as
everyone knows. He didn't come through with men on base, it's true,
but neither did Eddie Collins, and Eddie said to me, "Hell, Mickey, I
was the worst damn player in the club in that Series. I was awful. I was
bad in that Series."

But as I said, Buck did know about the deal with the gamblers. Buck
was smiling, and there was nothing in his conduct to cause any suspicion.
When he was out on third in infield practice, he talked it up and was full
of pep. I remember he made two, three beautiful stops on hard balls the
Little Skipper slammed at him. Maybe Buck was hoping that it wouldn't
happen, and that even if some of the others tried to lose the Series they
wouldn't be able to. I remember hearing him say on the ball field that
morning, "Hell, this ball club couldn't lose this goddamn Series, not even
if it tried to."

Or maybe he was hoping that the other players would double-cross
the gamblers, take their dough and then go out and win. I think it was
Chick Gandil who later said that Buck had suggested this idea—take
the dough and then go out and win the ball games.

Everything looked so right that morning, everything but the gamblers back there in the hotel lobby who had already started to lay bets for the sucker money. And I forgot them. I felt frisky and in fine form myself. I knew I had almost no chance of breaking into the lineup during the Series, but you never can tell what will happen in baseball, and I felt ready to go in there and play my best ball if the Little Skipper did have to call on me. I practiced at both second base and shortstop and performed as though I was in the Series, and making the crucial plays that spelled victory.

The players talked and cursed as they hurried through their showers and dressed. Some of us were going to the races across the river in Kentucky. It was a good way to spend the afternoon and pass the time, and the whole team seemed to be happy. I remember myself thinking how wonderful it was to be nineteen and on the White Sox.

When a season ends, you're glad it's over, especially if it's been a hard one. Most of the players could say they had had a good year. Red Faber had reason to think this. He was underweight because he'd had influenza in the navy the year before and he had not gained back his strength. If he had been in shape, we might have won, because he was as mean and tough a pitcher as you'd find in the League and there was no better man to send in to pitch a ball game you had to win. There was still talk of the Skipper using him in the box even though he kept tiring during the season after pitching four or five innings.

There was a chance of raises in pay for the next season, even though the Old Roman never believed in paying his ballplayers much. It looked like he'd have to give raises to some of the players. And they were looking forward to the winter. Buck was going hunting, and then he planned to go to California to take it easy and play a lot of golf. With the extra World Series dividend to come, he figured he didn't have to work in the off season. The Series was five out of nine games. The advance ticket sales had been big, and the first five games looked like sellouts.

I wasn't getting so much, but I counted on about $1,500 as a winner's share, and that was a hell of a lot more money than I'd ever seen up to that time. I was even thinking of buying a Ford, and I'd already become an important person in my neighborhood and parish.

Joe Jackson talked of going back home. He had some business in his hometown in North Carolina, and the extra dough was going to be handy for him. Eddie Cicotte talked of his farm, on which he was paying off the mortgage. And every one of them had plans. It was like life was all roses for everyone on that ball club. The veterans then seemed old to me, but they were all young men, and whatever group their age was, they could not have been in a better sport than they were on that day back in September 1919.

And think of it, it still wasn't too late. The deal could have been called off. They could have saved themselves. I can see them now, young and healthy and in their prime.

Buck later was supposed to have said that when he heard about the "fix," he told the other players, "It's crazy." And wasn't it crazy?

I enjoyed the races that afternoon and won $15. I took it as a good omen. I remember Buck happened to ride to the races in the same cab as Eddie Collins.

III

Around suppertime, the Sinton Hotel was like a madhouse. The lobby was packed and noisier than any bus station I've ever been in. It was almost as noisy as a ballpark during a World Series ball game. When I walked into that lobby after the races and saw that crowd, I got a kick. It was one of the thrills of my life. All kinds of important men were in that crowd. Stars of the game, owners, men from all walks of life, and they were talking, shaking hands, patting each other on the back, laughing, milling around, seeing old friends. The smoke from cigars and cigarettes was like a fog, or a smog, although that word wasn't used then.

That, I told myself, was the World Series. And just think, there I was, only nineteen, and a part of it all. I was a ballplayer, and even though I was still only a rookie, nobody could take it away from me that I was a big leaguer. I felt like I belonged in that lobby and at the Sinton Hotel. I had as much right to be there as anyone else. This was flattering, or so I thought. Just as I stepped into the crowded lobby, I saw Tris Speaker talking with Grover Cleveland Alexander, and not far away from them I spotted Joe Tinker and Johnny Evers talking with five or six others. I was mighty glad I had been recalled from San Francisco, even though it had meant my sitting on the bench instead of playing ball every day. I was part of the biggest thing in the world.

But in that crowd there were a lot of gamblers, and you could tell some of them were gamblers by the way they dressed and the looks on their faces. They had know-it-all, hard, cynical looks on their faces. They stared at you as if they didn't see you or else looked right through you. They made you feel nervous merely when you saw them drilling you with a stare, sizing you up and measuring you.

The betting was something I never expected. I knew that bets were made on the World Series and the papers always carried stories of the odds. I had read in the Chicago papers just before we'd left for Cincinnati that betting on the Series was light. That's what I couldn't understand, because they were betting all over the lobby of the Sinton Hotel. Men were waving stacks of bills in the air and shouting, "Two grand, even money on the Cincinnati ball club." I remember hearing a dark little fellow yell that.

And that's something else I couldn't understand. The day before the odds had been 5-1 on the White Sox. In less than twenty-four hours, the odds had shifted to even money, and the White Sox bettors could get all of the Cincinnati money they wanted to cover their own dough.

Then and there, I really knew, but I wouldn't admit it to myself. I couldn't admit it. I was still pretty dumb, naive, and with damned little experience, but I knew enough to know that the money being bet on the Reds was smart money. Gamblers don't bet the kind of money wagered on the 1919 Series unless they think they've got a sure thing. It wasn't hard to put two and two together, but I didn't do it.

"This is all goofy—even money on this Series, that's goofy. These guys must have holes in their heads," I said to Lefty.

"It don't make no sense to me," Lefty said.

"Lefty, gamblers ain't damn fools. They got some purpose betting like this."

"You can search me for it," Lefty said. Just like me, Lefty Sullivan didn't draw the obvious conclusion.

"They must have started the rumor that Eddie has a sore arm," I said.

"His arm ain't sore. If it is, it's news to me," Lefty said.

"I guess the gamblers must have spread that kind of rumor in order to shake loose some money. Now, when they have done this, they'll turn around and cover themselves by secretly betting on us," I said.

"That's more than I can understand," Lefty Sullivan said.

But I was even a little bit proud of myself for having thought out this angle. I believed it to be gospel and I even felt sorry for those in the Sinton lobby who were putting up big dough on the Reds. I had overheard some fellows in the lobby talking about the rumor that Eddie Cicotte had a sore arm just about five minutes or so before I'd figured out the angle and explained it to Lefty Sullivan.

Supper that night was an occasion. The big dining room was jam-packed all right, full up with celebrities, too. I kept looking about at some of them like a true rubberneck. I ate with Lefty and the two other catchers on our club, Birdie Lynn and Joe Jenkins. Except for warming up pitchers and catching batting practice, they were pretty superfluous in the club, the same as I was. Ray Schalk was in his prime then and he was a little workhorse who caught almost every day. Birdie would have been a regular catcher in most clubs, but he rarely got his name in the box score on ours. It was kind of tragic for him. In five years he got 115 games all told, and then he went back to the minors, forgotten. He's dead now. The two catchers were southerners and they roomed and palled together and never had much to say to me. I often ate with them on the road. They were good fellows, and Birdie didn't seem particularly bitter about the bum break he got in baseball. I guess it was because he knew that he was on a great ball club and he recognized what a great catcher little Ray Schalk was.

The four of us sitting at the table in the dining room of the Hotel Sinton in Cincinnati were as much spectators as ballplayers. I guess the others hoped as I did that somehow they'd get in the World Series and become a hero, but you feel a little rotten hoping that way, or at least I did. I was hoping that one of the regulars would get hurt, be put out of a ball game, or come down sick, and that's a rotten thing to hope about another fellow, another ballplayer. That's why you got to have confidence to be a big league ballplayer. If you hope something like I specified will happen, or if you try to take another man's job away from him and maybe even his bread and butter, why, you have to think you're good, better than he is. I wonder if all ballplayers coming up and sitting on the bench think like this? But I don't know. I don't remember ever having discussed this question with any ballplayer or ex-ballplayer. Of course a young rookie would have been kind of ridiculous, coming up and, say, thinking he could do better than Ty Cobb, but you don't only think, you also dream and hope. You come up and want to be greater than Ty Cobb was, or Babe Ruth, or Eddie Collins or Buck, or the stars of today, Musial and Williams and Kluszewski and the rest of them. I was dreaming and imagining that something would happen to one of our veterans or two of them, and that nineteen-year-old Mickey Donovan would go in there and win the World Series.

Since I didn't like Risberg and I was mainly a shortstop, I imagined him getting hurt, spraining an ankle or a finger or a wrist or getting a fingernail torn off, but that meant that McMullen also had to get sick or hurt or else one of the other infielders. When this all seemed too much, I resigned myself to being a pinch hitter and hitting a home run with the bases full one year ahead of Earl Smith of the Cleveland Indians, who did that in the 1920 series. He might never have performed that feat if my dreams of 1919 had come true and Clover Donovan had come from nowhere to win the 1919 World Series for the Chicago White Sox. For then we'd have won the pennant in 1920. It's a shame we didn't, and to this day I sometimes put myself to sleep imagining that we did win in 1920, with the stout bat and brilliant fielding and throwing, not to mention the base running of Mickey Donovan, of course, explaining why we did win.

And so, or anyway, to have seen me and talked to me, the busher of that great, unfortunate 1919 White Sox ball team, you never would have guessed what I was dreaming, not unless you wanted to be a ballplayer yourself.

I don't remember too much of what we said to one another, having dinner in the hotel on the night before the first game of the 1919 series. We talked baseball. I know we talked about the betting odds and how they had shifted from 5-1 to even money.

"I don't know how that happened," I remember saying.

"I only heard it when you told me," Birdie said.

"Make a sweet pile of jack if you had the money to bet," Joe Jenkins said.

I didn't like that because I was a little leery about betting on a ball game, even though I'd only bet on my own team. And I'm glad I was.

"There's some kind of rumor going around," Lefty Sullivan said.

"What kind?" Birdie asked pretty quick.

"I don't know—some kind of rumor that the other ball club is going to win the ball game tomorrow and this Series," Lefty said.

That sort of frightened me even though the last thing in the world that I thought or imagined was that any of our players was going to lay down and just lose, deliberately. And still, now I remember, the blonde, Annette, had said something about betting on ball games and tips and about how she had overheard plenty, she said, more than she would ever tell anyone. And she had said that she won five bucks a couple of times by making a bet on a ball game after she had overheard something said about a ball game. Maybe it was because of what she told me that I didn't want to believe any rumor and that I quickly said at the dinner table, "The rumor is that Eddie Cicotte has a sore arm."

"He ain't got no sore arm. He threw some pitches to me this mornin' in practice. Cicotte's arm, it ain't sore. Hell, long as I been with this club, and this is my fifth year, I can't remember him ever having any sore arm."

"Hell, the gamblers spread that rumor to get some sucker money," I said like a guy who knew what he was talking about from experience. That was about all we had to say about betting and gamblers at the table while we were eating.

I remember, too, that the talk had gotten around to Eddie Cicotte, and we talked about him, how he could pitch.

"He's an easy man to catch," Birdie said.

"Hell, how do you know he's an easy man to catch, Birdie? Quit bullshitting us," Joe Jenkins said.

"He's jealous of me. He's jealous. He catches as many ball games as me," Birdie said.

We laughed. That season, that is 1919, I think Birdie got into something like twenty-nine, maybe thirty ball games. Joe got his name in the box score maybe ten or eleven times. They roomed together and were always kidding about sitting on the bench or in the bull pen.

"His ass takes in slivers. He gets more slivers in his ass than I do," Joe Jenkins laughed.

"If they picked all the slivers out of his ass," Birdie said of Joe, "why, there wouldn't be no ass left. He's sat on a bench so long that his ass is all wood, all slivers."

But as I said, there was also talk of Eddie Cicotte.

"When he pitches, he looks weak in the knees. You think he's easy to hit until you hit against him." I remember Birdie saying this, and then pointing to his head with his left hand while he held his fork over his steak in his right hand. He pointed to his head and said, "He's got every hitter in the league up here."

"He ought to have this club eating out of his hand tomorrow," Lefty said.

"They ain't seen much pitching like his except maybe when they hit against Alexander," Birdie said.

"What I never realized until I got on this club was that he can throw a fastball," I said.

"Yes, Donovan," Birdie said. "Yes, he's got a good fastball. It comes in with a lot of life and the batter has a hell of a time hitting it. But the thing about Eddie is that the batter hits what he wants him to hit, not what the batter wants to hit. And he pitches an easy game. He doesn't tire himself out. He paces himself and throws down in the dirt, and not many of them ever get a good piece of wood on the ball when he's pitchin'. Do you know what he is? He's a beautiful pitcher."

"There he is."

We saw Cicotte coming into the dining room, walking to join Gandil, Lefty Williams, and Jackson at a table. He shook hands with a fellow here or there or waved to someone as walked to the table. He had that kind of wobbly-kneed walk, and he didn't look like a great ballplayer, if it means anything to say that someone walking across a hotel dining room looks like a great ballplayer or doesn't. He was thirty-five years old then, I think, or maybe thirty-four or thirty-six, but he didn't show the signs of having been in the American League for fifteen years. Like I said, he went twenty-nine that year while losing seven and was in forty games, and that was a 140-game season. I think he pitched something like thirty-six complete games. I thought as he walked across the dining room how he was at his peak, and what a satisfaction he must have felt, and how he must have thought and known that he was on the eve of his greatest of baseball achievements, being the outstanding pitcher in the World Series. He was figured to win two of the five games, three if the Series went to nine games.

Cicotte was a joker, and he laughed more than most of the other players who were barred on account of the scandal, except for Buck. He was a smart fellow and one of the most intelligent men on a ball field that I ever saw. He always knew what to do and did it and was a great fielding pitcher and a pretty good hitter for a pitcher, too. He was a switch hitter and he'd poke out a lot of base hits to left and right. I always pondered about Eddie. He was so smart that I wondered why he wasn't smart enough to stay clean.

Now I remember him, wearing a blue suit and a white shirt with a stiff collar and a polka-dot blue tie, walking across the dining room. It wasn't too late then, and if he had thought and said it was all off, he could have saved himself and the good name of baseball. I don't think he'd gotten the money yet. The money must have been put under his pillow while he was eating his supper.

Thinking of that, chills go up and down my spine. There was that crowded dining room with so much of the elite of the baseball world there—the Old Roman was at a big table with some of his friends, and Eddie Cicotte sitting with our Little Skipper, and Tris Speaker, Tinker and Johnny Evers who later was our manager and was mean and tough. I can't remember all who were there but the dining room was full of famous names, men who were household words to fans and kids all over the nation. And like I said, Eddie Cicotte was one of these famous men. Since 1917, he had come into his own and was known as a great pitcher. Despite his age, too. He had more good years in him. The next season, while he wasn't as good as in 1919, his record was 21-10, and in the last game he pitched on a muggy Sunday in September, he had Cobb and the Detroit club doing what he wanted them to do. I played right field that Sunday and got a base hit to center field. That was a tense, sad day to me, but let me tell about it in time.

I looked around the big dining room as much as I dared without seeming like a rubberneck. It was a big moment of my life. Like I said, I was nineteen and still a busher. My awe about some of the big league stars hadn't all been rubbed off. For myself to be in that company was like a miracle. I had dreamed of things like this happening to me, and when I found my dream coming true, I couldn't take it all as a matter of course. It was a great privilege and an honor to me, and I guess Lefty Sullivan felt the same way.

One thing happened in the dining room that night. Chick Gandil and Spoke, who had that fight early in the season, as I have mentioned, shook hands in the dining room to let bygones be bygones. Of course, if he had known, Spoke wouldn't have shaken hands with Gandil.

After dinner Lefty Sullivan and I took a little walk. It was a fine night and Cincinnati was baseball crazy. There were lots of people on the streets and you overheard snatches of baseball talk. Nobody recognized us as members of the White Sox, and we were amused to hear the names of players in our club in snatches of conversation. We walked to the bridge over the Ohio River leading into Covington, Kentucky, and walked out on the bridge and stood by the railing, looking at the shore on both sides and at the river, black and calm below. Lefty Sullivan smoked a ten-cent cigar for the occasion.

We didn't talk much. I thought of Mary, and Lefty must have thought of his girl, Isabelle. We stood there and it was calm and peaceful. The air was damp, full of the smell of the river, a damp smell, and there were lights on the shores where there were restaurants, and a few river boats and the big, black, quiet river, the Ohio River, which is historic and made me think of past times. Once there hadn't been a bridge, I thought, or buildings, and the Indians had been there. Indians had looked at the river at night. I wondered what the Indians had thought about. That had been before there was any baseball. I remember thinking that it was funny, kind of peculiar to think of a time before baseball had been invented, and I felt sorry for people who had lived in such times.

"Pretty, isn't it, Mick?" Lefty said.

"Yeah," I said. You never can talk and express what you think and feel seeing something beautiful like the river that night.

We stood on the bridge for a while, maybe twenty minutes or a half-hour, and then walked back to the Sinton Hotel. I was a lobby sitter in those days and thought it would be interesting to sit in the lobby and see the World Series crowd, because it had plenty of color and I'd see so many men, some of them men who were legendary to me.

But there was no sitting in the lobby that night. It was jammed, noisy as all hell, and the betting was so heavy at even money that it really worried me. I still didn't think that some of our players had been reached by gamblers, but I was uneasy and knew something was wrong. The odds were still even.

"I don't like it with all these Jew gamblers betting on Cincinnati." I overheard Clarence Rowland saying this to someone in the lobby.

I went up to bed early. I forgot about the gambling. I thought that on the next day the World Series would begin. I was afraid I wouldn't be able to sleep that night, but I was. Lefty and I talked a while in our room but we avoided saying anything about the betting, and I didn't mention what I happened to overhear Clarence say down in the lobby. We talked baseball and about the game the next day, but neither of us said anything about our being worried or concerned as to the outcome of the game. And I didn't have any real doubts. At least I can't remember that I had any. I was kind of anxious but I don't know about what.

Lying in bed and before I went off to sleep, I heard a few noises in the hotel corridor, voices, footsteps. I thought that there I was, in a hotel room in Cincinnati on the eve of the beginning of the World Series, and that, yes, it was true, I was on the roster of the White Sox, who were playing in the Series and were going to win. And yes, it was true, too, believe it or not, I was eligible, myself, to play in the Series.

I awoke the next morning seeing that the day was sunny, and that the weather for the ball game was going to be perfect. There wasn't any possibility of the games not being on the level. How could there be? And I just wanted time to pass until it would be time for me to be in uniform on the ball field practicing and then for the game time to come, and then, the ball game. Maybe I'll get in the ball game, I told myself, but I knew I wouldn't.

"Well, you nineteen-year-old goof, you'll get good dough today for any slivers you get in your ass working hard on the bench this afternoon," Lefty Sullivan said to me, kidding.

"Go on, you southpaw bastard," I said, kidding back, and I flung a pillow at him.

Lefty was happy, too. Like me, he was young then, and thinking of the future we both thought we had. Yes, we were young, and both at the beginning of our careers in the uniform of the Chicago White Sox, and that day was October 1, 1919, the first day of the 1919 World Series.

CHAPTER SIX

I

Most of the newspapermen who covered the 1919 World Series are dead. I mean, the Chicago ones, the ones I knew. There was a crowded press box that year. It was a big thing, that Series, coming as the first one after the war. I guess that there must be quite a few newspapermen still around who saw the Series, and there's twice or twice times twice or maybe twice times ten times as many who now say they were there. Some of them have written about the Series and there are others who weren't there, or who were too young even to have been around, who have written stories about what happened, but nobody seems to know the whole story. And lots of stuff has been written that didn't happen, even though the writers say it did happen just the way they say it happened. The writers are only making a living, and every man's got a right to make a living. But why do they have to keep raking up 1919? Look at all there is in baseball past and present to write about.

"Let sleeping dogs lie." I once heard Ray Schalk say that to a newspaperman after a dinner here of the old-timers. Ray was sore when he said it, and I can well understand why he was. That Series is best forgotten all right, and what's the use of raking it up and writing about it? It doesn't do baseball any good, and the kids reading it might begin to lose some of their faith in baseball.

I met Jim Cruisenberry the other day and was talking to him.

"Hell, Mickey, I don't want to write about it. I don't want to write about anything anymore. I'm seventy-five now and retired. But somebody is always asking me about that crooked Series, and young fellows who weren't around then write me letters asking me to tell them what I know or they ask me questions. I can't answer them. I'm an old man, Mickey. I'm seventy-five. I've lived more than my three score years and ten."

"You sure don't look it, Jim," I said, but he did look old.

"Thanks, but I know I'm an old man. It's all crap to say that a man is as young as he feels."

We were having a couple of drinks, and it was real good to see him. He was thin and getting silver-haired. Jim looked real distinguished though. Somebody looking at him who didn't know him might have thought he was maybe a senator and not a retired baseball writer.

"You knew it was crooked, Mickey, everybody did. How could you not know it?"

"I don't know what I knew, Jim, and I couldn't sort out what I knew then when it was happening and what I know from learning about it later. I was only a nineteen-year-old busher then, Jim."

"If the Skipper let you play and took a chance on pitching Red Faber even with his sore arm, maybe he'd have won it."

"I don't know, Jim."

"I knew something was wrong the day before it started. They write and ask why didn't we write about the crookedness then. I went to my publisher, oh, about the third day, and told him, 'This isn't right. This Series is crooked. Gamblers have got to eight White Sox players.' My publisher believed me but there wasn't any evidence and he was afraid to let me write what I knew because of the libel laws."

"Yes, it seems to me everybody ought to forget about it," I said.

"What did you say, Mickey?"

"I think it's well enough forgotten."

"Yes, it is. I know I have. I have closed my book on it in life, Donovan. Coming back here to Chicago, seeing old sights, what's left of the Chicago I used to know, and old friends and faces, is why it came to mind. And meeting you reminded me about it, since you were a member of that team."

"I was hardly on the ball club, Jim," I said.

"You were a member."

"I think I got in three or four ball games that season. Me and Lefty Sullivan, we weren't of any use to the club."

"Lefty Sullivan, is he still around? I haven't thought of him for years."

"Oh yes. He has some political job but he can't do much work. Lefty had a heart attack about a year or two ago."

"Did he? I'm sorry to hear that. As I remember him, he had a lot of stuff, a lot of promise, but he was no fielder."

"Yes. He couldn't field bunts, and if he did, he couldn't throw the ball to first base."

"That's it. He was at spring training two seasons, if I remember, 1918 and then he went into the army and 1919. They carried him in 1919. And he pitched around in semipro ball for years here."

"He once struck me out with the bases full when I played with the Miller Aces, and he struck Buck out right after me."

"Yeah. Buck Weaver is dead, isn't he?"

"Buck died."

"What a shame. I saw him right through his career. I saw him develop into one of the most beautiful ballplayers in the league. But he was as guilty as the rest of them."

"I never knew. I always sort of liked Buck especially, and he was the only one of those eight ballplayers I got to know at all. I never was sure about Buck."

"Hell, you remember the grand jury hearings?"

"Well, yes, Jim. Not everything about them, but I remember them."

"The grand jury called Buck's dentist, the one who fixed his teeth. What the hell was his name? He was a dentist on the South Side. Oh, what the hell was his name?"

"I can't remember. I know there was something said, some rumor, something that was said about his dentist."

"The goddamn thing about growing old is that you can't remember. Don't ever let anybody tell you that it's any fun to grow old and that it means a goddamn thing to grow old gracefully."

I didn't want to hear anything like that. No one does. But when I think about old age, that is, when the idea comes into my head, I, well, I don't think about it.

"Now I got the story clear, but still I can't remember the name of that goddamned dentist. I can't remember the name of the goddamn dentist."

"I'm sure I can't."

"Here, have another drink, Mickey."

"Yeah, I will, Jim."

"The dentist told the grand jury that McMullen, Fred McMullen, brought a package to Buck's home. He brought the package while Buck was in the dentist's chair. And when Buck came home, he blew his top. At first, he didn't want to take that package and he was sore. But then he took it. And the contents of that package were never revealed."

"Oh yes, I remember, there was a story about that at the time."

"McMullen is dead now. But he said it wasn't anybody's goddamned business what was in any package he delivered to Buck Weaver or anybody. He denied that it was money, but he never did reveal what was in the package."

"Yes, there was something like that," I said. I didn't like to be reminded of this because I now remembered more clearly. I remember how it had troubled me a number of times when I had thought about the 1919 Series and about Buck, and I wanted to ask him about it but I never did. It looked damning, I have to admit that, but now it's locked away with the secrets of the grave.

"You remember, we went to Cincinnati the day before the first game. We got into Cincinnati in the morning, I think it was, Tuesday morning. The betting and that shift in betting odds was peculiar. It wasn't natural. The experts, all of us writers, picked the White Sox, and there was that money being bet on the Reds. It didn't make sense. You could see something was wrong. Why, that evening, the evening before the first game, the odds had shifted from something like 5-1 to even money."

"Yeah."

"I inquired and so did other writers. And then, of course, there were those first two games. They didn't look right."

I guess I nodded and I thought I must have played those games over in my head I don't know how many times, dozens of times, and I'll bet some of the other players have done the same. At times I get mixed up on what happened in those first two games, not because I don't remember but on account of how I played the games over in my mind so much that I mixed up fact and fancy.

"Hell, the Little Skipper, Eddie Collins, Ray Schalk, and Red Faber were suspicious and they knew something was wrong. Every baseball writer, or damned near everyone in the press box, knew something was wrong. I knew the whole story by the end of three days. I knew the names of the eight players. So did the Little Skipper and the Old Roman. But what could they do? They didn't have any evidence.

"The Skipper came to me. He called me up in Chicago before the first game there, the game that Dick Kerr won 3-0. He phoned me and he said, 'Jim, can you come right over and see me? I got to see you.'

"I went to see him at his hotel on the South Side that morning and he was worried. He didn't seem to have slept for three nights. He told me, 'Jim, some of my boys aren't trying. Some of my boys are letting me down. They're throwing the ball games on me. I don't know what to do. I'm pitching Kerr today and he isn't in on it. But what can I do? The Old Roman knows.'

"That's when I first learned how the Old Roman couldn't sleep on the night after that first game and about four o'clock in the morning, he left his suite at the Sinton and woke up John Heydler, president of the National League, and appealed to John. He couldn't go to Gerry Herrmann, owner of the Cincinnati club, and he was having a bitter feud with the president of his own league. He didn't know where to turn."

"Of course I read and heard about that story, Jim."

"Well, it was true, and the Little Skipper told me about it on the morning before the third game. He named the eight players. He asked me, 'Jim, what can I do?' I asked him why he didn't pull the players out of the lineup, and the Old Roman told him to take any player he suspected out of the lineup."

That was a question that always puzzled me. Today, managers like Casey Stengel would have done just that, and in a hurry. But today a manager would have more of a bench because of the twenty-five-player limit. And of course, at the time I wondered about the same question and hoped, too, because if the Little Skipper had done that, pulled the suspected or guilty players out of the lineup, I would have played. But I often thought what kind of a lineup we would have had. I would have been at shortstop, and Shano Collins was a first baseman as well as an outfielder and played first on and off in 1920 for the Sox. Eddie Murphy would have had to have played third base, and that would have left us with one outfielder, Nemo Liebold. And the Skipper would have had to use Birdie or Jenkins or pitchers in the outfield.

"We couldn't have won any ball games if those players were pulled out of the lineup, Jim," I said.

"That was what the Little Skipper told me. He said, 'Jim, I can't win with substitutes, and what will the public say? I ain't got any evidence. I ain't got the evidence, and I know—I know that some of my boys are letting me down.' And then he got sore. 'By God, Jim, if I ever get the evidence, and I will as sure as I'm talking to you.' He said that to me and he clenched his fist. He did get the evidence. It was due to him and the Old Roman that the whole dirty mess was finally made public, but it broke him and shortened his life. When he died of a bad heart in 1933, it was a broken heart, too, Mickey.

"But he hoped on that morning of the third game. Kerr was honest. He said, 'I can win with this kid, Kerr, Jim.' And we figured, or we hoped at all events, that the gamblers had made their clean-up on those first two games. Maybe they'd get their dirty hands on the swag and were satisfied."

Sitting there and talking with Jim, I felt a strong wish that it had never happened. I have often felt this way. There wasn't any damned thing that I could have done about it, and yet I had the funny feeling that I could have done something to avert the whole thing, prevent it from ever having happened. And it brought back all over again those games. I half wished that I hadn't seen Jim Cruisenberry. Thinking back about the past, about the time you were young and full of beans, only makes you sad. You feel low and depressed about so many things, about all that you wanted to do and become but did not succeed at. It gives you a sense of having failed, of being a failure when it's too late. I felt that way talking with Jim and having a few shots with him. It wasn't just the eight players and what happened to them that gave me such feelings. It was me. I wanted to have my chance all over again, and it's too late.

It was already too late when Eddie Cicotte threw the first pitch of the 1919 World Series. It was too late, and I didn't know it even though I was still at the beginning of my major league career.

II

The first game in Cincinnati we played in our white home uniforms, and most of them were dirty. Some of the players wouldn't change their uniforms or even their socks or jockstraps when they and the team were going good. Ray Schalk was that way and so was Eddie Collins. Eddie was one of the most superstitious ballplayers I remember. I'd be superstitious myself if I could have been the ballplayer he was.

The ballpark was already beginning to be filled up when we took the field for practice. You couldn't say that it was a sportsmanlike crowd, but then how many baseball fans believed in the Marquis of Queensberry, that is, real fans? We didn't get much of a cheer when we went out on the ball field that day. Chicago rooters who had come to Cincinnati for the first game or the first two games gave us some yells and a few Cincinnati people clapped or cheered a little but nothing that would put a strain on them. They wanted us beat—and bad, real bad.

It seemed kind of funny to me, and not only to me but also to a lot of our players. The ballpark was too quiet. You don't hear the crowd so much when you're playing, or even sitting on the bench and watching a ball game, concentrated. You only miss the fans if they aren't there and the noise if there's really noise to hear. I don't know how this affected most of the other players, and maybe it made no difference in some cases. A busher will usually react different from a veteran. But the crowd is important in a particular kind of a way, the way I've just mentioned. The crowd's important when it isn't there and when you don't hear it. The stands kept filling up more while we practiced, and it wasn't totally silent. Shoeless Joe Jackson gave them something to think about when he hit one in the temporary stands in right field, a home run in a game, and I felt good watching his drive lift and fall over the fence. I felt sorry for those fans, thinking that they and their heroes weren't going to like what they'd soon be getting.

It was a crowd full of notables and prominent people, including the candidates for president of the United States, Harding and Cox, and a lot of others from all walks of life were also present. And everything seemed perfect, the day, and the team we had to beat, everything. I watched the other club on the field, and of course the crowd came to life for them. No sir, I didn't see how they could come near to us. But this is all history now. The score of that game was 9-1. In the last half of the first inning, Eddie Cicotte hit Rath, the lead-off man for the other club, with a pitched ball. It seemed to bother him, because he started toward Rath, but the little second baseman wasn't hurt. We tied the score in the second inning, but they made five runs in the fourth and Cicotte was taken out of the ball game.

He didn't say much on the bench between innings before he went to the showers. I remember Ray looked at him a few times, kind of puzzled, and asked him about a signal, if he hadn't got it, and he made out that he missed the signal. From the bench, he looked poor, like he didn't have any stuff at all.

And then we lost the second game 4-2 with Lefty Williams in the box. He didn't give as many as sixty bases on balls all season, I'd guess from memory, and he had fine control. He could bend a sharp curve over the plate on a batter with the count three and two, and he did it many times. But he was wild and gave up three bases on balls, and a triple and three runs were scored in the ball game. We out hit them, getting ten hits to their four, but with men on base, our batters didn't bring them in. And the players who were later barred didn't come through with needed hits, if I remember.

Those two days, they were almost like the end of the world. I don't know that I remember them clearly now. Certainly, I don't remember them as clear as I thought I did. After that first game, we walked in the clubhouse pretty silent, except for Ray. He was sore as hell, mad as a bull, ready to fight.

"I never played in such a goddamned ball game in my life," he said, walking under the stands to the visitor's clubhouse.

I happened to be right in back of him, and he slowed up until he was just on my right.

"You could have been blind in one goddamned eye and near-sighted and far-sighted and have no damned sight in the other and see my signals," he said, looking at me as if I was the one responsible for the ball game.

I didn't know what the hell to say, and I guess I must have turned pale.

"And a shortstop in a semipro ball club could play in position better than our man," he yelled, looking at me and so pissed off that I thought he was going to take a swing at me.

"What the f—— is that little crab talking about?" I heard big Risberg saying behind us.

"Some people ought to know goddamned well what I'm talking about."

In the clubhouse, Cicotte sat before his locker, looking at the floor. He was dressed, except that he hadn't put on his coat and vest. He looked up and didn't say a word when we all came in. Then he stared at some of us and at the lockers and the walls. He looked down, way down in the dumps. Ray walked by Cicotte without looking at him.

The showers were running and for a moment I heard them like they were the only sound. It was strange and I've often thought of this, of the falling waters and silence, and of something impending. Then Ray cursed, and others talked.

"I just didn't have it today," Eddie Cicotte said, but I don't remember who he was talking to or if he was talking to anybody at all.

He spoke quiet and his voice sounded almost despondent. He was depressed, and of course it wasn't just because he was a pitcher who had lost a crucial ball game. He must have felt guilty as sin and rotten about it. By that time, he had been credited with winning about 190 ball games and he had one World Series victory from 1917 to his credit. It was like he had thrown away all of those ball games, fifteen years of ball games that he had pitched and won honestly, all of these were thrown away, and the twenty-one victories he rang up the next season. Of course we didn't know this for sure then, and I still didn't suspect. And Cicotte couldn't have thought this. Only he will probably ever know what he was thinking, except maybe his friends and his wife might know a little of it. But he felt rotten, and after he confessed he said that he'd gone through hell many nights. I can believe it. I remember him sitting there, with his coat and vest off, just looking low and beat.

The Little Skipper seemed puzzled and hurt. Several times I saw him staring at some of the players and it seemed that he was going to say something and then changed his mind and didn't.

"Now, we'll come back tomorrow and knock their friggin' ears off," Buck said, but that fell flat.

Some of the players had already undressed and were taking their showers, and others were pulling off their clothes. I remember I went in for my shower just after Buck had said that about knocking their ears off. I was damned low myself, and I stood under the lukewarm

shower, feeling the water hit me, and I wanted to stay under that
shower a long time, maybe not forever, but a long time.

The way the team lost that first game stunned me, and not me
alone. The writers were stunned, too, and some of the others on the
club. We sat on the bench through that fourth inning, and most of us
didn't say much. Cicotte on the mound wasn't pitching like himself,
and it made some of us nervous. We couldn't believe our eyes, seeing
him out there and throwing as if he didn't have anything on the ball.
I don't remember for sure but I don't think he got knocked out of the
box all that season, and, if he did, it could only have been once or twice.
Suddenly, like overnight, he had seemed to lose all of his stuff. It didn't
make sense. A couple of the balls he threw seemed to float up to the
plate so soft and easy that a baby could have hit them.

When he was pulled out by the Little Skipper, he walked slowly off
the mound, his eyes on the ground. He neatly folded his black glove
and put it in his hip pocket. He sat down and said, "I didn't have it
today."

"It happens to the greatest," Fred McMullen said.

I don't think anybody else said anything. Williams was sitting near
me, slumped and morose. He was kind of morose anyway.

At this distance of time, I don't remember who was in the showers
with me, but not much was said.

The clubhouse was a morgue, all right. Maybe I'm reading into it
now because I know what was going on, but it seems that so far as I
can remember, the atmosphere wasn't the same as after a game when
a ball club has lost a tough one and the players are down in the mouth.
It was different. It was like the whole Series had been lost, or like a
tragedy had happened. That ball club of ours was good and knew it.
It didn't suffer over a lost game like some ball clubs have because it
knew it could come back fighting and win the next one. It had become
so good—hell, so great—that the players knew that they could almost
go out on the ball field any day they wanted to and win a ball game
against any club in either league. They were better in 1919 than they
had been in 1917 when they won the championship of the world. They
were better even though Red Faber was in a weakened condition and
not in the form he was when he won three games of the 1917 Series
against the Giants of John McGraw. Dick Kerr wasn't as good as Faber,
but Cicotte and Williams won sixty-two games between them, and the

club won the pennant that year with eighty-eight games of the 140-game schedule. There were days when I could have gone out there and pitched and we would have won the ball game.

It seemed that practically everybody knew that something unusual had happened and didn't quite know why or what it was all about. I don't think there were many who have said to themselves or who did say to themselves that the ball game had been sloughed. Even though there was talk of games being thrown like you couldn't hear nowadays, nobody on the ball club was ready and prepared to believe that this would happen on our ball club. That first ball game was lost in a way to make you kind of sick with surprise. That's about the way it was with most of those in the clubhouse after the game, except for the players who knew why.

They didn't let on to the rest of us how they felt. Cicotte had spoken to Pal Josephs in the lobby the night before the ball game and told him he felt fine and expected to pitch winning ball. Pal was a hell of a nice guy, a young fellow in business, I think it was real estate, who was prosperous and was an enthusiastic baseball fan and White Sox rooter. He knew the ballplayers and came around the ballpark a lot and saw the players socially. He was friendly to me but didn't pay too much attention to me because I was just a busher and he sort of took on the attitudes of the veterans who were his friends.

Pal must have wanted to be a ballplayer desperately when he was a kid because he was so keen about the game and such a strong White Sox fan. I first saw him on the train going to Texas for spring training in 1919. I thought he must be a rookie because he looked young, and then he was only in his twenties, but he was shaking hands and talking to the stars and veterans like an old friend, telling jokes with them, patting them on the back, and he couldn't have been a rookie and acted like that. I learned pretty quick what he was. Pal was good looking, and a friendly, warm guy, trusting and happy as a lark to feel he was so closely associated with baseball. He spoke of the ball club as "we" and "his" and of other teams as "them." Down in Texas he put on a uniform and practiced a few times, and I was afraid he was going to be hurt.

Pal bet a lot of money on the White Sox. He was supposed to have lost at least $3,500 betting on the ball club to win in the 1919 Series, and he was called to testify before the grand jury that investigated gambling in baseball and broke the story of the 1919 Series wide open. He bumped into Eddie Cicotte in the lobby of the Sinton Hotel the night before the first game, and that's when Cicotte told him he was in fine shape and let him go ahead and bet and lose his dough. I think he testified about this before the grand jury and also was the witness who told the jurors about that so-called mysterious package McMullen was supposed to have delivered to Buck's home.

I remember that Cicotte and Williams left the clubhouse together. And I remember the Little Skipper standing with his shirt off, bare from the waist up, still wearing his baseball pants and saying, "The ball game was played as if some of my boys weren't trying." He said that many times, they "weren't trying," they "weren't trying to win," they "didn't play like they were trying to win."

And I remember that Ray was still sore and talked about players not being in position and he and Risberg had angry words, but I think that it was after the next or the second game that they almost had a fistfight in the clubhouse. I believe that some of the newspaper writers later said that they did have a fight, but that wasn't true. It would have been stopped. Risberg most certainly should have been able to clean up a fellow like Ray, who was so much smaller and lighter, but Ray was a fighting little gamecock and he didn't take nothing from anybody, no matter who he was or how big he was.

I don't remember Eddie Collins saying much in the clubhouse. He wasn't on speaking terms with Gandil and scarcely with some of the others. They all, the eight players, left the clubhouse with one another. I left with Lefty. We didn't say much going back to the hotel.

"That was a lousy game today," I did say.

"I heard Eddie Collins say it was terrible. He said, 'This is terrible.'"

And the Hotel Sinton that night, that was terrible.

III

I didn't eat steak that night after the first ball game. I didn't have that much appetite. There was a prize fight in the Cincinnati ballpark that night. I think it was between Ritchie Mitchell and Joe Welling. I'd thought of taking it in, but I didn't feel like it.

On the streets coming back in the cab, I saw plenty of happy people on the street, and the sidewalk in front of the Sinton Hotel was crowded. I heard the newsboys shouting the extra papers as I pushed through a happy and buzzing crowd in front of the hotel to go inside into the lobby. The extra papers about Cincinnati winning the first game were already on the streets. The lobby was buzzing inside and the gamblers were already waving money, betting on the Reds for the second game. If I remember correctly, the odds had shifted and the White Sox were the underdogs. That was crazy, all right.

"This is all crazy," I said to Lefty Sullivan.

He just looked at me, sad, hurt, but he didn't say anything. I think that that was the moment that Lefty made up his mind that there was something definitely wrong with the Series.

There were happy and smiling faces and glum ones in the Sinton lobby, and there were a few drunks. Of course I saw a few dames here or there, like I did the first night, and I had an idea what they were there for. There were wives around, too, some but not too many. I remember that Ray's wife, for one, was with him at the Series. She's a nice woman and maybe it was good she was with him. Maybe she saved him from blowing a gasket.

Even to this day I get a little queasy or sick when I think of the lobby of that hotel in Cincinnati. Because there in the lobby were many of the bastards who pulled the job or profited from it by being in on it. I think of them and of some of them with greasy faces and cigars stuck in their mouths, and some of them seem in my memory like they had ratlike eyes. And there were some who were fat, and some in loud gray suits and wearing fancy silk shirts, and here and there, flashing a diamond ring or a diamond stick pin and waving wads of money, trying to get suckers. But after the first game it wasn't so easy.

A lot of people weren't like me, a nineteen-year-old rookie kid, and they caught the lousy smell of the wind quick enough, quicker than me. Some of the writers afterward said or wrote they were sure after they saw the first pitch when Cicotte hit Rath. I think it was the first pitch, anyway. Walking into the lobby, I wanted to get away from it, but I was held by some awful kind of fascination. You heard snatches of talk about the ball game, the players, the bets, and even a snatch or two that more than hinted that there was a fix, all right.

Outside, the fans and people of Cincinnati were beginning to make it a hot time in the old town, but in the lobby and hotel it was a little bit different, and while there were some fans or Cincinnatians, most of the people there were on the inside, baseball people and writers and gamblers, fans like Pal and quite a lot of Chicago fans, too. Some of these latter were glum, and others bet, and I heard one or two saying "wait until tomorrow." I heard one fellow, he was fat and had a deep voice, and he said, "Jesus man almighty, of all the days for Cicotte to have an off day, the opening of the World Series when I got five hundred bucks bet on the ball game."

"The worst I ever saw them play, the worst—why, they could have done better even with that kid, Donovan, in there," I heard Pal saying to somebody in the lobby.

It was a little early to eat and Lefty and I didn't know what to do. Neither of us wanted to take a walk, and so we went up to our room. The elevator going up was crowded.

We'd bought newspapers, and there was the headline before us. I don't remember what it was but it was something like "Reds Swamp Sox" or "Redlegs Trounce White Sox." I read a little about the game but not too much.

I flopped on my bed, and Lefty went into the bathroom and closed the door. I lay there and there was a buzz, the noise of the city, footsteps and voices in the hall. I heard the voice of Shoeless Joe Jackson speaking in his drawl, but I don't remember what he said or even if I heard his words or any more than just the sound of his voice. I closed my eyes to try and think about the ball game and the way we were routed. And I didn't and couldn't think of anything.

Bad as we had been licked, I wouldn't have been so down-in-the-mouth but for the atmosphere in the clubhouse, on the bench and on the ball field, and in the hotel. Of that, I'm pretty certain—in fact I am certain. I'm not what you call a psychologist or anything like that, but as I analyze it now, we were somehow prepared for what happened—even me, and that was why I was hit like I was even before the disastrous fourth inning when Cicotte was knocked out of the box. And I knew the ball club and the ballplayers least well of anyone on the roster because I was the newest man on it and the youngest, and even though I might have tried to pretend otherwise and did, I hadn't much experience in life. Hell, I was still only learning the ropes, learning to be big league.

If you're a ballplayer, you see a ball game different from a fan. You see a lot of little things that the fan never notices. Shortstop can be a few steps out of position, a few feet in or back, and the fan won't notice it, but you do, sitting on the bench and watching or playing on the field yourself. If you are playing the outfield, you see the ball from the minute the bat meets it and that's when you move. You can tell if an outfielder is on the ball or if he is slow, but not many fans will see this.

I'd had a little experience with the club in 1918, and I'd been with it in spring training in 1919 and then I'd sat on the bench and watched every game from early July onwards, and had even gotten into a couple. The way the veterans played was beginning to be like second nature or instinct to me. I'd begun to know what they could do and how they could and did play their positions because I was up there, determined to stay, and if I couldn't play but could only sit on the bench, well, I'd watch and learn, like a student. So I was, baseball-wise, different from the Mickey Donovan who was pulled from the Rocks to the White Sox just a little more than a year before in August 1918. In baseball, itself, as distinct from sophistication and knowing your way around off of the ball field, I was beginning to be big league, like I was able to prove in the latter half of the next season when I was put out in right field during a hot, hard pennant race because of injuries on the club.

I remember once hearing Buck talk to a writer who came to interview him when we were both winding up our active baseball-playing days in the semipro ballparks of Chicago and vicinity. Buck talked something like this. He was explaining how he played third base. "I knew my league. I didn't know nothin' about the other league. But I knew our league. There's a man on first. There's a man on second. There's a man on third base. I'm playing third. I know the speed of the batter. I know the speed of the ball. I know the speed of the pitcher. I know the speed of them runners. That's why I knew where to play on each goddamn pitch."

I learned how to play ball and get some polish, sitting on the bench and watching men like that out there on the diamond. So sitting on the bench with the sun on me in Cincinnati during the first innings of the first game of that unfortunate World Series, I could tell that there was something wrong. That was more conclusive than the way the betting odds changed.

Out in center field, Happy Felsch didn't seem to be in the right spot. Cicotte put his hands in front of his face, his left foot went forward, his right arm moved, and he pitched. Felsch or Risberg, they didn't move quick enough. Or take Cicotte. He hit the first batter and then started toward Little Morrie Rath like he'd hurt him seriously. There was something that didn't click in me. And the way he pitched. He didn't seem to have nothing, anything, not a thing on some of those balls he pitched. But I saw him throw in a fastball to one batter. I forget who the batter was, but he was a right-handed hitter, because we sat on the first base side of the field. He threw one pitch so fast that the batter couldn't get the bat around in time. I guess he threw that fastball just to show them what he could have done if he wanted to, a soothing of his pride. I like to think that that pitch was the best he ever threw. It was one of his best, and he must have thrown it just to soothe his pride. Why else would he have let go with such a fastball when he was trying to hit the bats of the Cincinnati players?

And even though the deal with the gamblers and then throwing the Series was so much of a surprise, now it seems to me that, in a way, it was all understandable. A team like ours shouldn't have surprised or shocked anyone, no matter what it did. There was no team spirit on it, and some of the time players would be playing against each other. This was all more noticeably so in 1920, the last season, but there were traces and hints of it coming before that. The outfielders sometimes would throw a ball more to make Ray look bad than to get the man out, and sometimes Eddie Collins could hardly have a ball thrown to him in infield practice except from Ray. The club disproved once and for all the idea that a baseball team has to have harmony to win.

I don't know if I told about what the Little Skipper and Eddie said when the Skip reappointed him as captain in 1919. Collins went to the Little Skipper a little while after that and said that there was no use in his being captain. Eddie, you see, called the plays. Well, he told the Skipper that his signals were being ignored, and he could never get some of the players to follow the signals.

Skip told him, "You got to use your head. If you want a hit-and-run play, give 'em the sign for a bunt. If you don't want a man to steal, give him the steal sign. Use your head. I can't think for you. You have intelligence."

Rowland said that he told the Old Roman, in 1918, that something was going to happen to the ball club unless there was a strong hand controlling them. It wasn't a team that raised too much hell by carousing. Some of them drank and got stewed, and Joe Jackson was a little drunk when he confessed, or at least the papers said that. He was supposed to have said he got "teed off" the night before he confessed. It was a team that played its own baseball and never paid much attention to the manager. Now looking back, it seems to me that something had to happen to that ball club. I guess you call it subconscious. What I mean is that somehow you knew without knowing that you knew, if that makes any sense.

But I was beginning to know that I knew after that first game. And it was hard to accept and believe anything like that about those players. Losing the first game seemed almost a relief on that night after it, because it seemed to justify the betting on the second game. This may sound like a goofy way to reason, and it is, or was, but I even had such thoughts.

The dining room was crowded again, and I saw many of the same faces. Lefty and I were ushered to a small table for two and we sat eating and not saying a lot. There wasn't much talk in us, I guess, because there was too much disappointment. The dining room seemed pretty much the same as on the first or the previous night. It seemed that we had been there at the hotel for a long time, longer than our second day. We'd not be staying there the next night, but we'd have to return for the sixth game, at least, unless the other club took the Series in a clean sweep of five straight.

"What the hell, one ball game," Lefty said, after we sat at our table, silent for a spell.

"Yeah, it might be the sort of thing this ball club needed."

"It just goes to show, even a man like Cicotte can be off. He didn't seem to have nothing on the ball. I could have hit him."

"It looked like you could see the seam on the ball while it was going up to the hitter," I said.

"Yeah, you could have read the trademark on the ball."

"He ain't pitched no game like that all year," Lefty said.

"It's out of his system," I said. We were talking to make ourselves believe in the ball club. I guess we even believed what we said, or at least we half believed it.

I said that I saw many of the same familiar faces on the second night at dinner as I had the first, but it was not quite the same. It didn't seem as gay in the dining room. It wasn't only the White Sox defeat but also the way in which our club lost that surprised so many. But while

I didn't know it then as I do now, the newspapermen and some of the baseball people at the Sinton Hotel weren't just surprised because the White Sox had played such a lousy ball game and looked off form so much. They were suspicious. And maybe I'm reading back now from hindsight, but at least as I remember it, I think there was a difference that you could feel and that I think I felt at the time. Men didn't talk quite the same as they had the night before. Lefty and I, we didn't.

Eddie Cicotte looked pretty down in the mouth at supper and disappeared right afterward, going to his room. I remember that one of the Cincinnati sportswriters wrote that he did that because he felt so bad, so rotten. I guess he did, because I remember reading how when he made his confession the next year, he said, "I suffered a thousand nights of hell." That night must have been one of them, the first one of those nights.

"A ball club like ours can't have two days like this one here today," Lefty said.

"Hell no," I said.

The Little Skipper was in the hotel dining room and he looked like he was taking it real hard, too. And Ray Schalk was sitting near us. His wife was with him, I remember. I heard his voice rise and him say, "My God!" Then his wife seemed to shush him a little, but I know I figured at the time that he must have been talking about the day's ball game, still taking it hard, still sore about it.

"We got Williams and I know we'll win our first one with him," Lefty also said to me.

"We can't have both of them off, two days in succession," I said.

Williams was eating and I remember looking across the room at him. I never had much to say to him, nor he to me, because I was a busher, and the next season the eight ballplayers stuck pretty much to themselves.

"What a pitcher he is," I said to Lefty.

"Before he hangs up his glove and is done for, he's going to go down as one of the greatest of them all, one of the greatest southpaws in the game."

"That's because you're a lefty yourself," I told him, trying to kid because a little kidding would have made me feel better. I took that defeat hard myself, as I guess I must have indicated already.

"You know how goddamn good he is," Lefty said.

"I'm glad I'm not batting against him."

"If the day comes when I can throw a curve or my spitter on a three-two pitch the way he does. He'll break that curve over on a three-two pitch, even on Ty Cobb."

"I seen him," I remember saying.

"Who we got in our league, what southpaws we got?"

"There's Ruth," I said.

"Yeah, I know. I don't take nothing from him."

"He struck me out last year and gave me a laugh. He couldn't remember my name or didn't know it and he called me Flack."

"Flack, how come?"

"Max Flack, the Cubs' right fielder."

"A good ballplayer, I hear, but there wouldn't be any room for him here on our ball club."

"I'm glad there isn't—I don't want room on this club. I like it in Frisco, but you know there's one place you're dying to be when you're a ballplayer and that's up here in the big leagues."

"Damned right, Mick—Mickey Flack," Lefty kidded, and he laughed.

"Flack, I guess he's a Jew," I said.

"Babe Ruth called you Flack," Lefty said, laughing.

"I heard he can't remember names."

"When you can pitch as good as him, you don't have to remember names. And Mick, he ain't no slouch as a hitter. Twenty-nine home runs this year, that's a record. He's not going to do as much pitching any more. He is a hell of a pitcher, but if I was a manager, I'd take Williams over him."

"You get a hitter, too, if you get Ruth, Lefty."

"This club's got hitters enough."

"It didn't have today. Jackson didn't look like a great hitter today."

"Tomorrow's another day."

"That's what my mother always says—'Tomorrow is another day,'" I said. Tomorrow wasn't another day, but I thought it was then, that night, eating my supper in the big, bright dining room of the Hotel Sinton with the shiny chandeliers and the linen and shining silver and the good food and the crowd, the World Series crowd. Yes, I thought that tomorrow was another day. Maybe the Little Skipper did too, and plenty of others.

I remember I saw Joe Gedeon pass our table and go on to sit down in a vacant chair at the table where Buck was sitting. Gedeon was the St. Louis Brown infielder and a friend of Buck's and the other players. He was with them in the Series a lot, and in Chicago I think he stayed with Gandil. If it wasn't with Gandil, it was with one of those eight players. He made dough betting on Cincinnati, I think, and he was almost called to testify before the grand jury. He was dropped from the game. Gedeon was a good infielder, and he had his best year in 1920. He hit over .290, almost .300, and he'd have had some more good years ahead of him. But he seemed to be a pal of St. Louis gamblers and he wrecked his own career. Gedeon was from the Pacific Coast. I think he played out there with Buck and that's when they became friends. He's dead now. It's as if it didn't make any difference. But he must have been a happy guy that night in Cincinnati because he was in on such a good thing and cleaning up.

Think of it. Gedeon thought he was in on a good thing.

IV

I got sore that first night, and I haven't ever had any use for Cincinnati and the fans there. I mentioned how quiet they were when we took our practice. It wasn't sportsmanlike and I never experienced anything like that in Chicago or in any other league ballpark. That night after the first game, the fans weren't quiet, not by a damned sight. The whole town celebrated and had a hot time in that old town on that night. They were milling and talking and shouting, and they were blowing horns and whistles, and the automobile drivers pounded their goddamned horns and put their cut-outs on. It was a goddamned racket to me and I couldn't have helped but dislike it.

I looked at some of the Cincy fans on the streets near the Sinton Hotel and hated their guts, and I would have liked to have taken a sock at some of them. And they bumped into you and they bumped into each other and anybody and everybody on the sidewalks and the streets, let out whoopees. There was a parade and some of them carried signs they had made, bragging about their ball club and making cracks at ours, and one guy was carrying an effigy of Cicotte. People looked at him and laughed and he went out.

Now that doesn't seem to be of any importance. Maybe many of the fellows who celebrated that night, getting everything off their chests and getting their kicks, maybe they're dead now. But it seems to me pathetic, the way they demonstrated and felt good for themselves and for Cincinnati on that night, making whoopee and whooping it up for their favorite ball club when our ball club just laid down and deliberately lost the ball game. I thought of them all as a lot of damned Dutch, but of course what I thought and what I felt and what I wanted to do was all colored by that ball game our club lost.

I stood in the lobby for a while. There was more betting, but I don't think as much Chicago money was to be found. I mean, of course, in the hotel. All around the country, there must have been plenty of money bet.

Pal Joseph was there and he came over to me. "Hello Clover," he said. He liked to call ballplayers by their nicknames even better than their first names.

"Hello Pal," I said.

"I never expected to see a ball game like the game I seen today," he said, shaking his head.

"The whole team was overconfident and had an off day," I said.

"Off day, Clover. I didn't think it was possible for me ever to see the boys play a ball game like that one today."

"Me neither. It makes you think," I said.

"What did you say, Clover?" he asked quickly.

"Cicotte didn't have his stuff and the team didn't hit Reuther. He seemed to have lots of stuff. He was throwing fast and some of the players couldn't get their bats around fast enough."

"Eddie told me he just didn't have his stuff," Pal said.

Lefty Williams passed with Gandil and Pal buttonholed Williams. They were just a couple of feet from me. I heard them talk.

"Lefty, how do you feel?" Pal asked.

"Oh, I feel all right," Williams said. He was born in the south and he talked with a drawl.

"Good. How's the arm?"

"Oh, my arm's good, Pal."

"It better be because I lost $1,000 today, and I'm laying a thousand on you to win that ball game tomorrow afternoon."

"Don't bet, Pal."

"Why—ain't that soup bone any good? Isn't it right?"

"Oh, it's all right."

"That's all I need to know. If your arm's good, that team of castoffs can't beat you, Lefty."

"I wouldn't bet, Pal."

"But why—your arm is all right?"

"Yes, nothin' is the matter with my arm. But don't bet."

"I got confidence in you boys, Lefty. That ball game today isn't enough to shake my confidence in you boys. I seen you enough and know you too well."

"I know we got the better ball club. But I don't know, Pal. I wouldn't bet."

"Since your arm is good, that's all I need to know," Pal said, slapping Williams on the back.

Williams and Gandil went through the crowd and left the hotel. That must have been the time they went out and Gandil gave the money to Williams in a dirty envelope. He gave Williams $10,000 and Williams gave half of that to Shoeless Joe Jackson.

There I was standing there and hearing that exchange between Pal and Williams, with the other pitcher trying to tell Pal not to bet. Pal didn't at all take the hint, because after Williams and Gandil had gone on across the lobby to leave the hotel, he turned back to me and he said, "I just talked to Lefty Williams and he told me his arm is good. I'm going now and bet another thousand dollars on your ball club. Hell, Lefty's a greater southpaw than even Eddie Plank was. This Cincinnati team of castoffs can't beat us two days runnin', not with the kind of ball club we got."

So, Pal went off to bet another thousand bucks, throwing bad money after good. It doesn't matter now and I think Pal is dead, but I still can't help feeling sorry for him. He was such a decent cuss, a hell of a nice fellow and a real fan. The White Sox never had a more loyal and devoted fan than him. The scandal just about broke his heart and he couldn't see another ball game.

I remember I met him on Michigan Avenue downtown, sometime back around 1926. "Clover, for Christ sake, how in hell are you? Gee, say, I'm glad to see you," he said, shaking my hand and smiling like he was real glad to see me. But also, he told me, "Clover, I couldn't see a ball game. I just can't go. I read about the games every day. I'm damned glad to see how you're making out, but I can't go out to the ballpark."

Hell, I have no bitterness against those players, but they didn't know the harm they were doing. They had no idea of what they were doing. They didn't know any better. At the time, I looked up to those players because of what they were. I thought of them as ballplayers and I didn't give any thought to their characters. Hell, if a man was a great or a near-great baseball player, or even a good one, why, that was like he had a good character. I learned that there isn't necessarily any connection between how good or how great a baseball player a man might be and what kind of man he is.

Some of those fellows were led, and I think that Lefty Williams was one who was led. He never would have done what he did by himself or have had the idea to do it. Sometimes he'd be morose and quiet, and now and then he'd get cocked, but only if he was with some of the other players and they were drinking. He liked to talk about pitching and sometimes he talked about farming. He was just a young fellow from a small town in North Carolina. He was a good friend of Shoeless Joe Jackson. They were roomies and palled together. He didn't know what he was doing.

No, I don't mean that. He knew what he was doing, but he must not have thought of the consequences of it, or that he'd ever be caught and barred from baseball. And his wife, she was a dark-haired southern woman, and I heard she didn't want him to take that money, and she cried and wanted him to give it back after he did get it. But he sort of went along. His friends were in on the fix so he got in. Why shouldn't he? I guess he figured it that way. Cicotte now, he said he wanted to win one game because of his next year's contract. But Williams didn't think of that, although he was making a hell of a lot less money than most of the other players he conspired with. There he was, the best southpaw pitcher in the league and he was making $2,800 a season, I think. Cicotte was getting more. Some said he got $10,000 but I don't think that's so. He made around $6,000, maybe a little less. Williams did try to warn off Pal, which Cicotte didn't do. Cicotte let Pal lose. But Williams did, too.

All of this doesn't mean much now, does it? Many things in the world would have been the same if those games weren't sloughed, wouldn't they? But in baseball it would have been different. And that night when

I stood in the lobby and Lefty Williams passed Pal, it wasn't too late. That lobby was full of people who could have done something about it. The Little Skipper was in the lobby for a few minutes, and many of the newspapermen, and if one or another of them had said something, that might have been enough to stop it. I thought of this many times during all of these years, especially after I retired from baseball.

Lefty Sullivan had gone out to walk around by himself and he came in smoking a cigar and we went up to our room to go to bed.

V

In the clubhouse before the second game, the Little Skipper stood in the center and looked around at us, and he said it looked like some of the players weren't trying. And McMullen blew his top at that and said he'd fight anybody who accused him. That was odd because McMullen was a sub and all he did was coach at first base and pinch hit. The Little Skipper didn't pick McMullen up, and we went on the field for practice. The Skipper walked out of the clubhouse alone, and his face was grave. But it didn't do any good, because like I said, we lost. The game was better than the first one, but it wasn't a good ball game.

The Cincinnati club didn't look like a real championship club to me and to many of the other players. That Roush was a fine player. I wouldn't have taken him over Felsch—that is, with Felsch trying—but he was good, a good hitter and good fielder. He made a good catch on a ball hit by Felsch, way out in right center, and he could hit. He led the other league that year but with an average of only .329. And that Groh at third base was a fine ballplayer, one of the best third basemen in the game. He used that funny bat, a bottle-shaped bat, and stood facing the pitcher and waving his bat forward, swinging it above his right shoulder. He'd step into the ball and he could hit. He was real good, even though I wouldn't have taken him over Buck.

The Cincinnati fans were out again like it was a picnic. And that's what it was for them. They saw their team win again over the White Sox that all the experts had picked to win hands down, and the fans couldn't not try to rub it in. But our club kept them on edge. We got ten hits and were threatening right down to the wire. Sallee pitched, and he was foxy and had a good crossfire, but those ten hits would have been more than enough to win if we could have moved the runners around. The players who were in on the deal didn't seem to do much with men on base, and, if a couple of them had come through, we might have knocked Sallee out of the box. That milk is long since spilled and dried up. Ray Schalk was fighting mad on the bench, especially after the last half of the fourth when the Reds scored three runs and issued three bases on balls.

"All season you get the ball over the plate. You throw me strikes, and now where are the strikes?" I remember him saying that.

It wasn't as bad in the clubhouse after the second game. It was like the second defeat was expected and could be explained. The Little Skipper took it hard. He thought a lot of all of us, and there never was a man in baseball who thought more of the players than the Little Skipper.

"My boys aren't trying," he said, and he said that many times.

"It's that sun in center field," Felsch said, explaining how he'd been misjudging fly balls. Happy looked like a high school kid out there in center field. And he was next to Tris Speaker in center field.

We went back to Chicago on the train that night after the second game, the White Sox Special. There wasn't any harmonizing, and some of the players turned in early. Lefty Williams was one of them. I sat in the club car with Sullivan and I said, "This is like a funeral train."

"It couldn't be anything else. We out hit them and lose, 4-2," Lefty said.

"Goddamn, they win two ball games. But this is only two friggin' ball games in five," Buck said at the other end of the car.

"Tell Buck to get a soapbox," one of the newspapermen said.

Ring Lardner, the sportswriter, walked through the club car with another reporter, I think it was Tubby Royal. They were singing a parody that Lardner or maybe both of them wrote. It was called "I'm Forever Blowing Ball Games." None of the ballplayers in the club car said anything.

I wanted to turn in, but I still sat in the club car. I didn't want to climb into my upper berth and lie there alone. Lefty sat there in the club car, too. I guess he didn't want to turn in either. They sang that parody again, "I'm Forever Blowing Ball Games." The Little Skipper came into the club car while the two writers were still singing that parody. He didn't look happy. Buck left the club car, passing by us and giving me a pat on the shoulder. Then a poker game broke up and

Gandil, Risberg, McMullen, and Cicotte left the club car. They didn't say good night to anyone. Eddie Collins sat down beside Eddie Murphy. I heard Collins say that he knew the Series wouldn't be like 1914, the year the Boston Braves took four straight from the Athletics.

"Say I'm a bad loser or anything you want, and I still insist, goddamn it, that the best team didn't win these ball games," the Little Skipper said to the newspapermen.

"We know that," one of the sports writers said.

"His wildness beat us," Ray Schalk said as he stepped near us to speak with a writer.

I felt lousy when I did hit the hay in the upper berth. I heard the wheels on the rails, the whistle, and then, a snore. If there was something wrong maybe I'd get in the Series, I thought. I dreamed of what I'd do in the Series and then went to sleep.

When I woke up it was morning. Now on our home grounds, we were going to even things up and then forge ahead. I felt a little rotten, too, because I had begun to grow suspicious. There couldn't be anything wrong, I told myself.

When the train stopped at 63rd Street, I left and took the elevated train to 51st Street. Walking home with my suitcase after I left the El, it seemed strange for me to be coming here from Cincinnati. But I was disappointed, too. I was glad I didn't meet anyone I knew. I think I felt a little ashamed about those first two games and didn't want to be asked by anyone to explain the way we lost. And I thought, too, that Pal had lost more money.

CHAPTER SEVEN

I

It's always been real good to get back to Chicago after I am away on a trip. It's coming home, where I belong. And with all of the traveling I've done, the cities I've been in in my baseball days, there isn't one I'd take over Chicago, not even New York. I might take the New York Yankees over the Chicago White Sox, but the way I'd like to take them is to bring them out here and send the White Sox to New York. But as I say, getting back home to Chicago always gives me a real good feeling. And it was certainly mighty good to get back to Chicago after those couple of days we were in Cincinnati at the beginning of that 1919 World Series. I felt something was over and I was back on safe ground. And the ball club was back, too, where the fans were all for it and with it, and it would play a different brand of ball. And as for something being wrong in the Series, I convinced myself that that would be different on the home grounds. Every one of our players would give his best and would try before the hometown fans. We had to win that third game. It was just in the cards that we do.

Getting home that morning, I realized how things were going on the same as usual, with the kids in school, the peddlers on the streets and in the alleys, the men working, the stores open, women shopping and some of them taking their babies or small kids with them, and other women doing their housework, and a hell of a lot going on besides the World Series. In Cincinnati, it was different because I was in the midst of what was happening, and so the World Series seemed like the only important thing in the world that was happening. I knew all of this but it hit me like a surprise, nevertheless. Only Ma was home, because Ruthie was at work and my kid brother and kid sister were at school, but I bought one of the tickets allowed me for Billy and he'd go to the ball game after lunch. I was just as glad he was away in school when I got home because he would have asked lots of questions about the Series and I wasn't in any mood for answering his questions.

"Mickey, did you let them beat you? I prayed, too, that the Sox would win both days."

"We'll win today, Ma."

"Let me make you some breakfast. You must be half-starved."

"No, Ma, I had my breakfast on the train. I'll just have a cup of coffee." I had that cup of coffee she gave me that morning sitting at the kitchen table. I can almost taste it now, at this minute. In retrospect, it seems that good.

I took a nap that morning, and I remember I dreamed I was playing regular and made an error with the bases full to lose the Series. I was leaving the ball field to get dressed, disgraced, feeling like all hell because I had made that error on purpose, and I couldn't find the clubhouse. I looked and walked, and there was a long passageway with no end, and I walked and walked, and I was in a panic, but my mother woke me up. It was time for me to go to the ballpark.

And I took my same old route, the 51st streetcar to Wentworth and then, the Wentworth Avenue streetcar. It was exciting as hell going to the ballpark. Excitement was in the air. The two games we lost in Cincinnati were nothing. We were home and with the stands packed, it was going to be like 1917 all over again, and the White Sox would be champions of the world.

Walking on 35th Street after I got off the streetcar, I thought how only two years before I had stood in line from five o'clock on, or maybe half past five, before it was dawn. And there I was, a member of the White Sox. I would have just about given my right arm to have played, too, especially in that third game when Dick Kerr set the other club down 3-0 and allowed only three hits. And of all of the times I stepped out on the White Sox ball field in the sunshine, wearing my glove and loosening up and going through the practice paces, there's no time I can recall when I got a bigger kick or a greater thrill than on that day of the third game of the Series. It was too early for the grandstand

and the boxes to be filled up, but there were a few people in those sections, and the bleachers and pavilion were just about full up. A big roar greeted us, and we began tossing the balls back and forth while Lefty Sullivan warmed up to pitch batting practice.

There was a band and music and the fronts of the stands on the infield were hung with bunting. Flags were flying and the day was fine. The World Series is a great event. It really is a classic. I felt that more on that day of the third game than I even had on the other two days. That was because we were home. That meant a hell of a lot to me, and I guess it must have to Lefty, too, but even more to me, because Lefty wasn't born in Chicago but in a small town in Wisconsin, whereas I was born and raised on the South Side of Chicago and had gone to see the Sox play. They had been my team, and then, I had become a member of the club.

Something happened between the gamblers and the ballplayers. The players had been double-crossed, and they didn't get all of the money that had been promised them. They were sore. Gandil was, I'm certain, because it later came out in the newspapers that Bill Burns had been sent out to see Gandil, who lived somewhere around 39th and Grand Boulevard, and Gandil had said he and the players were finished. He told Burns to go to hell. The plot was really thickening by then. In the clubhouse the players in on the deal didn't, so far as I can recall, say a word to Kerr. They didn't want to win for him, I guess, and that's the story. If they weren't winning for their own pitchers, Cicotte and Williams, they weren't going to win for a busher. So I'm inclined to think the story was right and Dick Kerr won with some of his own men against him.

In practice, the infielders gave the fans a demonstration. The way they handled that ball and threw it, and Buck at third was sure picking them out of the dirt in his best manner. I don't know if the other ball club watched us in practice, but if they did, they should have sat up to take plenty of notice. I had about five minutes, too, on the infield. When I ran off the field, a lot of the fans yelled my name.

Kerr pitched a beautiful ball game. He almost didn't make a bad pitch, and his control was perfect. He mixed up his stuff and his curve ball was breaking beautifully. He had the other team eating out of his hand. He was toying with them. And he had guts. He didn't seem the least bit nervous. Between the innings, Ray sat next to him on the bench and talked to him. Ray was like a new man. After two and a half innings, we were leading 2-0.

"We're going to win this game even if we don't score another run," Ray said coming back to the bench at the end of the first half of the third inning.

He was right, too, and every inning when the Reds went out and our players ran in from the field it looked better. That little fellow on the box had control of that ball game in his left hand and his left arm. He pitched an inspiring game, and I sat watching him out on the mound, almost like a midget, a real David and Goliath kind of battle. And that victory was heartening, leaving us only one game behind the other club. I felt it was really the beginning of the Series and that we'd win the game the next day and make the Series brand new.

That's how naïve I was, I suppose. I should have known everything about the Series, about the third game, I guess, because nowadays you meet people who say they did know everything, especially the writers. But it wasn't easy to catch on and know for sure. None of the players involved or supposed to be among the guilty came out and said that he was throwing the games. And even the best of them can make honest mistakes, commit physical or mental errors.

I remember once hearing some talk in the clubhouse about throwing games. It was in 1919, and I remember Eddie Cicotte saying that it was hard to throw a ball game, and it might be impossible. A player trying to throw a game might not have the ball hit to him. Or a pitcher might be trying to lose, but his teammates will make miraculous stops and putouts. Too many things can happen in a ball game. I remember Cicotte saying this in the clubhouse, and of course I heard him say it again the next season. So I was hoping all over again after that third game when I dressed and left the clubhouse. The Little Skipper wasn't. He hadn't slept for three nights, and the ball game Kerr pitched didn't allay his fears or suspicions at all.

Jim Cruisenberry, whom I have already mentioned, wrote later on, about a year or two after the Skipper died, I guess it was, that on the morning of the fourth game, about ten o'clock, the Little Skipper telephoned him to come and see him. Jim took a taxicab and went to see the Skipper and told about it. The Little Skipper told Jim he hadn't slept for those three nights, like I've just mentioned, and that he knew some of the players were crooked. "Some of my boys aren't trying on me," he is supposed to have told Jim.

They went driving for an hour and talked. The Little Skipper was worried but he couldn't prove anything and didn't know what to do. The Old Roman had told him to remove any player that he suspected, but there wasn't any proof. The Little Skipper told this to Jim. But Jim said that he couldn't do anything either. He went to his editor at the *Chicago Tribune* and said that he knew that the Series wasn't on the level, and he named eight players, including Buck, but the editor told him not to print anything because if he didn't have the goods on the players, then the paper could be sued for libel. They would have known more about that than I would have known, then or than I do now. And of course in Chicago, I didn't get to the hotels where the gamblers and newspapermen and the other ball club stayed, and I didn't see or hear anything the way I did in Cincinnati for the first two ball games. Being a busher and still really a kid, I didn't have much social relationship with the players off the field except for Lefty, and I didn't hear anything from them and none of them told me anything directly, insofar as to what they were thinking or what they were feeling. So all kinds of things were happening and I knew nothing about them. That's why for years I have been saying I didn't see much or hear much during that season, but nobody or almost nobody ever seemed fully to believe me.

I had to hear about a lot of things later on, some of them after it was all over. And you can't always be sure about what you hear after something has happened, especially years afterward, because people don't remember everything clear.

Even in Cincinnati, at the Hotel Sinton, things were going on that I didn't and couldn't know anything about even though they were happening on the same hotel floor as the one that we were on, Lefty and me sharing a room.

Nobody knew about the meetings of the players and gamblers in Cincinnati, and how Burns passed the Little Skipper in the corridor of the eighth floor of the Hotel Sinton when he had the money, $10,000, under his arm.

"Hello, Skip," Burns said.

"Hello," the Little Skipper is supposed to have said.

They each passed on. That was supposed to have been on the night after the opening game.

And Gandil is supposed to have sent a telegram to his wife from Cincinnati telling her, "I bet my shirt."

And Lefty Williams's wife is supposed to have cried and not wanted him to take any of the money that he is supposed to have taken, or else maybe I am wrong, and maybe it was Gandil's wife who cried. You see, even to this day I'm not sure about some details and can't be sure of what I remember hearing said or reading after the whole story came out in the newspapers and almost ruined baseball.

And Eddie Cicotte is supposed to have been talking with his brother at the boardinghouse where Cicotte lived in Chicago. His brother is supposed to have said something about how it was too bad that the White Sox had lost the first two games and that Cicotte had a bad day in the opener, and Cicotte is supposed to have said, "I don't care because I got mine out of it."

And then Burns went to see Gandil on the morning before the third game to find out what the players were going to do so the gamblers would know how to bet and be able to get even more sucker money than what they'd already roped in. And Gandil is supposed to have told Burns that he would see the people who sent him for their share of the money, and that he was through with them, Burns and Maharg and Attell. And Risberg came into Gandil's room and said that he was going through with his share of the bargain. And Gandil turned his back on Burns."Go to hell," Gandil said.

And like I said, the Little Skipper is supposed not to have been able to sleep for three straight nights, and he and the Old Roman talked, but they didn't know what to do. The Old Roman had not been able to sleep on the night of the first game and he got dressed and at four o'clock in the morning he left the Hotel Sinton and walked a couple of blocks to another hotel and woke up the president of the National League and appealed to him for help.

It was like all of this was going on and the gamblers were betting money openly and brazenly, and, I guess, many people must have heard it said that the World Series was in the bag for Cincinnati. And of course I heard some of these rumors. They affected me very much, and I guess that I've more or less indicated that I was affected by it, but that only left me confused. I almost said that it left me not knowing what to do, but there wasn't anything for me to do, anything I could do, because if all of the powers of baseball, the presidents of both big leagues and the National Commission and the Old Roman and the Little Skipper and the power of the press, couldn't do anything, why, then what could I have done when I was only a nineteen-year-old busher?

I don't think that I was in a daze or anything like that, but even so, I sometimes think that I was, or that I was dreaming it all. It seemed like I sort of resisted believing that it happened. Even when it was happening before everybody's eyes, including my own, you still couldn't exactly believe that it was happening, that it could happen. After all, it was the World Series, and not just a ball game, maybe a ball game that didn't make a hell of a lot of difference as far as the pennant went. And it wasn't one or two players but a whole group of them, eight of them, and it wasn't hard to guess who they were. If you were suspicious and thought that some of the players weren't trying, then you could make a good guess as to who they were, because the eight players who were barred went pretty much together. And it would have had to be them and you would have known that it was all eight of them because they pretty much hung together. And you hoped against hope that they weren't doing it and that they were going to turn around and win. And after the third game with Dick Kerr pitching such a beautiful and brilliant game, it seemed like things were going to be different, and we were going to win the Series.

I left the ballpark feeling good after that game, mighty good.

II

That Friday night after the third game, I went to the Collinses for supper, and then Mary and I were going downtown to a show. Her father and brother had been to see the ball game, and that's what they had on their minds. I had hardly gotten in the door when they were talking baseball. They were all set up and happy about the ball game and they wanted to talk to me about it.

"I'll bet the ballplayers were a happy bunch in the clubhouse after the ball game today, Mick," Mary's father, Jack Collins, said.

"Yes, they were," I said, sitting with them in the parlor. I couldn't say anything of what was going on in our own club. I didn't say anything of the dissension in the club. I felt that what went on in the clubhouse should remain there.

"I'll bet they congratulated Kerr," Jack said, smiling and plainly enjoying the idea that the players all should have been happy and have been happy as hell about the winning game and the brilliance of Dick Kerr's pitching. The clubhouse wasn't the same after that game as it was after the two previous ones, but there was nothing like what Jack imagined. Kerr was still a busher, despite the game he'd pitched, and I don't think some of the players cared that he won.

"How does the team feel now, Mick?" Pete, Mary's brother, asked me.

"Pretty good."

"The fellows expect to win now, don't they, Mick?" Jack asked.

"Yes, they do."

"Today was the turn of the Series, the break," Pete said, like he really knew what he was talking about.

"I hope so, Pete," I said.

I was more confident, I guess, but I was hoping more than I was believing the way I had believed when we went to Cincinnati before the beginning of the Series.

"I put $50 on the Sox to win," Jack said.

"Baseball's a tricky game," I found myself saying. "You never can be sure what's going to happen."

"Of course, a game's never over until the last man is out. But you could see today that the White Sox are a ball club with class, and that Cincy club can't come nowheres near to being the equal of it."

"Yes, I think we got the better ball club," I said.

"You could have knocked me over with a feather when I read about that first game. What was the matter, Mick? What did Cicotte have to say? I read in the newspaper how rotten he felt."

"He said he just didn't have it."

"Nothing's wrong with his arm, is there, Mick?"

"Not that I know of. I had the idea that he's going to pitch tomorrow's ball game."

"You would have heard about his arm if he had a sore arm, wouldn't you, Mick?"

"Yes, I guess so."

I felt shaky talking with Jack Collins and Pete. It wasn't that I was certain about the sellout and crookedness, because I wasn't. But I wasn't certain about the opposite of that. I wasn't so certain about our own ball club. I thought we were going to win and I was hoping we were, but I just wasn't certain, and didn't know what to say to Jack and Pete, especially since Jack was betting on the White Sox. I felt that I ought to say something but I didn't know what to say, that I ought to tell him something but I didn't know what to tell.

This was one of the times when I first felt different from people who weren't ballplayers or in the baseball world. It was like some kind of invisible wall was between us. Being a big leaguer made me feel different from them both. But I also felt badly, uneasy, worried about what was going to happen. I almost felt that if the ball club lost, I'd be to blame in their eyes, and maybe even in my own eyes.

We talked some more and we ate. I thought about the first time I'd eaten at the Collinses' home in June 1918, over a year before, the night when I felt that the Collinses didn't think I was good enough for Mary, and then I went to Washington Park and stained my Sunday suit imagining I was making base hits off Walter Johnson, and when I went home, I found out that my father had died of a heart attack. I knew that there wasn't any of that feeling about me that I wasn't good enough for Mary, and our engagement was an accepted thing.

Jack Collins was proud of me and liked to talk and boast about me to his cronies and business associates. That made me feel good because I was talked about by people I didn't even know. It made me feel I was somebody. And I thought of men like Mr. Collins and his friends as important businessmen, pillars of the community, although of course they weren't really that. I never knew much about such things, and I knew nothing about things then, business and politics, and I didn't have any clear ideas of the values of money.

A lot of young ballplayers are from the farms and small towns and I saw plenty of them come and go. I was a city kid, but still the neighborhood I lived in in those days was something like a small town with most of the people knowing each other or knowing about each other, and I didn't know a hell of a lot about the outside, big world. I learned what it means to be big league and what a great thing baseball is, taking young fellows and kids like it does and giving them a chance, putting them in the big league environment where they learn things and learn to feel pretty much at home in many circles.

But then, I was only at the beginning. Hell, I was just nineteen, and until the year before when the White Sox signed me up, I had never stayed all night in a hotel, slept in a Pullman, or anything like that. I was pretty green.

My God. Thinking back, remembering those days, and remembering how I was so full of dreams and confident of how I was going to become a star, a big star, one of the real diamond greats. I looked ahead to just wonderful years, wonderful years, and the time when I would have to hang up my glove and my spikes was so far away. It was something I knew would happen, but in the future, at a time so far ahead of me that I didn't give it any real countenance.

Hell, when I remember all of this now, I sometimes almost believe that I am thinking about a kid who was somebody else rather than myself. Myself, thinking I was going to be as great as Ty Cobb or Eddie Collins, myself dreaming and imagining all that I was going to do and all that I would be, myself kind of living with my head in a cloud, and expecting all sorts of things that were going to happen to me, things that I didn't see clearly or know what they would be like, the things that were supposed to happen to every baseball player who became a great star.

Yes, I sure did have my head in the clouds, all right. And even though I knew I wasn't going to get into any of the World Series games unless the totally unexpected happened, why, the idea of my being, at nineteen, a member of the team that won the championship of the world, that was a hell of a lot in itself. And I had already gained an importance with everybody I knew that I hadn't had before. People thought a ballplayer was very special then just as they do now, a hero, and that he lived a different kind of life from what ordinary people live, a life set apart and happier than other people lived. And I was expecting more to happen to me than could or that ever did. And I wanted, I wanted like all hell, for us, that is for the White Sox, to win that Series. But I couldn't really believe that I was a White Sox although I knew I was. Sometimes I would feel more like the batboy than one of the players. But to other people I was one of the players even if I was a young one and a sub. I was on the team with Eddie Collins and Joe Jackson and Buck and the rest of them. I saw them every day and associated with them, and I was really one of them in other people's estimation. This made me want to succeed all the sooner, and to stay up there in the big leagues. Already by the time of the 1919 Series, I began to think that it would be an awful thing for me, almost a tragedy for me, to go back to the minor leagues. I began to think of the next year when I'd go to spring training and how I would make a real do-or-die effort, but of course I had done that the spring before, and it had paid off. I was going to spend the winter, too, keeping myself in condition so that I'd be in shape the moment I stepped on the ball field in Waco for the first time in the 1920 spring training season. But of course, too, if the club won the Series, why then, my chances of becoming a regular next season would be so much worse. It made me understand why you had to compete in baseball, why you had to play to win and not be concerned about the fellow you beat.

That Friday night I had supper at the Collins home was one of the high points for me of the 1919 Series. Going there on the night after the ball club had won its first game, it did give me a real good feeling even though I was nervous about what was going to happen in the rest of the games. Maybe this isn't too clear, but I wasn't too clear either at that time. And others were like me. We were hoping that the players were all right, hoping that the things which caused suspicions were nothing at all.

But after all, I was kind of hoping. I was more hoping than worried or afraid that night at the Collins home. And I felt a little big and important. I felt that I was grown up and wasn't a kid anymore. I was a man, a ballplayer, and making good money with some confidence that I had a future. I had made good in the Pacific Coast League. And I felt that I was accepted in the family. That was why, however, I wished that I could have had more to say than I did.

After supper, Mary and I went downtown to see a show, and afterward we went to the Charles restaurant on West Randolph Street for a bite to eat. I was recognized on the street around 51st Street and near the ballpark, but when I went downtown, I wasn't recognized much. I kind of wished that someone would speak to me or that Mary would hear someone mention my name. I wished that someone in the restaurant would do that, but it didn't happen. But we had a good time, and we were looking ahead when we would be married and to our life going on, full of happiness, with no dullness, with nothing of the trials and tribulations, the day-by-day troubles of married folk. We talked about the future and about how sometime the next year we would be married.

"Yes, next year I ought to get a raise. And if we win, I'll get $1,500 World Series money, and of course my pay for the days the Series lasts. I'm not doing bad, hon, in my first full year in organized baseball. All told, I ought to knock down more than $2,000 in my full year of baseball," I remember saying.

I began to think of money because I was getting married, and of course I was contributing at home and had to think of money. And I heard lots said about money in baseball. When I was a kid, I thought of the glory and fame. When I got up there, I began to realize that in baseball there were men who were making their living and supporting their families, and I was making my living.

So we talked and then took the El train home. In those days, of course, I didn't have an automobile and didn't take taxis on a date with Mary, except on a special occasion. I think of those days. Mary was the only girl I ever courted. Some fellows had many girls, and I don't deny that I slipped now and then but that was different. And I remember those first days as some of the best days of my life. Those dates, walking with Mary on my arm, holding her hand in a dark movie or at a show downtown, going swimming in the morning in 1920 when we weren't married, sometimes meeting her by the clubhouse when she'd come to a ball game and then we'd go off and have dinner by ourselves, going skating in the wintertime. There are so many things I can remember. And sometimes I'd be recognized and I'd like that, especially when Mary was out with me. Once she said to me, "Mickey, you're going to be famous."

On that Friday night, I remember kissing Mary good night in front of her building and walking home, whistling to myself, and thinking how wonderful life was, especially when you were young and with the White Sox and in love. I was sure then that nothing could be wrong about the Series and that we just had to win.

But that fourth game is the one where Cicotte made those misplays in fielding a throw from Jackson in left field and lost the ball game, even though he otherwise pitched a good game, one that he should have won. It was a heartbreaking business, and with us behind 3-1, things looked more serious. Cicotte, one of the smartest pitchers and best fielding pitchers in the business, made two misplays in one inning, and we lost 2-0, and then, after the Sunday game was rained out, the Reds won the fifth game off Williams, 5-0.

That rainy Sunday was an awful day for me, and to this day I remember it because it was so dreary. I went to the ballpark and remember sitting there before the ball game was called off. It was like being in a morgue. Some of the players had a card game going, and Eddie Collins, who was very superstitious, blew his top, and Ray Schalk was as crabby as I ever saw him, and the Little Skipper looked hurt. And then when the game was called off, I went home and just slouched around the flat, doing nothing, looking out at the wet, black street and that dark, heavy sky and imagining that the breaks were coming our way and that we were winning the Series instead of losing it and just somehow passing a lousy day. I didn't call up Mary and go over to see her because I was ashamed.

There still wasn't any proof, of course, that things were wrong, but it was clear that something was the matter. And it was clear, also, that the Little Skipper thought so. He said so, speaking of the team as "my boys" and saying that some of them weren't trying. But it was all so bewildering. Buck and Joe Jackson were having a good Series and hitting the ball and Eddie Collins wasn't at all playing his best. Happy Felsch was so bad in center field that he was changed to right field.

There were all kinds of stories going around that I didn't hear until later, because, like I said, in Chicago I went to the ballpark and left and came home, and didn't see anybody in baseball at night. The newspapers printed rumors about the Series but denied that there was any truth or that there could be any truth to these rumors. And there was one story in one of the Chicago papers saying that gamblers tried to get to the Cincinnati players by giving a wild party for them and bringing girls for the party from Detroit, and when we won the sixth and seventh games in Cincinnati, that story was printed again and it was explained that the other club was out of condition and tired because of the party the gamblers had given them in Chicago.

There was something, all right, because before one of the games one of the Cincinnati regulars blew his top and raised hell in the Cincinnati clubhouse. He was supposed to have been tipped off that one of the pitchers on his club couldn't be trusted, and he made the speech to keep this pitcher in line. The players on our club got double-crossed by the gamblers and they seemed to have decided to double-cross the gamblers in return, and then there was this story of a triple double-cross. It's never been printed so far as I know, but I've been convinced that it's true. I got it from a newspaperman and he told me he got the story straight from the player who blew his top and threatened the pitcher on his own ball club.

After Cicotte lost the fourth game 2-0 and himself made the errors that cost us the game, I was mostly sure that something was wrong. I say that I was mostly sure because even right up to the end I couldn't absolutely believe that the Series was crooked. It was more than there not being absolute proof. It was too much and too shocking and too terrible a thing to believe, not only because of the players who might be guilty, but you just couldn't easily believe that anything like that could happen in baseball.

Just think of it. Those players had the baseball world right square, and nobody could do anything to stop them. I don't believe Buck did anything to lose us the games and believe that he only knew about it. But anyway, seven, eight ballplayers had the baseball world by the balls, and nobody knew what to do to stop them and to save baseball from a scandal that almost ruined it for good and forever with the fans and the American people.

The Little Skipper suffered from this. Maybe he suffered the most of all. It was his first year as a manager but he had been with the team as a coach and assistant manager. He knew all of the players and liked them. They were his boys, and he was mighty proud of them. Baseball had been his whole life, and he loved it and didn't know anything else. And he liked the way the team would go out and fight. He didn't seem to mind the players fighting with each other so long as they won ball games. He came from a fighting school of baseball. And during his time in baseball, ballplayers had fought on the ball field and off the ball field. Sometimes when players would snap and snarl away at each other, he let them and didn't say much, because he knew that the club would go out on the ball field and win the game for him.

And he had to see his boys do what they did, do it to him, too. It was just as much as if they told him to his face that they didn't give a tinker's damn for him. I already said that he didn't sleep for three straight nights because of what was going on. And he said in the clubhouse that some in the club weren't trying to win. The Skipper was one of the baseball people who was writing about the Series, but of course his stories about the game were written for him, just as baseball writers wrote the pieces signed by Eddie Collins and Ray Schalk. Ghostwritten columns were common. But the Skipper kept saying that the best team wasn't winning but that it would. His ball club would come back and prove that it was the best team, the one that had gone out and beaten and clawed every club in the American League.

He didn't dare pull the players he suspected out of the lineup because he didn't know how he would explain this to the public. He couldn't say in public what he was convinced of. And even if he had benched the players he didn't trust, he didn't have others to put in their place who could win for him.

On the bench, he sometimes cursed and sometimes was silent. When Cicotte made two bum plays in the fourth inning of the fourth game, he said nothing as the players came in off the field for our bats in the last half of the fourth. Cicotte came in and sat down. He didn't say anything either. He looked at the ground. He bent forward from the bench and retied the shoelace in his right shoe. The Little Skipper said nothing. He looked at Cicotte. He picked up a pebble and shot it off like a marble. In the next inning, he said, "Come on. Let's get some goddamn runs. Give me this goddamned ball game."

"We'll get it," Buck said.

The Little Skipper was always for the ballplayers, and even to this day, when he's been dead over fifteen years, ballplayers still talk about him with love. Buck always used to talk about him in after-years. There was nothing he could do. He couldn't curse the players into winning, or inspire them, or bench them. He had to keep hoping that they would change and go out to win, that with the gamblers having gotten their dough, the players could then play on the level. It was tragic for him.

Ray was the man who was mad, fighting mad, and he even took a punch at the umpire, Hal Borman, and was put out of one of the games. He never tried harder to win, and it was no use. Ray knew how to get a lot out of a team even though he sometimes would nag and curse it. He wasn't quiet on the bench or in the clubhouse either, and he kept saying that they had to play better ball than they were, and he cursed and yelled. But that did no good, either.

And Eddie Collins almost had a fight with the Cincinnati sub, Smith, who was coaching third base for them. He was rough and tough and I think he had been a prizefighter. He was pretty raw in the way he jockeyed our players, and Eddie said something to him. I think Eddie told him he shot his mouth off too much. He gave Eddie a shove. That was late in the fourth game, I think, when the teams were changing sides. The umpire got between them and the Little Skipper rushed out on the field, and I think he would have tangled with Smith. I cursed and called Smith a sonofabitch, and I thought he was going to come over and start swinging on me. I never cursed so much in my life and was using every foul-mouthed word I could on the Cincinnati players because I was sore. I wasn't so sore at them—I was sore and hurt because we were losing.

In that fifth game, Eller struck out five of our players in a row, and that was awful.

"He's got a drugstore on that friggin' ball," Buck said.

Eller was a shine-ball pitcher. In fact, I think that Cicotte taught him the shine ball or else he learned it by watching Cicotte in spring training, because he was tried out by the Sox and sent back to the minors. When doctoring the ball was outlawed, I guess that Eller must have lost his confidence because he folded up and didn't last long in the National League. He looked unhittable when he was striking out our hitters, but maybe they didn't try. I mean, some of them. He beat us 5-0 and that meant the Reds were ahead of us 4-1.

"I'd have said this couldn't have happened," Ray said in the showers after that fifth game.

"That little crab," Gandil said, but Ray didn't hear him.

But by that time, there wasn't much to say. We all had to dress and catch a train for Cincinnati, a funeral train. Just one week before, everything had been so different.

I just took my uniform off, went in, took a shower, came out, and dressed in silence. I kept telling myself that it had to be wrong and that the rumors must be true. I looked around at the players and wondered how they could be doing any such thing. I watched Cicotte lighting a cigarette and I thought of how he was such a hell of a pitcher and here he'd lost two games. It sort of hurt me.

He suddenly looked at Dick Kerr who had said, "Goddamned right I'll beat them again. I'll beat them as many times as the Skipper lets me pitch against them." Gandil used to call him "a fresh busher." He was.

"I just don't know—I pitch four, five innings and I'm pooped," Red Faber said.

"You dumb meat-ax. I wish you could go find some iron some place and pitch," Ray said.

"All I wish, Ray, is I could make you put that sponge in your glove the way I did in 1917," Red said.

"You could break my hand so long as you had your strength," Ray said.

"Sometimes I think there's nothin' like a farm in North Carolina," Joe Jackson said.

I noticed Eddie Collins wrinkling up his brows and staring across the clubhouse at Joe.

"We're gonna win this friggin' Series," Buck said. He seemed to be playing a hell of a ball game, and I just couldn't figure it, because he was associating with the other players. And by then, it was obvious that they were a group and were sticking together.

I happened to walk out of the ballpark close behind Eddie Collins and Lou Norman, the veteran sportswriter who was doing Eddie's articles on the Series.

"I don't feel like talking, Lou."

"I know how you feel, Eddie. I want to knock out your story on the train before I start drinking. Hell, I don't feel like doing my own story. I only feel like drinking and going fishing."

"I'll tell you in the cab," Eddie said. The story the next day praised Buck and Jackson. Both of them were batting over .300, the only two players on our club who were hitting that high.

I happened to ride to the station with Buck and Cicotte and Risberg and Lefty.

"Yes, I'm going hunting after the Series. Then when I go to California I'm going to take some money away from Babe Ruth playing golf," Buck said.

"It'll be a long winter," Cicotte said.

I was a little surprised at the way they were talking and taking the situation.

"What you gonna do, kid?" Buck asked me.

"Me—I'm gonna get a job. I'll probably go back to my old job."

"What's that—driving the horse and wagon?" Cicotte asked.

"Yeah."

"You're a baseball player now. You ought to get yourself a better job than that, Donovan," Buck said.

"I figure it'll help me stay in condition," I said.

"He'll make as much as a teamster as he probably will on this ball club," Buck said, looking at Cicotte and Risberg.

"I wonder what the Commission will do about Ray," Cicotte said.

"Yeah, he'll get fined," Buck said.

"Hitting an umpire in a World Series ball game isn't any light offense," Cicotte said.

"No, it isn't," Buck said.

"I don't think it's ever happened before. I'll have to ask one of the writers. Lou Norman or one of those fellows will know. He and Jim Cruisenberry have seen every World Series game that's been played since 1903."

"Hitting an umpire isn't good for the dignity of baseball," Buck said.

"I've never been put out of a ball game. The insult isn't worth the fine," Cicotte said.

"Now you're talkin' like a great ballplayer who plays on our ball club," Buck said.

"What's he gonna do with all his money?" asked Risberg. I knew they were talking about Eddie Collins.

"He'll probably own a ball club some day," Cicotte said.

"I hope I don't have to play for him," Buck said.

"Someday, he'll probably manage this ball club," Cicotte said.

"He can trade me," Risberg said.

As we got out of the cab at the station at 63rd Street near Jackson Park, Buck said, "Moran's probably pitching that Reuther tomorrow. I'm going to get my hits off him. He can be beat."

"Step into his curve ball," Cicotte said, but his voice seemed a little peculiar to me. I know why now of course.

Cicotte got out first and didn't think of the cab fare. We'd get it back no matter who paid for it, but Cicotte would let someone else reach first. Several times he let me reach for cab fares.

"You fellows got to take their pants off in Cincy," the cab driver said as Buck paid the fare.

In the station people recognized us as we walked through the station. We didn't have to carry any bags, of course. The club took care of things like that.

"There's Buck Weaver," a fellow called.

"That's Eddie Cicotte."

"There's the sub infielder, Mickey Donovan." I was thrilled hearing this talk and thought how I still wanted the ball club to win that Series.

A couple of fellows went up to Buck and one of them asked what the hell was wrong with the club.

"Read the newspaper tomorrow. We'll win," Buck said.

"That's the talk. The White Sox are down but they're never out," one of the fans said.

I ran into Jim Clancey who had played with me at St. Basil's and had graduated with me.

"They ought to put you in the game, Mick," Jim said.

"This is the big leagues, Jim, not the Catholic High School League."

"I always knew you'd get there, Mick. I mean it, Mick. Tell the Little Skipper to play you—there he is." The Little Skipper was walking through the station. Several men looked at him. The Little Skipper looked like a worried man. I talked with Jim for a few minutes. He had a job in an office of a wholesale hardware company.

"Yeah, I got a pretty good job, Mick."

I thought how I was already far away from St. Basil's. But I was glad to see Jim, and we would get together after the World Series and maybe take in a movie. He wanted to know what was wrong with the White Sox, overconfidence?

"It seems so—but it's not over yet. Kerr and Cicotte ought to win for us and Lefty Williams can't lose three games straight. He's too good for that."

"I got five bucks on your team, Mick. You tell 'em they better win."

I felt a little bad. No, I felt rotten as I said so long to Jim and walked on through the station to the platform.

CHAPTER EIGHT

I

The other club was winning 4-0, and the Cincinnati fans were gloating. It seemed all over but the shouting. We scored a run in the fifth inning, and then as the players came to the bench for the first half of the sixth, Buck, in the way he used to do it, said, "Come on, for Christ sake, let's win this friggin' ball game."

With benched kids, there was a regular White Sox rally. Reuther was knocked out of the box, and the score was tied. It was a new ball game and a brand new World Series. Dick Kerr tightened up, and those Cincinnati fans got frightened. For the first time in the Series, they saw the White Sox play ball. We scored a run in the tenth inning on a base hit by Gandil and that was the ball game, 5-4. And even though the other club has us 4-2, things looked good. After the bad start, the team had looked like world champions, fielding, hitting, playing their trademarked brand of baseball. Maybe now things were different and they'd win.

Even the Little Skipper was a bit cheerful after that ball game. And in the clubhouse, Eddie Cicotte said, "I'll win tomorrow." He patted his arm and said that it was good.

The Cincinnati writers were frightened despite the edge their club had on ours. They tried to explain how come their team lost the ball game after having a 4-0 lead.

The Hotel Sinton wasn't at all the same. There weren't as many gamblers there, and the lobby wasn't so crowded.

"We can still win this Series," I said to Lefty Williams.

"Hell, yes. Of course we can."

"It looks to me like this Cincinnati ball club might crack."

"Our club can always come from behind. It hit its stride today," Lefty said.

"It sure did," I said. We were both wishing. We weren't sure at all.

But the next day, Cicotte pitched a good game. We won 4-1. Cincinnati made four errors. Our team had the whole town worried, and the Cincinnati sportswriters were saying that their club could lose. They had been rabid when the club won, but they had heard all of the rumors and they had cause for worry. The White Sox had won two straight after the Series seemed to have been all over but the shouting. They knew that our ball club wasn't overrated and that the experts had had plenty of reason for picking them to win.

The trip back to Chicago had to be made, and if the Series went to nine games, the final one would be played in our ballpark. After losing two ball games, Lefty Williams seemed overdue to win, and then we had Dick Kerr, who had already won two ball games. The whole outlook of the Series changed, and it seemed that now the White Sox were playing on the level. That's all they needed to do.

All over again, I was sprouting my wings of hope. And I convinced myself that I wished so hard to win that we had to win. I also thought how up to then I had come up fast, and that I was lucky and had fate on my side. The way the Series was going, it was being set up just right for a rookie like myself to come in and be a real-life Frank Merriwell, delivering the historic blow that would make me the World Series hero of 1919. I convinced myself that my dream would come true.

The second trip back to Chicago was better than the first one. There's nothing like winning a ball game in the World Series to set you up and make you feel real good and a hell of a lot better than real good. And up to then, the Series was full of lessons for me. You can sit on the bench and live and die with every pitch. I learned how you have to have perspective, and how once you lose a ball game you've got to think of the next day's ball game and of winning it. This lesson stood me in good stead, because I played in more losing ball games than I did winning ones in my big league career. And a World Series that goes first one way and then the other is a real battle. I could see that, and I figured that I was learning plenty for the future, for those World Series when I would play as a regular. I remember looking at

Eddie Collins eating at the table across the aisle from me on that second trip back from Cincinnati to Chicago. I counted them and told myself that he was playing in his sixth World Series. That was the record for the number of Series played in up to that time, and I thought how I wanted to be the player who made a better record and played in more than six World Series. I thought I was going to, and I considered my experience getting slivers in my behind on the White Sox bench of that Series like being at school and learning baseball.

But it just occurs to me that I have said little about the other ball club. I've been thinking about our own club and trying to remember more about it and about how things seemed to me in 1919. I don't want to take anything away from them or their manager, Pat Moran. He's been gone for a long time, and some of their players are dead, too.

Their first baseman, Jake Daubert, is dead. I think he died of peritonitis after an operation for appendicitis while he was still an active player. That was a tragic thing, and nowadays few people die of appendicitis. But he was a fine ballplayer, an experienced veteran. He could field and hit, and he had even led the National League in batting before he had gone from Brooklyn to Cincinnati.

And then they had Groh at third base, with his funny bat and peculiar stance. That Groh, he was small but he was a ballplayer, too, and he was fast. He could run like a deer. He was one of the best third basemen of those days and almost any manager today would be glad to have him on his ball club. He could pull the ball down the third base on a line, and he made plenty of base hits. I wouldn't want him over Buck. Of course I didn't see too much of him, but I did play against him in spring training exhibition games, and he was one of the best men in the business.

And Roush, their center fielder, was a great ballplayer. He made some terrific catches in the Series, and he was a steady better than .300 hitter but not a long-ball or power hitter. He'd line the ball out to right and center field and he took a good clean cut at the ball and had good wrist action. They had a good pitching staff, and that, I guess, was what won them the pennant. Few of the Cincinnati ballplayers could have gotten on our ball club as regulars, except Roush and maybe Groh, but they had a pretty fair ball club. They couldn't have won that Series if our team had played to win. Almost all baseball people will say that.

Coming back, I thought they were done for and that they wouldn't recover from the two straight defeats they had suffered. That train ride was my real high point in the Series, but I sure was counting chickens that were never going to be hatched. Lefty Sullivan, he felt good. He was getting married and the winner's share looked plenty big to him.

The newspaper writers didn't feel the same as we did, and they didn't hope too much. All of them, I guess, were convinced that the Series had been fixed and they didn't care much by the time the eighth game rolled around.

Ring Lardner, the writer who wrote the stories and books, sat drinking and looking very morose and unhappy in the club car. He is one of the ones who had sung the parody, "I'm Forever Blowing Ball Games." Most of the time he wouldn't say much. He'd sit and never take any notes and he'd write the darndest things. I understand that the Series made him sour on baseball, but I don't know why it should have. Baseball is a bigger thing than any ballplayer and than the eight players who were barred for life, and it's certainly bigger than the writers.

Those two games didn't change anything on the club, and all I hoped for didn't come true. Lefty Williams got knocked out of the box in the first inning and three of our second-string pitchers labored through the game, which we lost 10-5. Jackson hit a home run, but with no one on base. In the first inning, when he came up and could have driven runs around, he struck out or hit a pop-up. In the eighth inning, it looked like we might do something, and I was on the edge of the bench, and on pins and needles wanting to get in the ball game. Roush made a great catch on a long fly Felsch hit and that put a damper on us.

It was over and the White Sox lost. You didn't know why and couldn't be sure. After the game, I just wanted to get away from the clubhouse and the ballpark. I took the defeat hard. And I felt a little bit foolish and goofy about the way I had had dreams of being the World Series hero. Some of the players left without saying goodbye to each other. The Little Skipper didn't say much but he took it to heart, all right. It hurt him so that he never got over it. The Series didn't at all look right, but it was done and 1919 went into baseball history.

I don't think anybody thought that the players were going to be found out and suspended from organized baseball for life. You didn't know if anything at all would happen, or if so, what it was going to be that would happen. And you didn't think about what should be done or what shouldn't be done. It was a hard thing to believe, but there it was and it seemed that you just about had to believe it because so many did believe it. I mean so many baseball people. After all, where there's smoke there's fire, and there was plenty of smoke already right during the Series. You just didn't know what to think and you didn't want to talk much about the Series.

You couldn't say to people that you were suspicious because you didn't want to spread rumors, and you didn't want to say that you weren't suspicious, and you sounded hollow and just talking through your hat saying you didn't know what happened or that the White Sox had been overconfident or that the Reds had been better than anyone expected them to be and had upset all of the dope. All that stuff sounded like crap. And you didn't want the public, the people, the fans to know because if they did, then what would happen to baseball? I'd heard sportswriters saying during the Series that now baseball was no different than horse racing or boxing and that it was crooked like just about everything else. Hearing sentiments like those hurt. They maybe hurt me especially because I was at the beginning of my baseball career and I had nothing else on my mind, no idea of doing anything else with my life but play baseball. It was a quandary, all right.

That Friday morning after the Series ended, I woke up feeling like there was a hole in my life. I was restless and disappointed, with most of the day to kill. I planned to go to the ballpark to get my belongings and my check. Like I think I said, the club paid us by the day as long as the World Series lasted. I was glad to be getting this money, which I hadn't expected, especially because I was only going to get about $800 as my share of the World Series money instead of something over $1,500 which would have come to me if the ball club had won the Series.

Riding to the ballpark, I kept telling myself that next year would be another season and that, after all, I had had nothing to do with the Series and that my days were ahead of me. But I was low. Some of the players were at the ballpark getting their things, but they were in a hurry. I got my things too, tipped the clubhouse boy, and went back home. I was restless and didn't know what to do with myself.

I read all of the newspapers and that was depressing reading, and I thought of how, if the team had won, the final game would be in progress at the ballpark, and Dick Kerr might have been winning it. But the whole question was if the best team had really won the Series, or if some of the games had been fixed. There was another story denying that there was any truth to rumors about the gamblers having gotten to some of the White Sox ballplayers.

I had no reason for crying over the spilled milk of other ballplayers, and I wasn't involved, but still the fear and suspicion that I had acquired did hurt. I kept telling myself and reasoning with myself that the Series was over, finished, and that I had to think of what was ahead of me, and of what a wonderful future I had. Mary's father, Jack, had said that to me. He had said, "Mick, you can have a wonderful future."

I saw Mary again on that Friday night, the night after the Series ended, and I talked a few minutes with Jack, her father, while I was waiting for her to get ready.

"I never thought the Reds could beat the White Sox, Mick. Hell, I couldn't imagine they could. So, I lost fifty bucks, fifty smackers."

I was glad it wasn't more.

"Now, some fellows are saying the games weren't on the level, but hell, I think that they're crying sour grapes and they're just damned bad losers. You can't fix a ball game, not very easy. And what the hell, it was an upset."

I was glad that he didn't ask me if I thought the games had or hadn't been on the level. And what Jack said was what I wanted to believe myself, because it was the easiest and the best thing to believe. It was all over, and I could only keep in condition and wait for February when the time for spring training would roll around, and that was what I was going to do.

Some of the players had left and the rest of them were scattering and the baseball season was over. It's now history, I told myself. I noticed a story about what the White Sox players were going to do. It mentioned me and said that I was staying in Chicago and working, and I was planning to keep myself in good condition and be ready to make my big try to stay on the team next season. And the story also said that Gandil had bought a new car and was going to drive home in it to California. Also the newspaper story said that the Little Skipper was remaining in Chicago to handle some odds and ends of business. Later it came out that the main item of that business was to check up and try to prove that his boys had thrown the games on him, because he was convinced of this as fact. And it was also said later that besides buying a new automobile, Gandil had stocked up on some new clothes.

That led to the suspicion that he must have got a lot of money himself, or made it by betting, but this has never been proven.

The end of the World Series left me wanting to play ball. For around three months I'd been receiving a salary as a big league ballplayer and I had hardly played at all. I was dying to play ball in a game, in any kind of a game at all, to stand up at the plate with my eyes glued on the pitcher and to keep my eye on the ball, swing, meet it, and know with the hearing and the feel of the crack of the bat that I'd gotten a base hit and to go tearing down to first base. One thing you never get tired of in baseball are your base hits. You love them, and even make them in your sleep and your dreams.

I remember that Sunday after the Series ended. It was an Indian summer day. I had nothing to do and there was only one thing I wanted to do, to play some baseball. I should have lined myself up to play with a semipro team and made ten bucks or so, but I hadn't done it, and I wanted to play ball. In fact, I was glad that I hadn't tried to get anything in semipro ball because I wanted to go out to Washington Park and play. I used to think of how after I had become a big leaguer I'd do just that, go back out to Washington Park and play ball with the fellows I'd known and played with over there. I'd electrify the crowd watching but I'd also prove that my head hadn't gotten too big for my cap. But that wasn't the only reason why I wanted to go to Washington Park on that Sunday. I don't know exactly what the reason was, except that I wanted to go and I wanted to play ball.

So I put on a pair of old pants, my Rocks shirt, and an old pair of tennis shoes and my blue White Sox sweater, but I took that off for fear it would seem I was showing off, and instead I wore my sweater with my high school letter sewn on it. I got my glove and spiked shoes, my gray Rocks baseball cap, and looked at myself in the parlor mirror. I missed the old days, only they weren't so old then. I found myself wishing I wasn't in the big leagues but was still only the Mickey Donovan who played over in Washington Park with the Rocks and in any ball game where a player was needed. I missed my old baseball playing.

Then I went out, and walked over to the park, the same as I had been doing for years. It made me feel that everything was the same as it had always been, and I felt good thinking that. It seemed goofy, my doing that after I was a White Sox, and I was sensitive about what people who saw me might think of me. I wanted them to think that I was the same as always, with no swelled head. I wanted them to say, "Mickey Donovan is one fellow who certainly loves to play baseball."

It was good walking over to the park the same as I had done so many times. I was on my way to my dreams. And I thought of how I used to walk along 51st Street, carrying my glove and my spiked shoes and sometimes a bat, and I'd be dreaming of the days ahead when I would be in the big leagues. And in Washington Park I'd feel more natural than I did on the diamond in the big league parks where I was a rookie, a busher, among the veterans and the greats of the game. I was conscious of them and the way they'd size me up. In Washington Park I would feel different. That walk was wonderful. I also imagined how fellows would be surprised, and about what they would say to me and I to them. And I was hoping that there would be a game, but I expected that there would be one. In those days, on a Saturday or Sunday afternoon, there nearly always were enough fellows around to make up two scrub teams and have a pretty fair game. Even on Sundays in October, when the weather was good, this was usually so.

When I reached the park, I got excited, but I also was a little concerned for fear that I wouldn't be welcome and that it would be felt that I had come out to the park in order to show off and have people see me. Maybe I'd be kidded, especially about the World Series, and I'd have questions flung at me and asked of me. But I felt better about the Series by Sunday and I was sure that talk about the Series and the upset of the White Sox would die now.

The park, too, was pretty. The trees were all bare and the ground was hard and the grass was dying. I looked at the trees with their black trunks, noticing size and shape and their bare branches, and it was pretty. I thought of Mary. And as I got near the diamonds, I heard voices, and of course there was the crack of the bat against the ball, which I had first heard faintly and then a little more loudly as I came closer. That was all swell. But I suddenly thought that if there was a game and if I played badly, I'd look pretty goofy. But then, I forgot that. I only wanted to play ball, to play in one more ball game before the cold weather set in.

I wasn't noticed as I sauntered toward a diamond where fellows were fooling around and flies and grounders were being batted out.

People were wandering about on the big field, and fellows sat on the grass. I guessed immediately that there were enough guys out for a game. And I sauntered up slowly, casually, I guess, just like I'd done many times before. Joe Hines was out catching ground balls and re-laying the ball back into a fungo hitter when balls had been lofted out to a fellow catching flies. Good old Joe, I thought. And I saw others I knew—Pete Glenn, Larry Morgan, Cal McMasters, fellows who had been coming out to Washington Park for a couple of years or more. A husky fellow I didn't know was doing the fungo hitting and I stood watching him a minute before changing my shoes and trotting out to catch a few myself.

Flinty came up to me, saying, "Well, for Christ sake, look who's here. Did the Little Skipper on the White Sox give you your walkin' papers?"

I said hello to him and noticed that he was all decked out and even wearing a silk shirt.

"What the hell are you doin' here?"

I talked to him and kidded, and soon Joe and other fellows I knew came crowding around me, and a few strangers came up to stare at me. Word had spread to men waiting to see a ball game. Mickey Donovan of the White Sox was around. I was greeted like a long-lost friend, and I felt plenty good.

"After what happened in the World Series, I'd think you wouldn't want to have nothin' whatsoever to do with a baseball," Flinty kidded me.

I shook hands with fellows I didn't know, and I was the center of attention of a little group that collected around me.

"I seen you in infield practice, Mick. And thanks for getting me tickets," Flinty said. "And goddamn your baseball team, I lost twenty bucks on it."

"Well, it wasn't Mick's fault, Flinty. Mick didn't play in any of the games," Joe Hines said. Good old Joe.

"The Sox couldn't have done any worse if he had of played," Flinty said.

"It was an upset," a fellow said like he knew and understood baseball mighty well.

I was asked questions about Lefty Williams and other players. Kids in short pants gathered around and stared at me. I guess they were afraid to say anything. I'd been like that when I was still in short pants.

Flinty, Joe, Cal, and the fellows were real glad to see me, and Joe told me that my ears should have been burning, because they'd been talking about me, and they'd been more than half-expecting that I'd show up, acting the same as usual, acting like the same old Mickey. That was what Joe Hines said to me.

"Hell, Joe, I ain't got nothing to brag about. All I did was sit on my can and collect pay for it. And I ain't quite got banker's hours, Joe, but I almost got them," I said.

"I wanted to telephone you—maybe to go to a show with you, Mick, but your bein' in the big leagues, I thought, hell, you'd be busy—maybe seein' the ballplayers, or goin' out with them," Joe said.

"Why didn't you call me, Joe?" I asked, disappointed.

"I was real sorry you lost the Series. I never expected the White Sox to lose, heck. I didn't, Mick."

"But you didn't lose twenty bucks on the Series," Flinty said.

"That's why they lost, because you bet on 'em, you bad luck, bad news little bastard," Cal McMasters told Flinty.

"Give me a bat, give me a bat till I break that blockhead," Flinty said.

"I sat in the left field bleachers the day Cicotte lost that heartbreaker," Joe said.

"It was a heartbreaker," I said.

"What was wrong with the White Sox?" a stranger asked.

"The team just didn't hit its stride," I said.

"Hey, Mick," Cal said. "Mick, wasn't it true that Happy Felsch and Greasy Neale had a fistfight under the stands and that Felsch knocked him up for grabs?"

"No, there wasn't any fight," I said.

"I'll be a Siamese twin of a horse thief," Flinty said.

"What brought you out, Mick?" Joe asked.

"I thought there might be a ball game, and then also I knew I'd see some of you guys," I said.

"You love to play ball, don't you Mick? I guess that's why you're on the White Sox," Joe Hines said.

That's the way it was, and I felt real good, real glad that I'd gone out to Washington Park on that Sunday afternoon. And there was a ball game, a pretty fair one, as I remember, with maybe a couple of hundred people watching us. I remember I played shortstop and made two or three hits.

"Just like old times," Joe said, as we sat on the grass when our side was at bat during one of the innings.

"Yeah."

"Hey, Mick, there's a scout from the Cincinnati Reds out here," Flinty told me one time when I went up to bat.

That was the last time I played in Washington Park. Sometimes I missed those old days. I still do. How I'd like to see some of those fellows again. Some of them are dead. Flinty must be dead. That's where I dreamed baseball, all right, as much as Young Stanky or any of those kids at Horace Stanton's Baseball School down in Florida ever dreamed baseball.

I went home from Washington Park feeling good but still feeling blue. And I thought how I wouldn't lose touch with Joe Hines but would see him regularly. But I did, just the same. I was going with Mary, and, well, we just didn't see much of each other. Good old Joe!

II

Once the baseball season ends, it kind of fades away as the fall comes on, and the weather changes, and there's Thanksgiving and winter coming on and Christmas and New Year, and then you think of the new year and the baseball season ahead. There was other news on the sports pages, and not much about baseball, except that Frank Houser wrote an article for one of the Chicago papers saying that eight White Sox ballplayers wouldn't be back with the team next year.

He didn't come out and say that the Series was thrown, but only hinted. He said that some of the players seemed to have done their best. Nothing was proven but the players wouldn't be back. That gave me some comfort. If nothing could be proved, then baseball wouldn't suffer. But what would the ball club be like without the eight ballplayers?

At the time, of course, I believed that the players would be traded, or at least some of them would be, and I figured that we would get some good ballplayers in return. That wasn't easy, because I didn't see what players most of the teams could trade for those ballplayers. Speaker was manager of Cleveland and we couldn't get him for Jackson, and I figured we couldn't get Ty Cobb either from the Detroit Tigers.

And I worried that if we lost those players, we wouldn't have a pennant-winning club. But my own chances of staying on and maybe winning a regular berth would be better. Even so, I worried and speculated. Some mornings, I opened the newspaper to the sports page quick and eager, looking for news about any possible trades or sales. Of course there wasn't any such news.

The idea of Buck being sold or traded to another ball club also bothered me. He was still pretty much my hero and my model. And he was too good a man, too great a ballplayer, to be playing against us. And it was hard to believe that he could have had anything to do with throwing the World Series, provided that was what had happened. I guess I really believed that some of the games had been sloughed, but I resisted believing this, and, like I have just said, I did especially about Buck because he had hit so well and played such bang-up baseball in those games. If the players, I reasoned, had made the deal with the gamblers, it was best not to have them around on our ball club. How could anyone ever know when they would be trying to win, and when they wouldn't be?

At that time, I didn't know that the Old Roman had had the eight players investigated and had held up the checks for their shares of the Series, but he couldn't get any evidence.

I didn't go back to work as a teamster, driving a horse and wagon. Jack Collins and Harry Grabiner helped me get a political job that paid me about $150 a month and wasn't hard work. It left me time to go swimming and take workouts in a YMCA gym to keep myself in good condition. And I got my World Series check for something over $800. I expected to stay in the big league the next season, but I knew that the worst that could happen to me was to be sent back to the Pacific Coast League or to be optioned to Clarence Rowland at Milwaukee in the AA. He bought into that ball club after leaving the White Sox at the end of the 1918 season. He wanted me. But I knew that the Sox considered me very promising, a good prospect. And the fact that I was a South Side Chicago boy and Irish was in my favor. That would make me popular, as it did.

Things looked good enough for my sister Ruthie to get married, which she did. That was one of the big things of the off-season, and there was much talk and preparation for it. I was led to thinking much about Mary and me, and I was wanting to get married myself. It was too hard not being married, and sometimes I'd feel guilty and rotten, almost like I was a bastard. We, Mary and I, talked of getting married.

There was much to look forward to, and somehow or other I was plumb full of confidence that I was going to stay right up in the American League. I guessed that other clubs would want me if the White Sox didn't, but that would worry me, because I wanted to stay right on with the White Sox. I also planned to do a lot of shagging of flies in spring training, thinking that I might make a showing for right field, where the club wasn't as strong as in other positions.

My mother met Mary's family when Ruthie was married. That affected her. She knew I was engaged but didn't think I'd be getting married for a long time. Ruthie's marrying put a big worry bug in her bonnet. She would tell me I was too young to marry, but that was about the only thing that was unpleasant, that and my feeling guilty about me and Mary, and just now and then a thought or question about the 1919 World Series that would pop into my mind. I wasn't shy like I had been, and I let Mary teach me to dance. I liked it and learned pretty fast, because I was always pretty graceful on my feet. We sometimes went dancing. Mary belonged to a sorority that gave a dance, and of course I took her.

The dance was at the Park Hotel, I think, over at 51st and Lake Park Avenue, and most of those at the dance were my own age. I knew a couple of the fellows there and met a lot more. I could see there that being a ballplayer meant something, and fellows wanted to meet me and talk with me. A couple of them had been high school athletes, but I was Mickey Donovan of the White Sox. That was the way I was introduced. That gave me some confidence. At that dance, and at other times I'd be with Mary and meet girlfriends of hers and the guys who were dating them, I'd feel older and different, more experienced and traveled. And I met some men in politics at City Hall.

"You're going to be famous, Mickey, but I'll love you just the same," Mary used to tell me, teasing of course. But she was proud of me, and every day she seemed to grow prettier.

That was a good winter, 1919–20. I was happy and healthy and full of my future.

Lefty Sullivan got married, and Mary and I sometimes went out with him and his wife, and they had us to dinner a couple of nights where we talked and played rummy. He was happy, too, and he had a political job as some kind of inspector. He expected to show more stuff in 1920 and to get into more ball games. He used to say how as soon as he got to spring training, he was going to work on his fielding. But he never mentioned the 1919 Series.

I didn't see any baseball people except that I ran into Ray once on the street and I saw Clarence Rowland two or three times. I read the news when the winter league meetings were held, wondering and worrying about trades. I saw Joe Hines a few times, and I developed a movie habit that I never lost. I must have seen every movie shown in Chicago that winter. I used to like Lila Lee as my favorite actress and always associated her and Mary. And since I was a ballplayer, I felt I was like many of the heroes and was going to do big and romantic things just as they did in the films. Sunday Mass was something I always looked forward to because I'd see people and talk to them, and I was treated with a lot of respect and pointed out. Then I became an usher in church. That made my mother proud, all right, and Mary, too. I joined the Order of Christopher and met some fine fellows and important older men, like Joe O'Reilly, who became a judge before he died.

It was sometime after the beginning of the year, that is 1920, that Harry Grabiner had me to the office at the ballpark and I signed my contract. I was hoping to get $250 a month and the $50 bonus for the option on my contract being renewed. All I got was $200, and Grabiner told me I was lucky to get that. He told me what great prospects I had if I could show enough ability.

"I'll show the ability," I told him, but I must confess that I was surprised to hear myself talk like that. The Old Roman came into Grabiner's office when I was talking with Grabiner and talked with me. But he was real nice to me. He seemed to know a lot about me, and I was kind of surprised at that, not cottoning to the idea that he checked up on me, unbeknownst to me.

"That'll be good for your legs," he told me when I said something about my doing a lot of ice skating. I didn't realize then that he and Harry Grabiner and the Little Skipper looked on me as insurance if the lid blew off the scandal.

And after New Year's Day, my mind was on spring training. I began counting the days. I went to bed at night thinking of spring training and the 1920 season, imagining and dreaming of myself as a regular. I had taken on a few pounds and felt wonderful, full of my own strength and power. I felt it when I just as much as walked down the street. I began to hate the winter days. Time couldn't pass fast enough for me. And I used to think that only two years before, I'd been a high school punk. And in those two years, I had become big league, because I was beginning to think myself big league.

I had dinner downtown with Tim Cahill one night not very long before spring training began.

"You got to stick up where you are, Mick," he said in the restaurant.

"I'm going to do my damnedest, Tim."

"I know you will."

"It's such a goddamned good ball club. It's hard breaking into that lineup." This was one of the first times I ever cursed in front of Tim.

"The hell with how good they are, you just be better."

"Yeah, Tim. But they're still good. It's one hell of a ball club. That's why I'd like to play outfield down in Texas. Maybe I could break in right field better."

"You can play any position—but I don't see why in hell they didn't keep you out there in the Pacific Coast League where you could play every day. You'd be better off back in San Francisco than you will sitting on the White Sox bench."

"I don't want to go back to the minors."

He looked at me, hard and straight, and that made me feel uncomfortable. "What the hell do you mean you don't want to go back to the minors, Mick?"

I got more uncomfortable. "Every ballplayer wants to be in the big leagues. And there's a chance for a World Series share, too."

He still looked at me.

"How old are you?"

"Nineteen. I'll be twenty next June."

"You need experience. You ought to be playing every day."

"Yeah," I said. "I want to marry Mary." He'd met her once.

"She'll wait. Listen, Mick, from the second or third time I saw you on the ball field at St. Basil's, I thought you could be a ballplayer.

'That kid's got it,' I told myself. But you've got to learn. Experience. And baseball comes first. Don't you realize it, Mick? It's your career, baseball."

"Yeah, Tim. You're right. I sit on that goddamned bench, and I'm crazy to play. I keep telling myself that I'll win a regular berth. I'll even fight Eddie Collins or Buck Weaver for it."

"You'd be better off on another ball club—with Connie Mack's team." I made a face, I guess. "He'll have more championship clubs. You won't get the call with the Sox."

"They'll decide. I did pretty fair every chance I got."

"You could have done as well as some of them did last October, Mick."

I got nervous.

"What did you think of the Series?"

I was slow in answering. "The ball club just had off days."

Tim raised his brows the way he used to when he didn't like what you said or did on the ball field. "There's a lot of talk, Mick."

"There was last October."

"There still is. You didn't notice anything or hear something?"

"I'd hate to think anything."

"I would, too. Millions of Americans would. How do they treat you, Mick?"

"Oh, all right."

"Do you go out with the regulars on the road?"

"I'm a busher to them."

"With all these stories, watch your step."

I was silent.

"I wish I was your age and had your ability. Mick, you got a big future."

"I'll try to justify your faith in me, Tim."

"You work for it, every day, and don't do nothin' to jeopardize it."

"I won't."

"It's a great thing to be a ballplayer, Mick."

Tim seemed sad. I felt sorry. I almost felt, well, guilty because I had gotten into the big leagues so easy, and Tim never had.

"I thought I'd make it. You know I wanted to be a big league ball-player, Mick?"

"I . . . I . . ." That's all I could say. I couldn't think of anything.

"I wasn't good enough. I can help kids. Some like you will make it."

"I'll try never to let you down, Tim."

"Mick, never let yourself down. Play every game up to here," Tim said, pointing to his throat.

"I will." He made me feel real good, like a father.

"We're proud of you at St. Basil's, too. If you stay with the Sox and have an off day in April or May, I'd like you to come out, hit 'em out, see us. I have some good kids."

"I will." I did, too.

Tim had a real love of baseball, and he must have strengthened my love of the game. But I couldn't help feeling that there was Tim, loving baseball, feeling like he did, and there was Gandil and some of the other players on our club, cynical. I felt real bad.

"I can coach, and I guess I got a couple of years of semipro ball left in my hide."

"I'm sure you have."

"We all dream of baseball, but most of us don't have what it takes. You have, Mick. Don't waste it."

"Heck, Tim . . ." He doubled up his left fist, reached across the table and gave me a soft friendly poke.

I loved Tim. I damned near cried when I was one of his pallbearers.

Often, like on that night, I thought how lucky I was. I think it would have broke my heart if I hadn't made the big leagues. I guess some of those kids at Horace's baseball school are like that. I see such kids, lots of them. Others, they don't care.

I remember, too, I met Rex a couple of days after that dinner I had downtown with Tim. He looked pretty seedy. We had a cup of coffee in a Thompson Restaurant.

"Jesus, boy, you're a big leaguer."

"I was lucky, Rex."

"Those goddamned bastards, they wouldn't buy me." He was bitter. "They brought up pitchers in the Western League. They were all Mel Wolfgangs. I threw my goddamned arm out, and here I am."

Of course I never saw Rex really pitch. Maybe he did have the stuff. I know because of my memory of Rex I always look mighty careful at every kid. It isn't only that I don't want to be beat by another scout, especially a Yankee scout or one from the other league. I don't want to overlook a kid.

Rex went to pot and several times I gave him handouts. He hit the bottle pretty steady and died in a cheap hotel, a flophouse on West Madison Street. In my playing days, I saw old-timers who reminded me of Rex. There was Alexander. I heard stories about him living in a flea circus in New York. But back in the winter of 1920, I was still nineteen. I told myself that I wouldn't end up like Rex, or like Tim either.

Now of course, the time of waiting for spring training seems to have been mighty short. But then, how the days moped and dragged their asses. But the day came for the departure to Texas, for my second trip on the White Sox Special. I felt almost like I was a veteran, too, when I went downtown to the La Salle Street Station. Gosh, that was all wonderful. You were too young to know how muscles can ache and how pooped you could get. You had all of the stored-up energy of the winter, and you felt like you'd found that well Ponce de Leon talked about and had drunk it all up. You knew that the reflexes go, the legs go, the arm goes, the wood goes—but not for yourself. You couldn't get that kind of an image of yourself fixed in your own mind. You were young and would always be young. The world was your oyster, all right. You were away from raw days and bitter winds, cold rain, and you'd play in the sun. You'd be with others like yourself, all of you ballplayers, getting into shape to play ball with the eyes of the nation on you. Yes, it was wonderful.

I kissed Ma and my kid sister goodbye. I gave my kid brother a buck and a closed-fist pat like Tim gave me. "You're the man of the house until April," I told him. I had said goodbye to Mary.

I took the El downtown. I pitied any young fellow who couldn't be a big leaguer. Columbus must have felt like I felt.

CHAPTER NINE

I

Right from the very railroad station, the dark clouds were over us. 1919 was gone. The 1919 Series was baseball history. The beginning of a new season is like New Year's. Ring out the old, ring in the new.

That's the way it seemed. Of course a lot of the players were going directly to camp. But some were at the station and there was a crowd to cheer us off and God-send. That meant all was forgotten. That meant the faith of the fans.

Eddie Cicotte showed up at the station. He hadn't been signed up. He was a holdout. But I always thought it was more than money. He must have begun having those thousand nights of torture. It seemed to me like he was afraid to come. Burns and Maharg said later that he went to them instead of them going to him. But he showed up. And just as the train was starting, the Little Skipper grabbed him and put him on the train, gave him a contract and a fountain pen, and Cicotte signed up. Of course there was no mention of the Series, I mean on the train. It was on that trip that I learned to play hearts. Happy Felsch used to win at hearts. He won on the train. The Old Roman wasn't on the train. He was driving down later, and his son handled things.

There were holdouts. Buck, Gandil, Risberg, and McMullen were holding out even though they all had a year to go on their contracts. It was a peculiar situation inasmuch as they all were signed up, and nobody would have lost money betting that, under the circumstances, they wouldn't get raises, not from the Old Roman. If four of the players could get more than they signed for, why couldn't others, even the whole team? They were all out in California and supposed to be in touch with each other, and in talking over their gripes, they must have thought of this. But anyway, they were officially holding out, because they hadn't shown up at camp or been heard from. A couple of the other players were late in reporting. As a matter of fact, Eddie Collins was a week or more late. But he had contacted the club and gotten permission to report late, as had Joe Jackson.

Few ballplayers carry out their threats about holding out to the bitter end. They usually can't afford to because most of them can't get jobs paying nearly as well in any other line of work. At least that was so back around 1920. There was nothing else most ballplayers could do. Baseball was all most of them knew, and while some could get jobs on the strength of their being ballplayers, the majority of them had to take what they could get and play ball. So you figured that a player would eventually come around if he was holding out and the club didn't meet his demands. Things didn't figure any other way, and so you'd naturally assume that our four missing infielders would be showing up at camp any day. But there was still fretting and worry.

The Little Skipper fretted about their absence, and he must have been afraid that they wouldn't show up. That would have been like a confession of guilt, but then, they seemed to be guilty even if they couldn't be convicted in a court of law. Without them, the ball club would be shot. Shano Collins was a first baseman as well as an outfielder and could take Gandil's job and handle it as credibly as he did that season, and there was a lefty busher up named Ford who was supposed to be ready, and I could play short or third. But the Sox infield was just a honey. And there was Buck. The club couldn't afford to lose him. The Little Skipper wanted another pennant and victory in the Series, and he wanted it bad because of 1919, and he wanted his players on the spot and getting into shape for a fast getaway when the season opened.

And while not much was said about the Series of the previous October, it wasn't forgotten or without its effects. You felt uncertain or not sure. You didn't know what to expect. There was a doubt in your mind about some of the players and you couldn't put that doubt to sleep and keep it dozing and snoring away. After all, if the players had sold out to gamblers, they might do it again, and they didn't care about winning, or at least you couldn't be sure—that is feel confident that they cared. Four of them staying away from spring training and sending no word to the club did look funny, peculiar, and that, also, could be a sign of things you didn't want to think about.

So right from the first day of spring training there was this source to make us anxious and to affect the Little Skipper. And after all, managing the club was his job. He was already old, sixty-one or sixty-two, and he didn't know anything else but baseball. He could take the rap for the lost Series in 1919 and if, after that, the ball club didn't make a good showing and stay up in the pennant fight, he could have been fired. If he lost his job, he might not ever get another one as a big league manager. And to the contrary, he had a good thing, maybe for the rest of his active life, if he won. He had a little saved up but nothing special and he needed and wanted his job. He was in a hell of a spot there. And it was worse because he was convinced the players had let him down for the gamblers. He needed them and had to rely on them, and he couldn't trust them.

The weather wasn't good those first couple of days either, but we started working out. And from the first minute, I felt real good and I must have looked good and like a much-improved young ballplayer over the previous spring because the writers sent back some stories about me, saying that it might not make any difference if Risberg and McMullen did hold out because of my playing, and that I might take Risberg's job away from him. But those first infield practice sessions were mostly makeshift.

The veterans and the rookies practiced separately, but I practiced as a veteran so as to help make up an infield for practice. Even though he was over sixty, the Little Skipper hit out the grounders and he slapped mean balls at you and made you move. And he did that to me particularly because he had to make up his mind about me so as to keep me with the ball club or send me back to the minors. He drove me to the right and left, sometimes making me race to get balls he'd slap over second base, but I only wish I made plays in league games the way I made them in those infield practice workouts.

Of course the players did show up, except Gandil, who quit the game. Good as he was, his not returning brought relief. Ford looked good and ready for the big leagues, and there was always Shano to fall back on.

But Risberg and McMullen showed up after a couple of days and I was shifted to second base until Eddie Collins put in his appearance, and then I changed to practice with the bushers or the Yannigans, as the writers always called us. The Little Skipper welcomed them quite cordially, and he seemed real glad to have them. And everybody else was too, I guess.

It wouldn't have made sense for me to wish they wouldn't come back just so I could play regular. I knew I had to win my place and I was giving a good old Harvard try. Risberg didn't seem worried about me as a rival and he hardly noticed me at all except that when I worked out at second base, with him at shortstop, he didn't make it easy for me and some of his tosses would be at my feet or over my head or wide of the bag.

I guess it was the second week, maybe the tenth day or a day or two more, when Buck showed up with his wife, and he had a new fur coat, some snazzy silk shirts, and his golf clubs.

Ray or one of the players kidded him about wanting to become a movie actor, a matinee idol. The Little Skipper saw him smiling in the hotel lobby, standing with his wife and all of his things around him, and the Little Skipper rushed to Buck, gave him a hug, and welcomed him like a long-lost brother. Buck was happy and tanned. He looked in good condition and said he'd been playing a lot of golf. He'd played golf with Babe Ruth. But then he said he wasn't reporting because he was a holdout and he was going to Chicago to see the Old Roman.

"Me and the missus, my hairpin here, drove from California. But more money or I don't put on a friggin' uniform." And he said he was offered a good selling job with a big Chicago company and he'd take that if he didn't get the kind of money he wanted. And he hadn't any word of Gandil.

Buck did go to Chicago but not for long. He saw the Old Roman and was on a train returning fast. He didn't get a raise, but he was promised a better contract for the next year if he had a good season. He looked good from the first day he was on the ball field in uniform. We had our whole team intact and were playing exhibition games. I was playing with the Yannigans, sometimes in the infield and sometimes in the outfield, and the newspapermen wrote a couple of stories about me. I hit a home run off a college pitcher in one game.

Of course I saw and talked lots with Lefty. He still looked good, but it wasn't the same as the year before when it seemed that Lefty and not Dick Kerr would be the rookie to stand out. He worked hard on fielding, and I even went with him a couple of mornings ahead of time along with one or two of the bushers and bunted and ran to first with him pitching and fielding.

We used to walk around the town or sit in front of the hotel or sometimes see a movie. We'd talk baseball and he'd talk about his wife, Isabella, and I'd talk of Mary, and sometimes I'd think of the years to come, of our careers, Lefty's and mine, and of our being friends and roommates, with Lefty becoming a star pitcher and myself a star, the two of us the backbone of the White Sox.

"A ballplayer has a good life if he's in the big league," Lefty said one night, the two of us sitting in chairs on the hotel porch, and the night nice and just cool enough, and the sky big and full of stars.

"It's not bad in the Pacific Coast League," I said.

"When you marry Mary, you'll think of the comforts of home, Mick."

"I guess so."

"The fellows who make a mistake are the ones who bounce around the minor leagues and don't make it. One day, they wake up old and the best years of their life are gone."

"I know. I told you about Rex."

"They can't do anything else, and what are they gonna do, become pick-and-shovel men?"

I hadn't thought much of that, and when Lefty brought up the subject, I was cocky enough and confident and was certain that nothing like that was going to be my fate.

"A married man can't buy a home for himself and his family and set himself for life as a minor leaguer, maybe playing in a different league every season. If you take your wife with you, you got to live double and you live double anyway. You got your furniture and your life set like I have now in Chicago, and you're away six, seven months and got to get a job in the winter, and leave it for the next ball season."

Lefty had gotten marriage hard, I thought. And, maybe, I also guessed or figured, he didn't have too much confidence in himself and was afraid he was going to be sold or optioned to a minor league club.

"And then what kind of life is it for a guy's wife and his kids, if he's got any?" Lefty went on.

"A lot of the ballplayers are married, Lefty," I said.

"Yeah, they're big leaguers now. Still, it isn't the best type of life for marriage."

I didn't like what Lefty was saying and I worried a little about him for fear that he was going to give up trying, fighting his hardest to make good. It wasn't that Lefty didn't make sense, but I only thought of succeeding in baseball and nothing else. It was all still pretty romantic with me, I guess, and I had been lucky and so far it had been easy for me. I was going to marry Mary, but I figured on making more than my $200 per month plus the $50 bonus and on World Series money.

"Hell, Lefty, you've got plenty of stuff. All you need is to pitch winning ball in this league."

"Oh, I think I have. I wasn't thinking specifically of myself. I was talking in general," Lefty said.

Sometimes there used to be harmonizing in the hotel and time passed. I liked those first spring training years of mine. Of course I was on my toes and trying and sometimes I'd worry, but I looked pretty good and my half-year with San Francisco had jacked up my confidence more than I realized. I'd keep telling myself, "Hell, I can play ball in this man's league."

II

It was exciting, getting back to Chicago for the opening of the season. It was my first big league opening, because in 1919 I'd been shipped to San Francisco before the opening day. Things had been pretty good on the ball club in Texas, and I had traveled most of the time with the Goofs or the Yannigans. My excitement and enthusiasm led me to forget about the 1919 Series and disharmony on the ball club. But I had my worries. I wasn't sure what was going to be done with me and I was divided in my mind as to what I wanted done.

If I was kept with the White Sox, I could be pretty certain that I'd be sitting on the bench. I remembered my talk with Tim a little while before going away for spring training, and what Tim had said made a hell of a lot of sense. And separate from what Tim said, sometimes I thought along this line on my own. I knew that my going back to the minors wouldn't at all have to mean that I had failed or slipped. There just wasn't a regular berth for me on the ball club.

But suppose I did go back to the Pacific Coast League, would I have any better chance in 1921? None of the regulars showed signs of slipping. And I thought how I would have a better chance on another big league ball club, and I'd hope to be traded or sold. But while I kept blowing hot and cold, my feeling underneath was that I wanted to stay with the White Sox. Sooner or later, I'd have to get my chance, and once I did, I'd make the most of it.

By the time we got to Chicago, I was pretty much convinced that I was being kept. And on my first night, Mary and I went to Lefty's for dinner. I felt a bit bad because Lefty had been sent to Milwaukee. I was sorry for him and knew that I was going to miss him. But Lefty seemed to be taking it pretty damned good. He didn't gripe or complain, or say anything, as a matter of fact. The girls did a lot of talking, saying how much they missed us and just talking and chatting. We had steak, because Lefty and I were steak-and-potato men. It was fun, and I liked it, but still I felt sorry and even kind of guilty because I was staying with the ball club and Lefty wasn't.

After we ate, Lefty and I talked in the parlor while the girls were in the kitchen. Lefty was puffing on a good cigar, and he suddenly said to me, "Mick, I'm not reporting to Milwaukee."

That almost bowled me over. It surprised me too much for me to say anything.

"I gave it a lot of thought. Isabella and me, we've discussed it, too."

"But hell, Lefty, you ain't quitting baseball?"

"No, just quitting Milwaukee."

"You'll come back. Maybe if you get a regular work up there, that'll be all you need for your fielding. Hell, I imagine I'll be joining you."

"No, it doesn't look like you will—not unless Gandil changes his mind and comes back to play, and it doesn't look like he will."

"You'll be with Clarence Rowland, too, and he's a real nice guy."

"I know, but I don't want to go away from here to a minor league ball club, Mick. I've got to think of my future. And Isabella is going to have a baby. I'll be a family man, and I don't want to be moving Isabella around with me."

"But Milwaukee's so near Chicago, and maybe you're giving up a future."

Lefty puffed on his cigar, and then shrugged his big shoulders. "I'll have my job here, and I can pitch semipro ball on weekends. Maybe I can get a job coaching one of the Catholic high school teams here next spring. We can save up a little money for rainy days, and we both think it's the smartest thing for me to do."

"I just feel sorry as hell to hear you say all this, Lefty," I said.

"I can't say that I'm not sorry about it myself, because I'm like you, Mick, I love baseball."

It seemed to me to be wrong for Lefty to do this. I didn't want to think he was giving up, but that's what it looked like he was doing.

"I don't want to spend four, five years, maybe six years or more, finding out that I'm just another ballplayer."

"You got plenty of stuff, Lefty. I'd hate like hell to have to hit you when you got that spitter of yours working."

"No, I'll do better, and it will cost me less money. And I never told anyone this, but now I can talk to you. Mick, you know the World Series last year, it didn't look right. It done something to me, almost took the heart out of me."

I almost wished he hadn't brought up the subject.

"I don't know, what the hell, Lefty," I said, not knowing how to go on and to say what I thought about it because I didn't really know what I thought.

"You must know, Mick. It didn't look like it was really on the level," Lefty said, knocking ashes in a tray and then taking a good big puff on his cigar.

"It worried me. I didn't know what the hell to think. I still don't."

"It's been on my mind ever since last fall. It was on my mind all winter."

"It's just something a guy can't believe."

"Yes, you can't, and it still didn't look right. Tell me, Mick, it didn't look right to you, did it?"

"No, it didn't," I admitted after hesitating.

"If things like that are done once, they can be done again."

"But we didn't do nothing. Nothing can happen to us, Lefty."

"I know, Mick. But that's not what I'm getting at. It's that I began feeling different about baseball. Some of the fellows on our club are heroes of mine, and it hurt me like it would if my own father done something rotten. Well, it has just made me feel different about baseball.

It made me feel that I don't want to pitch my heart out and throw my arm out for four, five, or maybe six years trying to get way up there at the top of the baseball heap."

"But it's worth it, Lefty."

"Yes, to you Mick, I think it is, but I don't for myself. I don't believe I'll be good enough, and my feeling has changed."

"I hate to hear you tell me all this."

"I hate to hear myself saying it, but . . ."

"Why don't you give it another year?"

"One year leads to another, and I want to live here in Chicago with Isabella. We can build something, build ahead. I'll pitch every weekend, on Sundays, and make twenty-five bucks. And I like to play, Mick. It's the playing I love, and so long as I'm playing it doesn't matter if it's semipro or the American League. And look at Walt Hunt. He was all finished and let go last year. He didn't have much to show."

"I still wish you weren't quitting. Hell, I know you'll make it."

"That's all I could do—make it. The best I could ever be is a second-string pitcher, and I don't want to lose my years being that."

"You don't rate yourself high enough, Lefty."

"No, I know what I can do and what I want to do. It's the best thing for me. But you son of a gun, I'll miss not rooming with you."

"Me too."

"But I'll be seeing you—I'm gonna be the best man at your wedding or there ain't gonna be no wedding."

"You'll come back, Lefty."

He just shook his head, and then the girls joined us. There was a movie both of them wanted to see so we all went to the show. But I felt sad about Lefty's decision. Now, looking back, I don't know but what he made the sensible decision. Except that he did have a lot of stuff, and he could have learned to field. Anyone can learn to field, except maybe a few like Ike Boone and Smead Jolley.

Most of the players didn't say anything about Lefty quitting, except Ray Schalk. "What the hell's he want to quit for? He's got enough stuff to pitch winning ball in this league."

I missed Lefty. We've been friends from that day to this, and I used to see him quite a bit. But I haven't seen him but only once in the last year and a half or so because Lefty had a heart attack and he doesn't get around much any more. I think he often regretted that decision, but he never said so. He pitched semipro until he was about forty or so, and he was damned good in semipro ball.

But it was the spring, and the opening of the season was a time of all kinds of hopes. I think that the opening of a new baseball season is one of the most thrilling times in a ballplayer's life. You're starting fresh and your record is clean. The new season is going to be your big year, the one in which you get all of the breaks. You're in condition and feel strong and full of enthusiasm. It's a beginning after the winter. You've been excited about opening day ever since you can remember, and then you're a ballplayer yourself on opening day. It's a thrill.

I was still on the club, and I felt it in my bones that something was going to happen so that I'd get my real chance.

"We're going to win this pennant," I told Mary, and also her father, Jack.

III

I don't know that I'd like to go through another baseball season like 1920. I used to tell that to myself while I was still an active player. That 1919 World Series was a ghost whistling all year. From the first day of the season on, the Series was haunting our ball club. The story was all over the league and it was believed. The players on other ball clubs threw it up to us, and they were pretty rough. Cicotte got it real hard, because he doctored the baseball and that made some of the ballplayers sore. It's easy to dislike a pitcher you can't hit just like it's easy to dislike your dentist. They'd shout at our bench and at players on the field and ask if the game was on the level or if anyone on our club made an error. They'd ask if he'd seen a gambler.

You had to know it now, because you heard so much. Sportswriters talked of it, too, and I was beginning to know some of them. And I found out that the World Series checks of eight of our players had been held up by the Old Roman. Sometimes on pay day, players on the other ball clubs would ask our players if they had gotten their pay. All of this razzing and taunting and bench jockeying wasn't criticism of the suspected players. Many ballplayers weren't sore at them. They were just taking advantage of an opening, and a ballplayer will attack your mother on the ball field if he can rattle you or make you sore.

The suspected players stayed mostly together and didn't associate very much with the rest of us. Of course I was still considered a busher, and some of them even continued to treat Dick Kerr as a busher despite the two games he won in the Series.

The suspected players didn't show any real signs that they felt guilty or apologetic, and Risberg and McMullen were pretty tough. If anybody would have accused them openly, they'd have fought the man. Joe Jackson didn't seem bothered by anything that was said, and sometimes he acted like he didn't understand a man. He couldn't read, although he sometimes said he could, and often you would see him sitting in the lobby of a hotel with a newspaper before him, opened to the sports pages, and he acted like he was reading and understanding what he read. He could make out names, and especially his own name, in the box scores, and he knew what the box scores meant. In 1919 he hit .351, and he had a terrific season in 1920, ending up with an average of .381, his highest ever with the White Sox and his best since about 1912.

Most of the time he was quiet, and after a game, when there would be talk in the clubhouse of what happened in the field, he wouldn't say very much. He was not an articulate fellow and never could tell you how he did things or explain how he hit. But he was just about the greatest natural hitter there ever was. If he was playing today, you wouldn't be hearing so much about Ted Williams or Musial or Mantle. He was the kind of man you couldn't help liking and he meant no harm to anyone.

And Buck had the best year of his whole career, hitting about .330 or .335. He was put third in the batting order and Eddie Collins was moved from that spot to second. Buck was with the suspected players a lot, but he seemed to like everyone except Eddie Collins. He was going to win a big raise for himself and had been promised it if he had a big year.

"They're talking crazy," he used to say sometimes when the fellows on one of the other clubs would be riding us about losing to Cincinnati.

Ford petered out fast. He couldn't hit, and Shano played first and hit over .300. Ford saved my spot on the roster, because when he couldn't come through, then it was a sure thing that I was going to stay on the club. And Red Faber had his strength back and took his regular turn pitching so that we had four starting pitchers, and all of them were twenty-game winners, Cicotte, Williams, Kerr, and Red. Once Shano went in at first base in place of Ford, our ball club was as good as in 1919 and better in pitching, thanks to Faber.

Cleveland was improved and, of course, won the pennant, and the Yankees, with Babe Ruth hitting fifty-four home runs, were in the pennant race. But our club was the best. Every regular man in the lineup except Risberg and Ray hit over .300, and Gandil wasn't missed. I think some of the players were glad he wasn't back. He was supposed to have been the ring leader, and that's my opinion, although it's said that Cicotte was the man who started it. Cicotte blamed Gandil, however. Cicotte wasn't as good in 1920 as the year before, but he was 21-10.

But I don't know, and nobody else but the players themselves knows, about the games in 1920. Lots of things didn't look right, and you were always wondering and asking yourself what was going on. Doubt is a terrible thing, and you had doubt. Every time you put it to sleep or thought that you had, it would pop back at you, or something would be said or would happen in a ball game and you just wouldn't know.

That's a reason why I think our ball club was the greatest one of all in modern baseball. What is a great baseball club? I'd say it's a club that doesn't need anything more than what it's got and is good in every position. Our club was like that, even if right field was the weakest spot. Liebold and Shano were not great ballplayers, but they were day-in and day-out ones, and Risberg had all the makings of a great shortstop. The three greatest ball clubs I ever saw were ours, the New York Yankees of 1928, and the Philadelphia Athletics of 1929–31. None of these clubs needed any improvement. And ours was the greatest of these three. If it hadn't been, it couldn't have come so close to winning the pennant in 1920.

My God! Think of the strain, if you can. Those fellows knew they were suspected. After all, their World Series checks had been held up, and a detective had investigated them, and they were ribbed and jeered at on the ball field.

"This is the busher who didn't have to get paid for strikin' out," a catcher said the first time I went to bat in 1920. And that was mild.

And the strain wasn't only on the suspected players but on every one of us. If seven or eight players had been bought by gamblers, why couldn't others also be bought? And with rumors floating everywhere in every city in the league and all through the National League as well, other players could be mentioned and talked about. I felt the strain, myself, and sometimes, when I was in my neighborhood or going to or coming from Mass on a Sunday morning, I'd begin to think that somebody was going to see me and think that I had something to do with ball games being sloughed.

Before the season was over, Ray was catching Cicotte and Williams when they didn't have much to say to him, and the team was divided off into groups. You felt something had to happen. But the suspected players seemed to settle down with the conviction that nothing was going to be done to them. They knew they were good ballplayers, and I guess they believed that the Old Roman didn't want to wreck a ball club of stars. You couldn't believe that all of them would be kicked out of baseball. It was like actually believing in your own death. You felt, and in a way knew, in your bones that something was going to happen, and you couldn't believe that it would happen.

Early in the season we were riding to Cleveland and there was talk of Hal Chase. "He used to test the bats with his teeth. When he was with our club, all of the bats had his teeth marks on them," Ray said.

"He's playing outlaw ball now," Jim Cruisenberry said.

"They say he cleaned up a lot on bets last fall," Lou Norman said.

"McGraw merely suspended him with nothing said," Robby Allyson said. He was another of the writers.

"I saw him in Cincinnati. What could you prove?" Cruisenberry asked.

"There are some goddamned things you see and you know," Lou Norman said.

"Hal just has a bad character," Robby said.

"That stuff comes out. It did on Chase, didn't it?" Cruisenberry said. I noticed him looking down the car at Risberg, Cicotte, and Felsch, who were playing cards.

"I never noticed or suspected anything when he was playing with our ball club," Ray said. "In those days we didn't have much of a team, and he didn't have to go out of his way to get a ball game lost. The team just lost."

"You can tell on the ball field. When I played on the Pacific Coast, I knew. A man gets one, two feet out of position. A pitcher just misses the corners. An outfielder hesitates just long enough not to get the jump on the ball," Lou Norman said.

"You writers can second-guess anything," Ray said. "I couldn't say I ever saw one play I could be sure about. A thousand things can go wrong on a ball field. Even Ty Cobb is human."

"Yes, Ray, I know it," Jim said.

Ray left, and the newspapermen went on talking about throwing ball games. Lou told a story about a Cincinnati player who'd been dropped for throwing games. In the ninth inning in Boston with the score 1-0 in favor of Boston, this player came up to bat with two out and none on base. He couldn't end the game because he was hit by a pitched ball. The next batter hit the first pitch out of the ballpark. Instead of trotting around the bases, he ran full speed, right on the heels of the crooked infielder. He told that infielder, "Run, you sonofabitch. You're gonna work for the money you lose on this ball game."

The newspapermen laughed. Then Buck joined them and they changed the subject.

I thought of gamblers. If one ever came to me with a proposition, I decided that I'd slug him on the spot. And I thought of Hal Chase. He'd been a favorite of mine. And he'd been dropped for throwing ball games. Why had he done such things, I asked myself, and I thought how you just lose some of your illusions. That hurts, too. Ballplayers were just men, not heroes. I told myself that. It must sound naive, but we are naive until we get around.

In Cleveland, then, I heard a stranger in the hotel lobby say something about the last World Series being crooked, and I thought for a minute or so that I was going to slug him.

IV

By June, our ball club looked like it would win the pennant. We were wobbly early in the season, and Cicotte lost a couple of games, but then the team began clicking and winning regular White Sox victories, with a sudden attack, bunching hits in rapid-fire succession, and sewing up the game.

"Come on, put this friggin' ball game on ice," Buck would say in the sixth or seventh inning as he came in from the field at the end of an inning.

And plenty of times that would be done.

A pennant and World Series victory would have been a redemption. It would stop the talk about the 1919 Series. I thought so, anyway.

And I wanted the talk to die down. It was damned hard for me not to believe that something had been wrong in the Series. But I didn't want the players to be exposed. I just hoped that it would be forgotten. I was afraid. It seemed to me that if the story got printed in all of the newspapers, that would be terrible for baseball. It would almost be like the end of the world.

In the latter part of June, the eastern clubs went west, and our club was clicking nicely. Even with the talk, things looked good. And since the opening day, the home fans had been wonderful, and 1919 seemed to be forgotten. Attendance was good and they cheered us and rooted for us. If any of them had heard the rumors or were suspicious, they didn't show it. They were for the White Sox 100 percent and with powerful lungs. And after the games, there would be small crowds waiting to see the players leave the clubhouse.

I was a familiar figure, and as I left I'd often hear a kid or some adult fan saying, "There goes Mickey Donovan." "There's Donovan." "Clover Donovan." I got a thrill out of that. I was popular because I was Irish and a Chicago boy, even though I was still spending my time sitting on the bench. I got tired hearing someone I knew from my neighborhood telling me that they'd seen me on the ball field in practice.

I was seeing Mary a lot, and we were usually in a daze of hopes and plans. I told her that I was getting very confident that the White Sox were going to win the pennant. And if we did, we were sure to win the World Series. With the World Series money, we could get married and go to California for our honeymoon. That made quite a baseball fan out of her and she began really learning about the game. Sometimes she'd come to the ball game and wait for me, and I'd feel mighty proud having fans see me walking away with my girl. The future I saw for Mary and myself reduced my being concerned about the 1919 Series, and so did the ball games the club won. Now and then, I convinced myself that rumors were just rumors with no foundation.

Things looked jake, and there was only one source for complaint. I wanted to be in the ball games. It's rotten to hope a player will be hurt, but sometimes I wished that bad luck on Leibold or Risberg and McMullen. And I wished Eddie Murphy would sprain a wrist. He was one of the greats when it came to pinch-hitting, and that year he was terrific. He wound up the season with an average of something like .436. I went to the ballpark each day thinking that it would be Mickey

Donovan's day. And I got my kid brother passes, and he came to the games a lot and waited outside for me. I was his hero.

Eddie Collins kept watching me in practice and giving me tips and helping me, and now and then Buck told me something. My isolation as a rookie was breaking down, and I began to feel that maybe I really did belong with the White Sox. I began now and then to smoke a cigarette after a ball game, because even though I only watched, it was a tense experience and wound me up. And I was getting to know the league, storing bits of knowledge and information away for the time when I would need it in a ball game.

A reassuring story I heard happened in Cleveland. A sportswriter in that town, Elmer Vogt, was a good friend of Cicotte. He and another newspaperman saw Cicotte and asked him point blank about the Series. Cicotte told them that there was no truth at all in the rumors and stories. He had pitched in that first game, and he had made that error in the fourth game. A man couldn't be sure of succeeding even if he wanted to throw a ball game. They believed him.

A couple of times things were said in front of Buck. "For Christ sake, look at my record. This talk is crazy," he said.

And Risberg once said, "All kinds of sons of bitches talk. Talk is cheap."

McMullen was ready to fight anybody who accused him.

Joe Jackson would look at a person with a kind of dumb or sleepy look and say slowly, "When Ah go up there, Ah don't know what Ah'm gonna do. Ah go up there and Ah teed off on the ball."

Lefty Williams said, "They ain't talkin' about me."

Happy Felsch would say, "I don't know what the hell it's all about. I play ball and I can't talk like a Philadelphia lawyer."

I think Risberg told them to sit tight and keep their mouths shut. He was tough and hard-boiled. "As long as you keep your mouth shut nobody can do nothing." And when some Cleveland players went at him, he told them, "That would be the only way you bastards could beat us."

From time to time, we'd lose a ball game that would leave a doubt in your mind. Lefty Williams lost one in St. Louis.

But as I said, it began to look like we were pennant-bound, and there's nothing in baseball like being a winner, even if you're still a busher sitting on the bench.

Then on July 4th, Cleveland came to town and we won two, the second on a screaming pinch-hit triple over third and along the foul line, which Eddie Murphy hit. That was the last time I saw Ray Chapman play. He was the Cleveland shortstop who died after being hit by a pitched ball thrown by Carl Mays. He was a hell of a good ballplayer and a friendly, likeable fellow. That tragedy seemed to assure us the pennant. Nobody wanted the pennant that way, and when I read about the accident or when I thought about it or when it came to my mind, it gave me a sick feeling. Of course I don't know if Mays threw that pitch at Chapman's head or not, and I'm sure he didn't mean to hit him, but throwing bean balls was something I didn't really encounter until I played in the big leagues. There it was done so regularly that you accepted it, and the batter was expected to keep his eyes open and duck. And I did, plenty of times.

I didn't know Chapman really, but the players liked and respected him and they were affected. Some of them were down on Mays and some weren't.

"I'm not letting that batter crowd the plate on me," Red Faber said in a clubhouse discussion.

"I know you aren't, Red. But you're a pretty mean pitcher," Ray said.

"No batter is going to stand on top of that plate on me," Red said.

But of course Chapman and the unfortunate, tragic accident were discussed more than bean balls.

"According to the story I read, Mays says he ducked into the ball," Eddie Collins said.

"Then it must have been a curve that broke," Ray said. "Did you say he ducked into the ball?"

"That's the story," Eddie said.

"Always go back, not into the ball," the Little Skipper said.

"Or fall flat on the ground," Ray said.

"Sometimes I've seen fellows who seemed to be hypnotized. They couldn't move. That must have been the case with Chapman," Eddie Collins said.

"We had this kid, Corhan. He looked like a good prospect," Shano said. "I seen him fall like a log, a felled log, and the sound just made me sick clean down to my belly. That kid Corhan was never any good after that. That must have been eight, nine years ago, 1911, 1912, back there."

"Oh God, it makes you feel rotten," Ray said. "He was a damned fine fellow and a hell of a good shortstop. God, it just makes you feel rotten."

"I'll get out of the way of that friggin' ball. My head ain't hard enough for it," Buck said. "And such a fellow to get it, one of the goddamn swellest in the league."

"He wanted to retire and go into business. And a nice wife. He has a damn fine girl for a wife. One pitch," Ray said shaking his head.

"He got up after he was hit and then he became unconscious, I read," Red said.

"That's wrong. Never got up. You can't move if you got a concussion," Collins said.

"I was hit once. The ball done went and bounced away, but I must not have got what you called it a—what you just called it," Joe Jackson said.

"Concussion," Eddie said.

"Yes, I didn't get nothing. Next time I come to bat, I hit for two bases."

"Never take your eye off the ball," Eddie said.

A collection was taken up and we sent flowers to the widow, and Eddie wrote a letter to Speaker for our team. That was an awful thing, and no ball club wants to get a break that will give it the pennant by any such tragic happening.

We came into New York after that tragic accident and there was more talk of it. There was bitterness against Mays and a movement even to drive him out of baseball. But nothing happened. In our series with the Yankees, we rode roughshod over them, and were in first place, way out in front, something like three, four, five games. It looked like we were heading for our second straight pennant. The way the club knocked off the Yankees, it looked like it was at its peak. And none of the players was hurt or ailing. Cleveland had lost its great shortstop and the Yankees had lost a series to us. We went to Boston, a second-division club, to play a five-game series. They had some good pitchers—Bush, Jones, Waite Hoyt, who was a young pitcher then, and Pennock. But the club had been sold to New York and Boston was easy for us.

We lost five straight ball games. It was a nightmare, and to this day I don't know what happened or if there was any skullduggery or not. Red was beaten, and so was Kerr, and I remember that Eddie Collins made some fatal errors. Ray was fit to be tied, fighting and scrapping to win just like he did in the World Series. I pinch hit in one of the games and Bullet Joe Bush struck me out in three pitches.

The Little Skipper took it hard. At the time I didn't know it, but I later learned it from Jim Cruisenberry, and the story was also printed a couple of times. But all season the Little Skipper was still trying to clear up the facts about the 1919 Series. And in New York, while the team was knocking over the Yankees and our pitchers were keeping Babe Ruth in check, the Little Skipper got the story straight. Here's what happened.

He knew that Abe Attell, the retired prizefighter, had been in on the fix and knew the whole story. He saw Abe, he and the writer Ring Lardner. The Little Skipper told Jim Cruisenberry to be at the bar in the saloon they went to and just to listen. So Jim went to this place and stood having a drink near the table where the Little Skipper sat with Abe Attell and Ring Lardner. Abe told the story. The players had gone to Bill Burns and Burns had gone to him. He had talked with Cicotte in the Ansonia Hotel in New York. He had brought in a big New York gambler and that had clinched the deal.

Jim had heard this, and the next morning he and the Little Skipper had taken an automobile ride so that they could talk in private. "That's it," the Little Skipper had told Jim. And he told him that Cicotte was weak and that he had been working on the pitcher all year. He said Cicotte would talk and tell the story.

So that happened during the New York series and, like I said, we then went to Boston in first place, looking like sure things for the pennant. And the ball team loses five straight games. Overnight it looked like a different team, just the same as it had in Cincinnati when the 1919 World Series got under way. I don't remember the scores of those games, and, in fact, I don't even remember much about the games. It's all blurred now in my memory. There was one doubleheader in that series, and that was the worst of all, dropping two at once.

"What the hell—are we going to give away the goddamned pennant?" the Little Skipper asked in the clubhouse.

There was no answer, at least not right off. The players were undressing, showering, dressing. Cicotte had pitched and lost that ball game, and a couple of errors had helped us lose. He went and lay down for a rub without saying a word.

A little later Buck said, "We're still gonna win this pennant. We got ball games with New York and Cleveland, and we know we can beat them."

"We got more games with Boston, too," somebody said. I forget who it was.

Those days must have been rotten ones for the Little Skipper. He was managing a ball club and he was convinced that he knew that eight of his players had been involved in this deal that had sold him down the river. And now they could be doing the same kind of thing over again, and after losing him the World Series, maybe they were losing a pennant for him. He'd been so proud of the ball club and had called us all "my boys," and still often did at that time. He still called us "my boys."

All through that season he really wasn't down on the players, even the suspected ones, and blamed not them so much as the gamblers. After it was known and the players were gone, he'd always blame "the dirty gamblers" whenever this matter came up in conversation. He was just as friendly to the suspected players as he was to the rest of us, or that's the way it seemed to me. He felt that he had such a stroke of good luck in being made manager in 1919, getting the club just when it was great, and he'd been proud of the club all through the 1919 season. Then, he kept driving and, I guess, hoping during the 1920 season.

But he knew what had happened, and then in New York, just when the ball club seemed to be hitting on all cylinders and was in first place and looking like a sure thing, just then he gets the proof right out of the horse's mouth about the World Series "fix." And on top of that, the ball club goes to Boston, drops five games, and falls from first to third place.

In Boston, we heard more and took more jockeying about the Series. After the Red Sox won the first game, one of their players asked, "Say, did we win yesterday?"

"I don't know, they took the score off the scoreboard. I never can remember anything about your ball club," Buck said.

"The score shows we won, but did we win, Buck, or did you crooked bums just lose?"

And the Little Skipper was called a YMCA secretary, taking care of such good boys.

Of course, jockeying don't mean much, and if your skin isn't thick and you can't take it, you don't belong in baseball and you won't last long in the game, either. But sometimes this kind of jockeying was different, and it did hurt, more than anyone let on. "You guys can get rich losin' ball games, can't you?" Stuff like that was pulled.

So, we lost that five-game series in Boston and came home. It was a lousy trip and I was only glad that I got to sleep quickly. They were still giving me an upper berth of course. I was glad to be home because it meant that I wouldn't be around the players so much, living with them practically all of the time as I did when we were traveling. That's what the five straight defeats in Boston did to me. It had been something that was growing, accumulating. The cracks on the ball field, in the hotels, this all added up.

"I can't understand it," Ray had said to Eddie Collins in Boston.

"It doesn't look right," Eddie then answered.

And Ray and Red had been talking.

"You can't do nothing," Red said.

"Christ, I'd like to."

"What are you gonna do, except try to win anyway. Every time I pitch, I think that, I got to win it myself because I don't know if there's any other way I can win," Red said.

It was like 1919. The suspected players had us all at their mercy. They had baseball at their mercy. No one seemed able to do anything to them and everybody seemed to think that there was nothing to do because there was no evidence. That made it hard, harder than any one of us seemed fully to realize at the time. And sometimes when the club won a ball game, you were almost surprised. At other times, a ball game on the won side of the won-and-lost column would raise your hopes and put back to sleep any rising doubts that you had.

"If the Little Skipper doesn't do anything, what can a ballplayer do?" Eddie Murphy said.

"He's only the manager. It's up to the Old Roman and the authorities," Red said.

"Hell, the Old Roman must be suspicious of something," Ray said.

"Yes, he's suspicious," Collins said.

"It doesn't seem like him," Ray said.

"What's that?" Shano said.

"He's never stood for anything before," Ray said.

"Hell, we think we know, and we do know, that it looks terrible. It still doesn't look right. But what the hell do we really know? What could we say if we had to talk?" Collins said.

"How can a ballplayer go and spill on another ballplayer, or a whole bunch of 'em?" asked Shano.

"But how in hell can we do anything? What the hell can we do?" asked Ray.

And what could the other players have done? Eddie Collins, Ray, and all of the players not suspected or involved? If one of them spilled the beans, he was taking a chance himself and might be ostracized by other players, and some of them might have called him a stool pigeon. Nobody wanted to stick his neck out or knew how much the Old Roman and the baseball bigwigs knew or what they wanted to do or would do or if they even wanted to do anything.

This of course wasn't the only thing on everybody's mind. You didn't even want it on your mind at all, and tried to forget it and keep it off your mind. It was forced on you just when you thought you could forget it. It came back. The pennant race was the main thing, and each day's ball game in that race took up your attention. And on the road, I went to some shows, did some sightseeing, and I played poker a couple of nights, and I sat in lobbies and talked baseball, and I kept thinking and dreaming of the future. The doubt about the 1919 Series was just there in everybody's mind. And even though it seemed that it was all more than smoke, that the Series had been thrown, well, it hadn't been proved. And that's what made it worse. There was the uncertainty about the game every day. Then a game or a couple of games would be won, or the White Sox would lose a game that seemed to be on the level, but you couldn't go on being sure.

I was still a busher even though it was the third straight year I was on the club and I was spending my first whole season as a White Sox. I didn't have much to say. And if I had, nobody would have listened much. I had been respectful, maybe over-respectful when I broke in, and that attitude wore away only slowly. I was beginning, though, to be sore and resentful about some of the players. I felt this way after the disastrous Boston series. If the suspected players were not trying their best, they would be affecting and hurting me. The loss of the World Series cost me some odd $700, which was nothing to sneeze at in those days. I even thought of asking to be traded. That's how I was beginning to be affected.

We came back to Chicago, and then, with the end of August almost on us, the last stage of the pennant race was reached.

V

We got back home on the morning of a weekday. No game was scheduled, but the Little Skipper ordered the team to report for practice
that afternoon. The players griped like hell.

"Get sore as hell at me, and I don't care. Win me ball games and you
won't have to work on an off day," the Little Skipper had told them.
This was on the train. He saw Risberg with a surly expression on his
face and said, "I can get as sore as any man on this ball club and don't
think I ain't got reasons for it."

There was a long workout that afternoon, and the team snapped into
it real well. It began winning ball games again. But it was in August
that the rumors began to fly once again, and there were stories and
rumors about the other league. Bush Herzog of the Cubs was accused
by Rube Benton of the New York Giants. And there was a story about
a Cubs ball game. Gamblers in Detroit were betting on Philadelphia
to beat the Cubs on a day Claude Hendrix was supposed to pitch, and
a note was sent to the Cubs president, Mr. Weeghman, telling him to
pitch Alexander because of the gamblers. This was done. Alexander was
pitched out of turn and he pitched real hard but lost the ball game.

This was the snowball that began rolling. There were stories in
the newspapers. These made our ball club nervous, but little was said
about these rumors affecting the other league. And we had a pennant
to win.

Leibold turned his ankle going after a fly ball in practice and he
gave his ankle a bad sprain. This happened in practice on the day we
got back home after losing those five ball games in Boston. It didn't
seem bad right away, but then it started swelling and there was fear
that he'd broken a bone. We had practice the next morning and Leibold
was in bad shape and didn't even put on a uniform.

"You bat in Leibold's place this mornin'," the Little Skipper said.

"Yes! Yes, sir," I said, so taken aback that I said "sir." But I was
happy as all hell because I knew this was the main chance. Right field
was the sun field and hard to play, but that didn't worry me at all. I'd
go for everything out there and break my neck to get it. That's the way
I felt. I took fielding practice in right field, and I kept looking into the
sun, with my sunglasses on of course, and walking around the field,

studying and observing. And I asked Shano questions about the field. Just like that, in a couple of minutes, I lost all my feeling about being a rookie and a busher. I thought of Leibold and told myself, "I'm going to take his job."

That day Ray took me across the street to Mrs. Kelly's for lunch. "Come on with me and I'll take you to Mrs. Kelly's to lunch, kid," he said.

I had heard of her. She lived across the street from the ballpark and many of the ballplayers went to her house. Before Prohibition, she had run a saloon. Her husband had died and she had kept his saloon going. With Prohibition, she closed up, but there was always beer and drinks for the players, and food, too. They could sit down with the family and leave whatever they wished on the table. She was a friend of the Old Roman and his family and of Harry Grabiner and the Little Skipper. She washed towels for the White Sox, and many of the ballplayers loved her. She had three daughters and a little son named Mike and was supporting them.

"Ma, this is Mickey Donovan," Ray said, introducing me.

"Make yourself at home, boy. It's about time you came to see me," she said.

She was a tall, thin woman with darkish skin, gray hair, and wonderful brown eyes. "You should have come over to see us before this, and you on the White Sox since the war."

I was kind of surprised at what she said.

"I didn't know you."

"Man, you have a tongue. Any ballplayer on the White Sox is always welcome at this door."

She turned to Ray. "Ray, he reminds me of you when you were first brought to me by the Roman." Ray smiled. "He was a boy like you, and the Roman brought him over here and said, 'Ma, this is Ray Schalk. I want you to feed him and take care of him.'"

"And you're still feeding me."

Shano came in and soon we sat down to eat. Mrs. Kelly kept telling me to eat more, and I didn't want to because of the afternoon ball game, but I didn't want to say this in front of Ray and Shano.

"He's playing this afternoon—at least I think he is, Ma."

"Well, goodness, what's happened?" she asked in surprise.

"Nemo Leibold sprained his ankle," Ray said.

"He turned it in a hole in the outfield," Shano said.

"That's a shame. Is he hurt bad?"

"It looks like a bad sprain," Ray said.

"That's too bad. Will he be out of the game long?"

"I don't know. It's a mean sprain."

"So you'll have to play, Mickey."

I grinned.

"You look big and strong enough."

"Sure. Sure, Ma, the kid will fill in," Ray said.

"I'll try like h—like the devil," I said.

"You can say 'like hell' here, Mickey, and don't ever stand on ceremony under this roof," Ma Kelly said.

I was quite thrilled. Ray later told me he did it to relax me in case I might be nervous about playing. He did lots of things like that to relax a player and to get the best out of him. That's one of the reasons why he was such a great ballplayer. He had a kind of instinct as to what to do.

I went back to the ballpark feeling like a million dollars. Now I was really on the ball club.

We were playing St. Louis, and Red was pitching that day. There weren't many fans in the stands when we walked on the field but they gave us the usual cheer. I kept telling myself that I was going to stay in the lineup now that I was breaking in. I stepped up to batting practice feeling different. If I hit the ball, it meant twice as much as the day before. And it may seem peculiar or surprising to some, but I was less tense than I often had been when I had been just a sub and a rookie who had almost no chance or hope of breaking into a ball game.

I stood near the batting cage when Sisler came up from our dugout onto the field. This was a thrill. I was playing against him and would have to be on my toes when he came to bat. He often hit to right field and on a line. And to be in a game with such a man, a game that counted in the pennant race, these were the things I'd dreamed of. He talked to a few of our players and the other Browns came out. Buck made a date to have dinner with Joe Gedeon, their second baseman.

"I want to talk with you," Buck said.

When I went out to right field for fielding practice, some of the fans in the bleachers gave me a cheer. I was, of course, familiar to them, and now I was playing. This was my chance.

We won that ball game. I didn't get any hits but walked and scored a run, and I hit a couple of balls hard but on the ground and straight at Sisler. I caught three or four balls in right field. I wanted to get hits that day and didn't. But I was sure I'd be back in the lineup the next day. The Little Skipper had won with the lineup he played, and Leibold was limping badly. I'd be back, I knew that, and I was back.

We began winning ball games again and playing championship ball. Cicotte's pitching was as good as at any time in 1919, and since we had three games each with New York and Cleveland, we were very much in the pennant race. And we had the best club in the league and knew it.

The stories about gambling were in the newspapers every day but the White Sox weren't mentioned. Herzog and that game I spoke of when Alexander pitched out of turn were being mentioned. Around the end of the month, the news was printed that a grand jury was going to investigate the rumors about gambling in baseball, but still, the World Series wasn't referred to, and I don't think anyone on the club thought that the Series would be investigated also by the grand jury.

On Labor Day we beat the Detroit Tigers twice. The second game was pitched by Shovel Hodge. He was a big dumb yokel from Alabama. He pitched the second game, and for seven innings the Tigers didn't make a base hit. They kept saying that he didn't have a thing on the ball, but they weren't hitting it, and made their first base hit only in the eighth inning. Shovel wasn't much of a pitcher, and while he did last two more years with us, he wasn't much help. Ray and he had a fight the next season, and even though Ray was so much littler than Shovel, he cleaned up on him. The best game Shovel ever pitched in the American League was that first one on Labor Day.

I made four hits in the Labor Day doubleheader, one a double, and had already won my place, at least until Leibold's ankle healed. I knew this and I was getting my chance to contribute to winning a pennant. What better chance of breaking into the lineup could a young ballplayer ask for? I had really run in luck ever since graduating from St. Basil's, and I was still running in luck. I took this as a good sign, and while I wasn't particularly superstitious, I believed that this was a sign that I was under a lucky star.

I was playing good enough not to have Leibold missed, and all I needed to do was to play the same way and then Mickey Donovan would walk out of the dugout carrying two bats, the crowd would be roaring, and Mickey Donovan would be the first White Sox batter in the 1920 World Series. My picture was in the paper twice and the writers mentioned me in the accounts of the games as much as they could. The fans took to me quickly when I was put in the lineup and played good ball and hit major league pitching at a time when every hit really counted. By Labor Day I was getting a good hand when I stepped up to the plate to lead off in each game.

And the way we came out of that Boston slump was encouraging. The team was now playing ball. It was mad, too, and every man on the club wanted to win that pennant. Those rumors, even though the World Series hadn't been as yet mentioned in connection with them, were a tonic. None of the suspected players could afford to take chances. We were in a good position, playing all but six of our remaining games at home, and our four starting pitchers were in top form. This all was baseball at its best, where every play counted big and every pitched ball could have thousands of dollars on it. The fans were with us and there were good crowds. You don't think of the crowds in the game but you know they're there, watching you, and it is a tonic.

I was at Mary's on that Labor Day night.

"Good going, Mickey," Jack Collins said to me.

"I knew you were going to get your chance, Mickey dear. I prayed all summer for it for us," Mary said.

"You ain't out of this pennant race, not by a long sight, Mick," Jack said.

"Hell no, we ain't out of it. We'd be way out in front but because of our slump in Boston last month," I said.

"It's all just what you kids needed to start you off," Jack said.

Mary and I had made our plans. We were going to get married right after the World Series and then go to California on our honeymoon. The World Series was again going to be five out of nine, and a winner's share promised to run over $5,000. Since I'd stepped into the lineup and made the grade, I was certain I was going to get a raise in my next year's contract.

"You got as many hits today as Ty Cobb," Pete Collins said.

"If I could do that every day, I'd ask nothing more."

"What's Cobb like down there on the field?" Jack asked me.

"He's more than they say he is. Even out in right field you get a little nervous when he steps up to bat. The worst thing is to get him mad. We all flatter him when he comes out on the field. We don't want him mad."

"Now that's interesting. The usual thing is to get a fellow mad. When you get his goat, then he's liable to make errors and mistakes," Jack said.

"But when you talk about Cobb, you don't think of the usual thing, Jack," I said.

"You go on and win the pennant and the World Series, and that'll put a stop to all the talk about last year's Series," Jack said.

I kind of froze up at that. Especially then, with myself in the lineup and the club playing winning ball, I didn't want to talk or think about the 1919 World Series.

"Haven't the players ever said anything about these rumors, Mickey?" Jack asked.

"They say there's nothing to them."

"Don't they get sore?"

"Oh, yes, they do. But rumors will die down."

"Yeah, when you play winning ball like you did today."

"Hell, if they did get some dough last year, who wouldn't get dough when he can?" Pete asked.

"It ain't an honest way to make money, and Pete, you know damned well that it ain't," Jack said.

"Everybody else seems to be out to get theirs. Look at what the papers say about graft and the governor," Pete said.

He was referring to a political scandal and graft that was all over the front pages. It involved something like a million dollars, but I don't remember it clearly. I didn't pay much attention to such things then.

"Damn it, Pete, baseball is the last sport. A man can't believe that racing and prizefighting is on the level.

"Oh Dad, everybody's human."

I didn't want to say anything and wished that they would change the subject.

"You wouldn't want Mickey to take money from a gambler, would you?" Jack asked.

"I'd never do anything like that," I said.

"I want to see Mickey get all he can get. After all, he's going to be in my family, and I want to see him give Sis here everything he can."

"Mickey will give me enough," Mary said.

"You got the wrong attitude," Jack told Pete.

Pete sort of smirked. His attitude was no different than many people's, and you have to get what you can, but not by doing wrong in baseball.

The subject of the conversation was changed then.

"I'd like to get five tickets for that Saturday game when Babe Ruth is here. Can you get 'em, Mick?"

"I'll try."

We talked about Babe Ruth, and then about Mary and me and our plans. We took a walk that night, and people recognized me and talked to me on the street. I had really become a celebrity in my neighborhood.

"I'll be so glad when the baseball season is over," Mary said.

"Isn't it exciting, honey?"

"That's why—it's too exciting, and you're not all mine while you're playing baseball."

"But it's my living, dear."

"And you're my lover," Mary told me.

That made me feel so damned good. It was one of the happiest times of my life. A year before, like I said, I was only a rookie sitting on the bench, and two years before I didn't know for sure if I'd be signed up by the Sox after the war. I was certain that I was a big leaguer and felt that I didn't have to worry about my future. I saw myself going up and up. I loved baseball. And I loved Mary.

And besides the excitement of baseball, there was the fuss and the excitement of the wedding, the planning and talking, and Mary's excitement and happiness, and the way her folks all took me into the family and were proud of me. And all of that was mine and I was only twenty.

We walked on Grand Boulevard. That was the best street in our neighborhood and the people who lived on it were mostly all rich. I felt that I could even hold my head up on Grand Boulevard. My life was turning out so close to the way I dreamed it. And how many kids of my age had what I had gotten in just a little over two years after I got my St. Basil sheepskin? And it was not only what I had, but what I was going to have. We could be on top of the baseball world and live for a few years in a row the way Connie Mack's Athletes had, winning four out of five pennants between 1910 and 1914.

And I think that it was the next day that the grand jury began its investigation of gambling in baseball.

VI

We kept playing good baseball and being right on the heels of Cleveland and the Yankees, who were first and second, in that order. I was kept in the lineup and I hit at a .300 pace. I was hitting big league pitching as well as I had hit in the Pacific Coast League. I even got a hit off Walter Johnson, but I owed that to Eddie Collins. He said to wait for the curve. I got it the first time I faced him and hit one on the ground between first and second. The next time I waited for the curve I didn't see the third strike. The big climax of those first days of September 1920 came with the Yankee series in the middle of the month. We made a clean sweep of the series and advanced to second place, and Babe Ruth didn't hit anything out of the ballpark except in batting practice.

I remember especially the third game, which we took 10-5 before a crowd that just about filled every seat in the ballpark. Babe Ruth came into his own that season as a home run slugger. He hit fifty-four home runs. The previous record was twenty-nine, made by him in 1919, and he packed them into the ballparks all over the American League. Crowds waited for him and almost mobbed him with adulation after the ball games, and he took the place even of Ty Cobb as the outstanding ballplayer of the time.

It's always said that the Babe saved baseball after the scandal, and there's no doubt that that's true, but this might not have happened if the Babe had not already captured the imagination of the fans before the scandal was busted wide open. The sportswriters were calling him "the Bambino," "the Bambino of Swat," and "the Sultan of Swat" before the eight "Black Sox" were in the headlines on the front pages of the newspapers, and the fans were swarming into the American League ballparks all that season to see the Babe hit one. The Babe had come into his own by September 1920.

So when the Yankees came to play their last series of the season with us, there were two attractions, the pennant race and the Babe. We won the first two games with Lefty Williams and Red Faber pitching, and Red set the Babe down nice. So did Lefty Williams, but I think here of Red because he was a mean kind of pitcher who didn't care who he was facing. He just stood in there and pitched his heart out, asking no quarter and giving none.

I never knew a pitcher who hated to give an intentional base on balls as much as Red. Some years after 1920, when Eddie Collins was our manager, Red beat Pennock 1-0 in Yankee Stadium. In the ninth inning, the Babe came up with two out and either one or two men on base. Eddie told Red to give the Babe intentional base on balls. Red got sore as hell but had to do it because he was ordered to. He struck out Pipp who was a pretty fair hitter.

Eddie Cicotte was pitching the last game of that Yankee series, and the Babe had never hit a home run off him so that this was a third attraction for the fans, the duel between Cicotte and Ruth.

But things had been happening outside the ballpark while we were still making our big comeback after that fiasco of a series in Boston. The grand jury investigation was under way, and players had testified for Herzog and he seemed in the clear. He was a good fighting ballplayer. I never played against him but the ballplayers all talked of him in that vein. The Old Roman and a few others had testified, and there had been mention of the World Series in connection with all this. The 1919 World Series should be gone into. That was what was being printed in the news stories and some of these were on the front page, too. It was getting real serious, too serious for us to speak much about it in the clubhouse and on the baseball field. Ban Johnson, president of our league, was going to testify, too, but he had been quoted as saying that he was making an investigation of his own before he came to Chicago to go before the grand jury.

A few things were said among us. I think it was Risberg who said, "There's not a goddamn thing to find out."

And a couple of times I remember Eddie Cicotte talking about his past in baseball.

"I weighed about 121 pounds when I came up from Augusta. I brought a pretty fair young ballplayer with me. His name was Tyrus Raymond Cobb. I was wilder than a March hare then. Talk about these wild southpaws. They weren't near me. I practiced on my control for hours. Hours and hours and hours. I just threw that ball. I threw and I threw. I'd try to hit the catcher's glove in the center of the plate. I aimed for dead center. I learned how to pitch. I wasn't born with it like Johnson. Detroit shipped me, but after I went to Boston three years later, I was different. I weighed a little more and I was getting my control."

He'd talk like that.

"Next year I'll be fifteen years in this league. Hell, the horse cars were going out when I was coming in. In 1912 when I was on a good ball club, they were loaded with pitchers. That was Joe Wood's big year. They didn't need much else with him."

"Jesus, I told him to quit playing like Walter Johnson. I was batting right handed and not hitting my weight that year. It was my first year up," Buck said.

"Yes, I've put in many good years in this game," Cicotte said, kind of wistful. And then, I caught him looking around the club with something in his eyes, sadness.

And Joe Jackson talked about a business he had back home and farming. "Ah wanted to go home. Ah told Mr. Mack," Joe said, speaking of his first days when he was too lonesome to stay with Connie Mack's Athletics.

"I don't want to be no goof like I was when I came here," Buck said. "I didn't know nothin'. I was a goof, that's all. You come up and you don't know nothin'."

"They don't ask you to trade hits on the sandlots, do they, Buck?" Risberg said.

And one day Lefty Williams picked up a dirty ball in front of the clubhouse and he kept turning it in his hand, looking at it, examining it. He said, "Look at that dirty little old ball. It sure can cause a man a wagonload of trouble."

Eddie Collins told some newspaperman, "It looks like an effort to distract us in the thick of a pennant fight."

But Eddie and Ray and the other players who weren't suspected were getting worried too about something. They could be subpoenaed and forced to testify under oath. It dawned on me that I'd be subpoenaed too. And I thought that, hell, I wouldn't know what to say, I wouldn't know what in the hell to say.

"Who the hell wants to read a newspaper? Think of what you're going to do out there on that ball field," the Little Skipper said.

He was trying to keep morale high for the pennant drive, because the Indians were on fire and winning game for game with us to hold their lead. Joe Sewell joined them and took poor Ray Chapman's place, and they got Duster Mails from the Pacific Coast League. He was a house on fire in September 1920 but never any good after that.

During the Yankee series, the newspapers had printed stories pointing the finger of suspicion at the White Sox. One story spoke of five players. People wondered who the players were before the suspected players had been named, and this placed a load on all of us. Fans wondered who the players were. Nobody knew what was being said or what was going to be said behind the closed doors of the grand jury room. An innocent player could be accused and ruined. That fate threatened Buck Herzog.

"I'm worried, Ma," Ray said to Ma Kelly.

"Ray, you have no reason for being worried. It wasn't you and everyone knows it wasn't you," she said.

Suspicion and rumor can do terrible things and a man can be ruined for life. He can be accused and how can he prove he's innocent? How can he prove he didn't slough a ball game and that an error he made was honest? The fans did stand by our ball club. That's for sure. But you couldn't know, and suddenly you come to realize how important the fans are. No fans, no baseball. You walk out on the field and ten, twenty, thirty thousand of them are watching you, and if you make an error, suppose they all shout, "Crook! Crook! You dirty crook!"

I sometimes told myself, "I didn't do it." I didn't like to be seen by my friends for fear they'd ask me questions or be suspicious of me.

"Mick, it says in the paper that five White Sox ballplayers were reached by gamblers last fall," Mr. Collins said.

My first reaction was to say to myself that I wasn't one of them and that I couldn't be because I didn't even play a third of an inning of any Series game.

"Yes, I saw it."

He looked at me kind of hurt and puzzled.

"I didn't think anything like that could be true."

"Nobody knows, Jack."

"Is there anything to it, Mick?"

I felt almost like a man.

"That's the whole question—it's hard to prove."

"Did you suspect it, Mick?"

"I was afraid to say anything because I didn't know what to say. I was afraid to say anything even to you, even to Mary."

"But then you knew something?"

"Just rumors, just the rumors that everybody knew."

"When did you have any suspicions?"

"Well, that first game didn't look right. Things didn't look right during the Series."

"And you really think that there's fire behind this smoke, Mick?"

"I'm afraid there is, Jack," I blurted out. I found great relief in saying this, a relief like I still get after I go to confession.

"You can't be named in this in any way, can you?"

"Oh no, I didn't even play. No, I had nothing to do with it."

"You had nothing to do with it? There was something?"

"There might have been. It seems there is. There's a lot of suspicion." I somehow remembered Bill Burns. He hadn't been named then, but his name came to my mind, and I recalled also that he had been in Cincinnati at the Hotel Sinton.

"Have the players talked about it?"

"In a way, they have. They stick pretty much together."

"Who does?"

"The players, the ones we suspect."

"You really suspect some of the players, Mick?"

"Yes."

"Who are they?"

I named the eight players, and it was like telling him that somebody dear to him had dropped dead in the street. He was stunned.

"Jesus Christ, I can't believe it."

"There's no proof of course."

"Do they act guilty?"

"No, not that I can notice."

"What do the rest of the players think?"

"I think every one of them thinks that there was something wrong. Players on other teams ride us about it. They give us a rough time."

"They can't say anything against you, Mick?"

"Oh, no, Mr. Collins—Jack."

"The Little Skipper must know it."

"I think he does. He hasn't been the same since the first game of the Series."

"God, this will ruin baseball."

That made me feel like ice. I hadn't really thought that baseball could be ruined by the "fix." I hadn't thought really what would happen. And I had really lived with this knowledge for almost a year, so that I was accustomed to it, more so than I realized. I say that I lived with this knowledge even though I was not sure or convinced that it was true. I knew without knowing I knew. I know a lot about baseball the same way. When I was put in the lineup in 1920, after Nemo Leibold sprained his ankle, I knew how to position myself for many of the batters and had an idea about many of the pitchers. I had gotten this and stored it away as if it was forgotten while I was warming the bench. That isn't exactly the same, but it gives some idea of what I mean. I was like a man pretending he isn't sick when he is, or like a washed-up ballplayer who thinks or tries to think that he isn't washed up.

And Jack Collins's reaction as well as the newspaper stories made me realize how serious this affair was. It isn't that I didn't think it serious beforehand. I did. But I didn't realize how serious it was, and what it would mean and what would happen. I had read about scandals but had never known anyone in a scandal, anyone in trouble so that he got his name in the paper and the whole city or even the whole country was talking about him. I never knew anyone who was afraid to walk along the street for fear of being seen and asked questions, but I was beginning to become afraid myself in this respect.

And I never really thought that it could wreck and ruin baseball. So much seemed the same before and after those World Series games. Those eight players didn't seem to be any different. They didn't show any guilt the way you would expect them or the way they would in a movie or a story. They didn't think they would be barred from baseball for life. At least, I don't think they did. They didn't think they could or would be caught.

Well, there it was. And this was all only beginning during the series with the New York Yankees. All of us had something on our mind and our conscience. All of us were carrying some weight of guilty knowledge. And I don't think that any of us knew just what we thought about it or what we thought ought to be done. Jim Cruisenberry told me that in the winter after the 1919 Series, the Little Skipper went to the Old Roman and said he could trade those players, and that the Old Roman said no, that they would handle the problem themselves. The Little Skipper didn't seem to think of just kicking them out of the game.

Of course you knew that was what would happen to any player caught throwing a game. But you knew this and thought about it theoretically. You thought it was wrong, and yet you didn't know if you should condemn those players. It wasn't for you to do anything about it and you didn't know what the powers that be did think about it. And you had to live with them and play with them. This all put the load on you, and the load was starting to become a heavy one in September 1920.

And at the same time, you were fighting to win the pennant. It would seem funny that any of us could have played ball like we did under all of these circumstances, but we did. It isn't funny, either. Baseball was our job. And we all get used to our job, to working at it even when we have a lot on our mind. When you get out on that ball field, it usually takes a load off your mind. At least that's the way it seems to me.

And there was the pennant. When we started cleaning up the Yankees with Babe Ruth and their Murderers Row, I told myself, "The pennant is ours."

And winning the pennant and then the World Series—that would somehow take care of the 1919 business once and for all.

VII

Like I said, we took the first two games from the Yankees, and Cicotte was the pitcher for the final game of that series. Fans were streaming into the park and crowding the sidewalk and street outside when I reported for the game. It was all as exciting as a World Series. Babe Ruth and the pennant race was uppermost in people's minds, not the grand jury investigation. It was a wonderful day, too, warm, sunny with one of those big blue skies and white clouds.

I saw the crowd as I walked from Wentworth Avenue. Men in short sleeves, men with their kids, plenty of kids, groups of young fellows, many young fellows around my own age, all moving to the ballpark, some of them running, going double-quick, walking fast. I heard snatches of conversation, mentions of Ruth, and I heard one man talking about Mickey Donovan. It was a real thrill. Hell, I told myself, baseball's wonderful and it's great, just great to be a ballplayer.

"Sure is a crowd today, Mickey," the Irishman said.

"It's going to be an overflow crowd."

"It's that big fellow. He just got here."

"He did?"

"He's just after arriving. The kids outside, have mercy on my soul, I thought they have to be calling out extra police. I never saw the likes of it for any other ballplayer, including Mr. Collins himself."

"It's something, all right," I said.

"He's like an overgrown kid himself, but you'll have to beat him today."

"We will." I went in and a few cops called to me. I was getting very popular around the ballpark. I climbed the steps to the clubhouse telling myself that I was going to have a big day.

"Hello, Mick," the Skipper said as I entered the clubhouse.

"Hello, Skip," I said.

He was sitting by the locker in his shirtsleeves. He didn't seem happy at all despite the way the team was playing.

"I was putting on one of these things before you were born, Mick," the Little Skipper said.

"I only hope I can be putting one on as long as you, Skip."

"Play the game and you will. Baseball's come a long ways in my time. It's given me many a laugh and many a heartache." He started getting undressed to put his suit on.

"You're still wearing the same socks, Donovan?" Eddie Collins asked me.

"Yeah, I got them right there in my locker."

He was superstitious and when we were winning didn't like anything changed. We wore the same dirty socks and uniforms when we won in them.

Cicotte was already in uniform. I watched him shake talcum powder on his pants and make a dusty white cloud of it around him. He did that for his shine ball.

"Put plenty of that on your pants, Eddie," Buck said.

"I got enough of it."

"Put twice as much on as you just done. Put so much on that it gets in his eyes when you pitch to him."

"I'd rather pitch to him than to Mr. Cobb," Cicotte said.

"The only son-of-a-gun I don't want to pitch to isn't in this league anymore," Red said.

"Huh?" someone exclaimed.

"That Barry, I never could get that son-of-a-gun out. And he was only a .250 hitter," Red said.

"All he's got to do is hit to the left," Buck said.

"Let him. He won't hit with power," Eddie said.

This was in reference to the shift for Ruth that Collins invented. It's the same as the Boudreau shift on Ted Williams, only Boudreau wasn't the first man to think it up. To the best of my knowledge, that man was Eddie Collins.

Dick Kerr came in. He sat down beside Lefty Williams but didn't say a word to him.

"There's our midget," Shano said.

"There's more people in this ballpark than you'll ever see in Paris, Texas," he said.

"This is the big leagues, boy," Shano said.

Dick looked at Risberg and then said, "Yeah."

Risberg said something about bush league towns. Ray walked by Cicotte but said nothing. I watched Cicotte and he seemed very relaxed to me. I was nervous inside and thought how these players had all been through the grind of pennant races before. I imagined every one of them was relaxed and envied them their experience. I smoked a cigarette and it made me less nervous. Soon we were on the ball field with the big crowd cheering us, watching, and there was a steady roar in the ballpark.

It was a thrilling, beautiful sight, that big ballpark, the grass with the sun shining on it, that big clear sky overhead, the people in the stands, the packed bleachers, the white shirts and dark suits and an occasional touch of color from a woman's dress, the stands filling up with more color in them because there were more women in the stands, the steady roar of the crowd and the outbursts of louder and thunderous roaring, the shouts of the vendors, the crack of the bat—all of this seemed really wonderful to me. It made me think of what a fine thing baseball is.

That Saturday the crowd was so big that the overflow was let out on the field and fans stood packed and roped off in left and right field. It was the first and only time I played with an overflow crowd on the playing field, and it was the last time that this was done at the White Sox Park. Our infield put on an exhibition in the session of fielding practice, and while I was catching fungo flies in right field, the fans kept calling to me as they did all during the game. But I didn't hear any of them yell anything about the rumors of the scandal. That big crowd was with us, with us pretty solidly, and they supported us with lungs as mighty and as powerful as ever came within my experience.

The Old Roman used to say that Chicago was the best baseball town in the world, and he must have been right. All during that season the crowd came out to see us and cheer us, and on that Saturday it gave a big demonstration. It wanted to see Babe Ruth and wanted to see him hit a home run or two, but it wanted us to win, and we did. I think I said the score was something like 10-5, but it was more like 13-6 or 13-7. The game was one-sided, and the Yankees scored their runs toward the end of the ball game when Eddie Cicotte ease up because of the big margin he had to work on. Miller Huggins sent in Bob Shawkey and we got to him in the first inning.

I was lead-off man. It was quite a thrill for me to take two bats and walk toward home plate, swinging them while the fans roared, thousands of them, shouting my name and giving me an ovation.

"I'm going to pop a ground rule double into the right field crowd," I told myself as I stepped into the batter's box, and I did on the third or fourth pitch. The ball sailed high over the Babe's head, and I knew it was gone for two bases the moment I connected. In a minute I was home standing up on Collins's single, and then Buck and Shoeless Joe Jackson hit doubles. We knocked Shawkey out of the box and scored four runs in that first inning and went ahead 4-0. Cicotte had got the Babe to hit a high fly to me to right field in the first half of the first inning, and that was one time at bat and no home run for the Babe.

I think it was Thormahlen who was in the box in the second inning when I again led off. If it wasn't Thormahlen, then it was Mogridge, a southpaw, and I batted right-handed and hit a high fly that was just out of reach of the left fielder. I think it was Duffy Lewis. Twice up, two innings, two doubles, and I came home on a triple that Buck hit to the flagpole in center field. At the end of the second inning, we were ahead 7-0. The game was one-sided. I got two more hits, a single and another double, and Shano made four doubles. The Babe got a ground-rule double but no home run. It was the last time he faced Cicotte, and that ball game was the last time that I played against the New York Yankees on a ball club that was better than the Yankees.

In those days, a ballplayer didn't get half-mobbed by kids seeking autographs. Some of the fans and quite a lot of kids would stand to watch the players leave the clubhouse and the ballpark, and maybe some of the kids would say something, a hello or a few words about the good game you played, but that was all there was to it. If any of them followed you out of the ballpark, they did it at a respectful distance and didn't pester, let alone molest, you. But that was all there was to it. The change came with Ruth. I don't know what it was originally about the man that so captured the imagination of America, but it was something. He was a great man and a genius. He seemed almost like he was superhuman with the things he could do and the way he could do them. There'll never be another like the Babe. Hell, he didn't have to abide by the rules and standards of ordinary people because he wasn't like them. He was the Babe, Babe Ruth.

But to come back to that Saturday ball game. Mary had seen it and waited for me under the stands, near the steps leading up to the clubhouse. That was a thrill, a big moment, my coming out of the clubhouse with Mary down there waiting for me. I had invested in a couple of good suits of clothes that I'd bought at the Hub down in the Loop, and I was wearing a light-brown covert cloth suit that Mary liked and so did I. I felt good, real good. And of course the crowd recognized me, and some of the fans and the kids called to me about the ball game I had played, and I walked up to Mary, and she was all smiles and all dressed up in a pretty dress, a lavender dress, and we walked off, with Mary taking my arm. You can guess how set up I was without my having to elaborate on it.

As we came to the front exit-entrance gates, there was the Babe in a swirling mob of short-pants kids, his big moon face looking bewildered. He couldn't move with the kids crowding around him, a shoving, yelling mob of them. They were pushing and driving the big fellow, and he rolled and swayed with them. The little mob of them passed us and shoved toward the gate. They kept yelling and shouting. "Babe." "Hi Babe." "Babe Ruth."

A big barrel of mustard had been overturned near the gate, with the mustard oozing over the stone floor. The Babe was almost shoved in that mustard by the mob of kids. Then they and the big fellow passed out of sight on 35th Street outside.

"That's Babe Ruth," I told Mary, thrilled even to see him.

That day, and that ball game, was a high point of my baseball career.

"We'll win the pennant, Mary darling," I said, and I believed that we would.

CHAPTER TEN

I

After that Yankee series, we took two out of three from Philadelphia, and that left us even with Cleveland in the win column but three behind them in games lost. After an off day, we had a three-game series in Cleveland, and if we could take those three games, we could go ahead of the Indians by a game and a half. After Cleveland, there was a three-game series at home in Chicago with Detroit, three days of rest, and then a final series of three games in St. Louis to wind up the season.

All year we'd knocked off Detroit and St. Louis with regularity. We could beat them again with the pennant at stake, and, in addition, Cleveland had to play three more games than we did. The heat would be more on them than on us, and with our four starting pitchers going great guns, we stood a damned good chance of coming home with the bacon. This of course makes it clear what those five games lost to the Red Sox on our eastern trip did to our chances. If we'd won those five games, or four of them, we'd have been the league champions come hell and high water and everything. And what was so strange about this is that from that day to this, who knows if those ball games in Boston were lost honestly or otherwise.

Like I have already said, the newspapers already had begun to print rumors and suspicions about that 1919 Series in the week that we beat the Yankees three straight and knocked them out of second place. Finally on that Saturday morning, I think it was about September 17th or 18th, the newspapers had stories about the grand jury which claimed that the Series had been crooked and that eight White Sox players

were involved. But the players had not been named. The grand jury
didn't hold any session on Saturday, the day of the game that Cicotte
won, and so the Sunday and Monday morning newspapers didn't have
any further information about the investigation. There was news or
rumors alleging that gamblers in St. Louis, Detroit, Pittsburgh, Des
Moines, and Boston had been in on the fix, as well as those from New
York who had arranged the whole seamy business.

The eight suspected ballplayers had not been mentioned. Of course we
knew who these players were. But the clean sweep against the Yankees
gave us false hopes and cushioned the anxieties we felt. It was so near
the end of the season, and the three-way pennant race was so torrid, our
minds were more on the ball games and the fight for the pennant than
on the grand jury. And we expected that nothing would be done until
the season ended. This was more of a hope than it was anything else.

The crowd at the Yankee series, and especially for the final game,
gave us confidence. The fans had turned out in droves, cheering their
heads off and yelling out their lungs, and they'd gone home highly
satisfied with the results of the ball games. That weekend was a lull-
ing one. The Sunday morning newspapers didn't have anything new
about the baseball scandal. And there wouldn't be anything new, any
further development over Sunday and Sunday night.

Maybe something would happen or something would be done to
quash the whole business. After all, it could hurt baseball, and the owners might get the whole thing quashed. With the fans getting worked
up by the hot pennant race, they might be distracted away from the
rumors and alarms of gambling. Anyway, everything was the same as
usual over Sunday, and look how the White Sox had played.

I guess the suspected players must have been talking amongst themselves, and they were more affected and worried than they seemed to
be. With Gandil gone, Risberg seemed to be the main one among them,
and I think that he was already telling them, or at least some of them,
that nothing could be done or proved so long as they didn't talk. The
word of any one of them was as good as the word of any other man and
without evidence nothing could be proved.

On Sunday, when we beat the Athletics with Kerr in the box, nothing out of the way happened or was said by the ballplayers, at least
not that I saw or heard. And none of the Athletics jockeyed or ribbed
us about being crooks.

I woke up that Sunday morning dreading the prospect of facing people even though I should normally have wanted to see and to be seen after my big day at bat with three doubles and a single. I remembered that the newspapers had carried the story charging that professional gamblers had reached eight White Sox players. I was afraid that people would stare at me suspiciously and ask me embarrassing questions. They might even think that I was one of the eight even though I hadn't played in the Series. I most especially didn't want to run into Joe Hines or other fellows I knew. I didn't know what to say to people. I worried needlessly because nobody asked me anything embarrassing, although I did talk to five or six of the parishioners. I went to the ballpark telling myself to think of the ball game and of nothing else.

"All that stuff is horseshit. Last year is dead. It's horseshit. What about this year?" Felsch said in the clubhouse.

I think everybody would have liked to think this. The other players, let alone myself, couldn't do anything. They were all sort of powerless. This thing had been there with the team all season. A shadow had hung over us. It had been like we had a ghost with us. It seemed to have something to do with our being comfortably in first place and coasting to the pennant.

Like I said, we couldn't be sure but what the same thing wasn't being done to us again in the regular 1920 season as had been in the 1919 Series. Some games we had lost should have been won. And then, when we had blown those games in Boston and had seemed to have blown away the pennant, the ball team came to life. It was just at that moment that I stepped into the lineup, too.

We all were playing our hearts out, fighting every minute, fighting in every play. We were coming from behind after we could have been counted out, and we were playing baseball the way it's supposed to be played, the way the fans want to see it played. On the ball field, all thought and worry about what was going to happen just faded away. The possibility that anything could happen, a big scandal disrupting us, and the pennant fight and all of the baseball world—why, that seemed out of the question. But after the game, riding home, at home, or when I was with Mary, waking up in the morning, reading the newspaper in the morning, then I would have worried thoughts and fears.

And I suddenly realized that if the suspected players had been guilty, they had done something to me. If any of them had had anything to do with throwing games during the season that was still on, they had done something to me. I was beginning to get mad, to get sore at them. And it occurred to me that since there were all of these rumors and so many people seemed to believe that the Series had been crooked, then the Old Roman and the Little Skipper must know a lot and they must have known a lot all along. And of course it came out that they had known a lot but said they didn't have the evidence really to prove it. And so we came up to that weekend like I have described it.

Then came Monday, and we had morning practice.

"Now, we got to win. We can't afford to lose. We don't know what the hell can happen if we don't keep winnin' ball games," the Little Skipper said.

"A ball club can only try to win the goddamn games," Risberg said in a fighting, a rather snarling manner.

"Yes, try, try like hell."

"Who the hell ain't trying?"

"I didn't accuse no man, but I'm sayin' we can't afford to lose a ball game."

"The whole goddamned business and the goddamned cheap rumors was engineered to embarrass us when we're fighting for the pennant. If the moguls weren't out to cut each other's throats, there wouldn't be all this horseshit," Risberg said.

"Talkin' doesn't win ball games. Let's get the hell out on the field for some practice."

But we lost the ball game that afternoon. And in the afternoon papers, the district attorney was quoted as saying that the World Series of 1919 had been crooked, that gamblers had conspired with eight White Sox ballplayers, and the eight of them were named: Chick Gandil, Joe Jackson, Happy Felsch, Buck Weaver, Swede Risberg, Fred McMullen, Eddie Cicotte, and Lefty Williams. These were the players everybody suspected. No one was sure that all of them had been involved in any double-dealing, but it was among these, at least, that the double-dealers were to be found.

It was awful, coming home after losing the ball game and carrying the newspaper with that story in headlines and all over the newspaper, spread out there on the front page. Yes, it was awful. Something would now be done, and with this scandal hanging over our heads, how could we go out on the ball field and win games? And the next day we were leaving for Cleveland for a three-game series that would decide the pennant. We had to take all three games or else we'd only have a slim chance of ending up in first place and meeting Brooklyn in the World Series.

"Newspaper talk proves nothin'," Risberg said in the clubhouse after the game.

By then it was clear that something had to come out, and that weekend feeling was only a deception, a kind of wishing away of the exploding bombshell. The situation was strange, all right. Hell, everybody on the club really knew, and nobody would come out and say point-blank to the suspected players that it was so. And the suspected players naturally wouldn't start admitting anything. They weren't saying much anyway to the rest of us, except Buck. He said a number of times, "What can they say about me, when I hit .330 and fielded 1.000?"

But with the grand jury already digging, they would be certain to go in deep and to keep digging, and it began to seem that the ballplayers would all have to testify. That didn't promise to be pleasant in any sense of the word at all, not at all, and the very idea of testifying under oath was frightening. The newspapers had said that White Sox players would be subpoenaed, but not until the end of the season, when this wouldn't interfere with the club's fight to win the pennant. But what would you say when the grand jury put you on the witness stand? What would you say about the other players on the ball club? You could easily be tripped by the men from the DA's office because they were lawyers who had learned their business of tripping people up. I spent an awful time that night and the next day until I boarded the train for Cleveland. I went over to Mary's and spoke with her and Jack.

"This can't touch you in any way, Mick?"

"I don't see how it can, Jack."

"Anything can happen now when the thing's gone this far."

"Do you think so?"

"Hell, how could I think anything else? And when the names come out, and that fellow from the district attorney's office wouldn't be making the kind of statements he is if they didn't have the goods on those ballplayers."

"Yes, I guess that's what I think."

"And if they have the goods on them, I say run them out of baseball," Jack said, bitterly.

I didn't feel that bitter myself, or rather my own bitterness hadn't come out as yet. "Of course, they won't admit it."

"Who won't?"

"The players."

"What do they say?" Jack asked me with quite a bit of interest.

"They don't say much about it, actually. It's rumor, they say, and it ain't true."

"But isn't it true?"

"Yes, I guess it is, Jack."

"But why hasn't anybody said so?"

"Well, I guess there wasn't the proof."

"Looks to me like they're getting the proof now."

"It seems like something was wrong. But you couldn't put your finger on anything and say this proves it. And it was hard to believe. I guess it was especially hard to believe because you didn't want to believe it or to believe or think that it could even happen."

"My God, didn't any of the other players say anything?"

"They said things, but it was all suspicion."

"It isn't anymore. Hell, this is a big thing now. It's on the front pages of the newspapers all over the country. I can't understand how them players would have the courage to walk out on a ball field, but that's what they've been doing."

It was still sinking in deeper on me. I knew that the investigation was news all over the country but I hadn't thought much about that or what it meant. I thought of men in homes in every part of America talking about the investigation as Jack Collins and I were arguing, condemning the players, some maybe defending them, while many others were wondering if it was all true or not and hoping that it wasn't. Faith and trust in men dies hard. And thinking of this while I was talking with Jack, I began really to be afraid for what might happen. I didn't know for sure or have a really clear idea of what would exactly happen of course, but I could see that it was going to be something pretty awful and tragic.

"If you win the pennant and go into the World Series, with your team playing these eight players, what are people going to think?"

"I don't know. I think we're going to win the pennant. We can beat Cleveland. We got a better ball club than they got."

"You think you're going to win even after all of these stories have been printed in the newspapers?"

"Yes, we can win. Somehow, when you get out there on the field in a ball game, Jack, you forget everything else."

"I don't know how they can forget what they did."

"I don't know what they really think to themselves, but they don't act like they felt guilty. Of course they stick pretty much together and don't have too much to do with the rest of us off the ball field."

"Mickey, what are you going to say when you're called before the grand jury?"

I must have looked blind and dumb. I didn't know what to say to Jack, and the very question made me nervous. I knew I didn't want to be subpoenaed, and I was afraid that I'd be so nervous and so bad in answering the questions asked me that I'd make those jurors and the district attorney suspicious of me even though I was innocent.

"You'll have to tell everything you know, Mick."

"I guess so, but the thing is, I don't know much. I don't know nothin', anything about it."

He found it hard to believe me. I could see that he did by the expression on his face.

"I didn't see or hear any players with gamblers, or receiving any money, and you ask me about how they played in those games, I don't know what to say. Any player can have an off day or a couple of off days. Some of the players sometimes seemed to be playing a bit out of position, like Happy Felsch, and he played way below form. And in that first game, Cicotte didn't have nothin' on the ball. But they can say that about any player when he has an off day."

"Didn't you hear anything said?"

"Oh, well, the Little Skipper said they weren't trying. He said that many times."

"He did? What did he mean?"

"I guess he meant they weren't trying to win. And Ray Schalk was sore during the Series. But I don't know what to say."

"Maybe some of them will confess if they're guilty."

"Maybe. I ain't seen any signs of that from any of them, the eight players I mean, wanting to admit it."

"Now they got to say something. They've been named as crooks in the newspapers before the whole of America."

And of course they had. That's what happened and what the newspaper stories meant.

"I don't know how they could face themselves in a mirror if they are guilty," Jack said.

There were all kinds of popular reactions, and I guess there was plenty of excitement over the investigation. It was a real shock to fans, but it was a shock to me and to other baseball players. It was now outside of the hands of baseball. It was all in the hands of the law, and that made it so much worse.

I was thinking of this when I went to the La Salle Street Station to take the train for Cleveland on Wednesday. We left around one o'clock. The station was crowded but there wasn't a big crowd to give us a sendoff. The ballplayers got lost in the regular station crowd. I'd been glum and felt uncertain all morning, nervous, wanting the time to pass and wondering what was happening. A couple of times I thought I heard kids and men in the street on Prairie Avenue shouting about an "extra" paper, but it was only my imagination. But that will give an idea of my own state. Something could have already happened, a confession or testimony that proved beyond all doubt that the players were guilty, and I didn't know if something like that had happened. I didn't know what was going on of course in that jury room or what added information the newspapers had gotten hold of, and I just felt something was impending.

Already, too, the investigation was drawing my mind a little bit away from the pennant race. I didn't think so much on that Wednesday morning of the pennant race, not as much as I did of the investigation. I kept thinking, too, that a net was closing in on the players and I wasn't sure what it all was going to mean to myself, to the other players on the team, for the team or even for baseball itself.

And so I walked into the station carrying my grip. I thought how proud and confident I'd be feeling that very moment, bound for Cleveland to play in the series that would settle the pennant race. Yes, how proud and cocky and confident I would have been feeling except for the investigation. I hoped I wouldn't be recognized, at least not by many people. People recognizing me might think I was involved, or in some way feel hostile to me, and it would have made me jittery just to be stared at too much. I even felt like I might not find the team or at least all of it, and that some of the players might be at a police station arrested instead of getting ready to board a train.

There was a crowd around some of the players and I was surprised. Nothing had happened as yet. Maybe nothing would happen. There was Buck Weaver smiling and talking to a fellow who must have been a friend. And Joe Jackson stood with his hands on his hips, looking like he didn't have a worry in the world. Maybe my fears were exaggerated.

And I saw the Little Skipper. He was about two feet from me and he was talking to a newspaperman. I heard the Little Skipper saying, "It's all hearsay. No, there's nothing to it. That's what the entire thing has been, hearsay. If there was anything behind this thing, it would have come out long before this."

The newspaperman jotted down what the Little Skipper had said and then asked, "What effect has this had on the players, Skip?"

"It's made them fighting mad, so mad that they're determined to prove their innocence by knocking the stuffing out of Cleveland."

"I hope they do, Skip."

"They will. Right now, this ball club of mine is the best in this league, the best in either league."

That reassured me, but only for a minute. I had heard the Little Skipper talk different. I remembered that I'd heard him saying something quite different. It was during the World Series. "I can't believe that the gang that worked for me great all summer would fall down like this. I'm just sick at heart, absolutely sick at heart. I looked at all of them as my boys. I felt like a schoolteacher might for his pupils. I loved my boys because of the way they fought for me all summer and I'd have staked my life that they'd have gone through with me in the World Series. But something has happened to that gang of mine. They're not playing baseball."

I knew the Little Skipper had been talking for the newspapers and the public, but it still didn't make me any too confident. Soon we were on the train for Cleveland. The ballplayers were quiet, not at all talkative. They didn't want to say anything, especially to the baseball writers with us. They weren't like the baseball writers today and they didn't print quotes, except only occasionally, and they didn't try to keep writing about rhubarbs or trying to get a player in an unpopular light and quote him to the player's disadvantage before the public. But even though we kind of trusted the writers, we didn't want to talk much, and the suspected players were pretty quiet.

Buck did say on the train, "Goddamn it, a man who hits .330 in a series and fields a 1.000 has got to be a trouble to the other side. What the hell do they mean saying that about me? It's crazy, and they can subpoena me and I'll tell them it's crazy."

And Cicotte did say, "In that first game, they swung at everything I pitched and hit it. But the ball didn't go at somebody. It went between them."

The ballplayers were mad, especially the suspected ones, and I could feel myself getting mad, too. Why in hell did all of this have to be dragged into public and just at the boiling point of the pennant struggle? This sort of thing could hurt us, wreck our pennant chances. Why did they do this to us just when that pennant battle seemed to be coming to its knockout climax? It wasn't right and we had to show them, but show them on the ball field. Speaker never did anything to me except play ball against me, but I found myself starting to hate his guts.

I had other thoughts, too. I looked at Joe Jackson snoring in a Pullman car seat, his mouth open, his lean face looking kind of stupid in sleep, and I told myself that Joe could go to jail as a result of the investigation and so could the other players named and suspected. That didn't seem right, or even possible. Joe Jackson, Shoeless Joe Jackson, we often called him the General. The General was one of the greatest hitters in baseball and at that time and for my money I'd have taken him over Babe Ruth. He couldn't go to jail. No, that was crazy, all right, crazier than almost anything I'd ever heard of.

By the time we hit Cleveland, we were sore, all right, or we had at least kidded or rationalized ourselves into being sore and determined to go out to the ballpark and scalp Spoke and his players.

And by then, things were worse. The Chicago grand jury story was bigger than life in the Cleveland papers, and the same eight players were named. The words "Crooked World Series," it hurt to read them in the Cleveland newspapers, reading that eight White Sox players had been named. And then, the president of the American League, Ban Johnson, had made charges in the newspapers, which made things worse. He had said that in the season then current, some members of the White Sox had been forced to lose games because they were in the power of certain gamblers. This made everything worse, and it got us mad.

Ban Johnson and the Old Roman had been good friends and were two of the men who had started the league. Then, they had become bitter enemies, hating each other, and their feud had begun over a joke one had played on the other while hunting. Ban Johnson had played a joke on the Old Roman, or the Old Roman had played one on him, or one or the other of them had said something and they had never spoken to each other again. When Ban Johnson heard that the Old Roman was afraid his team was selling him down the river in the 1919 Series, he is supposed to have said, "It's the whelping of a whipped cur."

I didn't know what it was all about then, and I still don't know what it was all about. But they had no use for each other and that fact was no secret at the time. And so with the ice breaking under us as a ball team when we were trying to win a pennant, Ban Johnson came out with his statement, charging that games had been thrown in the regular 1920 season which was then still in progress, as I have indicated. Well, it was a cause for suspicion on the ball club, and all of us, or most of us anyway, had been worried about just that danger.

I have mentioned the Boston series, and there were other games, some in St. Louis, when Cicotte and Williams pitched. Ray Schalk had complained that things didn't look right, and the Little Skipper had kept saying that some of them weren't trying, and at times you didn't know where you were. Sitting on the bench in all of this and dying to play and thinking that maybe some of those who were playing weren't doing their best when all you wanted to get was a chance to do your best—that was disheartening.

It seemed that maybe Ban Johnson had the goods and could prove it, and I guess that most players thought he could. But saying it when he did was like a body blow, and it seemed that we were going to be pawns in this feud between the Old Roman and Ban Johnson. It wasn't a cheerful thing to read when we got to Cleveland and saw the news of what he said along with the headlines, and the pictures of seven of our players and Gandil.

If anything like that should happen today, you can imagine what it would be like with the reporters and television and radio people on everybody's neck, and the gossip columnists printing juicy rumors, and it wasn't as bad as that but it was rotten enough. The baseball writers in those days stuck pretty much to baseball and hardly anything of the investigation was printed on the sports pages, at least at first. It was handled as news, as general news, and printed along with other general news.

The writers weren't breathing down our necks to find things out, questioning all of us to get copy, trying to get one of us to say something for print, attacking the other players, and making accusations. There was nothing like that. Maybe it was because the newspapers hadn't wanted to print much about the scandal. In 1919, when the Series was going on, they hadn't wanted to, and afterwards writers said that it was their editors and owners who quashed the story.

I don't know about this and I don't care much. I am merely trying to describe. And all I want to make clear here is that when we got to Cleveland we didn't have to run away from the press and hide on them. They didn't make our life more miserable. A couple of the writers with us got instructions by telephone or mail to get statements from the Little Skipper and they did that.

"I have already said that these stories are all hearsay and I say it again," the Little Skipper said to the reporters. "If Johnson has got any concrete evidence, it's up to him to give us the cold turkey. They have none. If they had anything, it would have been told long before now, and I am sure Johnson would have given out anything he had long before this if he had the goods on any Chicago player or any player on another team."

And Eddie Collins said, "It sounds to me like a bad statement that Johnson made, if he hasn't the proof with which to back it up. I'm certain I know nothing about it, and I'm sorry to see Herzog's name mentioned 'cause I've always thought him a great ballplayer."

And Ray told the baseball writers, "I hope the news and stories continue to have the same effect on the players that it has, then they'll win the pennant. I don't know anything about what's been printed."

They had to say this and not what they thought and were afraid was the truth. How could Eddie and Ray have come out and accused their own teammates in print and in the heat of a pennant battle at that?

"I don't want to get dragged into this. I don't want my name dragged in this scandal," Ray told a couple of writers.

I guess that most of the players felt that way. I had Roy Wilkinson, a second-string pitcher, rooming with me on the road. Roy had been with the ball club in 1919 and had gone in as relief pitcher in the first and last games of the Series. Roy was a quiet young fellow, desperate to be a great pitcher, which he wasn't. He worked hard as hell and tried his damnedest. He had a fair curve and a fastball but it wasn't enough stuff to keep him up in the big leagues. Roy was the kind of pitcher who had a better chance as a second-string pitcher with a club like our 1919 and 1920 teams than he did as a starting pitcher on the club we had the next year, that is in 1921. He just didn't have enough stuff and baseball intelligence. But he used to sing the blues to me a lot because he didn't get enough opportunity to work.

"Hell, man, I could have beat that Boston club," he complained after the Boston series. "And they'd have known that they had in that there box a man who was trying."

"What do you mean, Roy?" I asked.

This was on the train when we were returning to Chicago after our disaster in Boston.

"I ain't saying everything I know, but come on, Mickey, you know what I mean." I'm sorry to say that I did. "If the Skipper would let me pitch against St. Louis, them Browns eat out of my hands. Last season, I struck Sisler out. I struck him out on a low curve that broke inside."

"He caught a low curve of Faber's and hit a triple."

"He's not a curveball pitcher. He throws the spitter, but me, I'm a curveball artist. And when I throw Sisler a low curve, breaking my ball in low, he won't look like no rival to Ty Cobb, Tris Speaker, and Mr. Jackson on our ball club."

Roy believed that he should have been used as a starter in the 1919 Series, thought that he might have won that last game. The Reds hit him hard when he did go in, but he forgot that. He had hinted to me right along that he was fully aware of what must have been going on during the 1919 Series, and he used to say, "It was a crying shame, Donovan, a goddamn crying shame that we lose the Series."

But after the grand jury investigation began, Roy started to worry, "Hell, man, the country's full of crooks, and nobody does anything agin' 'em. Why are they singling out baseball players?"

"I guess they think there's something wrong, Roy," I answered.

That was early in September, right after Labor Day. And I was half hoping then that the grand jury investigation would do some good. I thought particularly that if some of those Boston games were lost because all of our players weren't trying their best, then it was obvious something had to be done. Like I said, I was pretty sure the Little Skipper and the Old Roman knew the score, and it later turned out that they knew a lot and suspected more. And like I said, the Little Skipper heard the story pretty straight in New York just before we went to Boston to play our last games of the season there.

And the Little Skipper and the Old Roman didn't seem to be able to do anything, so maybe the grand jury investigation would get something done. It was already a big private stink. And so I was kind of glad about the investigation, even though it sometimes worried me. I must add that I hadn't visualized or imagined what it would all be like. I was really still a kid and pretty naive.

Roy didn't like the investigation from the very beginning. "Them men will take the bread out of a ballplayer's mouth," he said.

"I don't know much about the damned thing, Roy, but if they had crookedness over there in the other league, something had better be done about it. Crookedness and the gamblers can wreck baseball."

"There's other ways of doing it besides politics. Them politics in these big cities, I tell you, they'll even steal or graft the hole in a gray-haired widow's last doughnut."

I had begun to have a little of this same feeling. It wasn't a question of my thinking that the politicians were all crooks, and after all I had been helped by being given a political job the previous winter, but it was the fact that outsiders were sticking their noses into baseball. I was in my third season in baseball and by the time that the scandal started breaking, I was playing regular and batting over .300. I had begun to feel myself as a part of baseball, and the grand jury and the DA, lawyers, and some of the newspaper people were outsiders and they were coming in and investigating, like strangers coming into a man's home and looking into all of the closets. I had begun to develop some of that feeling.

"Mickey, I don't want no subpoena," Roy told me in our room when we got to Cleveland.

"Maybe you won't get one," I said, because I was hoping that I wouldn't be served also.

"Oh no, they ain't gonna miss one of us, not one of us that was on the ball club last year. Before them bastards is through, they're gonna try to make us tell every time every ballplayer on this club farted during the World Series last October."

"They can't make you say what you don't know, Roy," I said.

"But they can twist what you do know. They can twist it any way they want, and if you don't answer their questions, they can send you to jail and say you are a liar. Ain't that what they call perjury?"

"But we weren't so important. It's Ray and Eddie Collins, Shano, the veterans they'll want more than us."

"I don't know, I don't know. All I know is they might make us go down to that jury room and sweat and talk. I don't want to be no stool pigeon."

"Maybe it's all going to blow over."

"No, not now, not with all that's been in the newspapers, not with all that publicity."

I didn't have anything to say. It was one thing to think about this scandal as it affected others, the players who were guilty, and it was another thing entirely to think about it when it affected me, and I would have to make up my mind as to what I would have to say and do.

"Suppose we say the wrong thing?" Roy asked me.

"If we tell them what we know or what we don't know, that can't be the wrong thing, can it, Roy?"

"It sure can. We're just young ballplayers, bushers, we don't know all of the ins and outs of this here situation, or how them moguls feel."

"By the time they would get to us, hell, this thing will be investigated and everybody will have an idea of what it's all about."

"I don't want to go and sweat in that room with no grand jury," Roy said.

And neither did I. I was getting afraid of this aspect of the situation.

We beat Cleveland in our first game with Red pitching and throwing a mean ball. The team was mad, fighting mad. That much of what the newspapers printed was true all right. There was a big crowd out at the ballpark and naturally they were a hometown crowd, rooting for Cleveland. They were pennant hungry and they cheered and roared for the Indians but were silent about us. They weren't completely silent. When Joe Jackson went to bat he got booed, a pretty mean Bronx cheer. I never heard him get booed like he did in Cleveland that day.

"They've done gone mad on me because I used to play here and was sold," Joe said on the bench.

"Who cares about 'em. Let 'em rave," Risberg said.

We took some ribbing from the Cleveland players and fans from the bleachers yelled at us from the outfield. "Hey Jackson, won't you look handsome in a striped suit," one fan yelled from the left field bleachers.

It wasn't pleasant at all, but victory was sweet, and if we hadn't won, then it would have been thought that we hadn't tried, and the Cleveland fans might have felt that the victory of their ball club was tainted, just as was that of the Cincinnati Reds the year before. Already, some had begun to demand that if the White Sox won the pennant, the World Series should be called off because there were crooks on the ball club, and they might sell out and throw another World Series.

It was producing an awful tension, and you had to hide it and not let it get you, either. I never played ball under such a strain. The strain, of course, wasn't so great in the actual games, that is, when I was playing, because then, and like I said, you forgot and concentrated only on the ball game. But you felt it before and afterward, at night, when you went to your room, in the dark when you turned out the lights and lay in bed falling asleep, and in the morning when you woke up, in and around the hotel, and when you'd look at other players on the team. Then it would come to mind. And it was hard at Cleveland because we were away from home and living twenty-four hours a day in a baseball atmosphere. And one of the worst things about it was that you had no power to do anything about it. None of the players had. The only power the seven of them had was to confess and say what they knew. It was too late for them to save themselves.

Well, we won two out of three in Cleveland. The rookie Duster Mails beat us. We couldn't touch his speed, and he struck out five, six, seven of us, something like that, while he was pitching shutout ball. I struck out twice and didn't do so well in the Cleveland series. I only hit two singles and made an error on a throw. And that didn't make me feel any too good because our chances for winning the pennant were so much less, and the net was tightening around those seven players.

All week there had been more headlines pointing the finger at them, but there still had been no conclusive proof revealed. And they were sitting tight and refusing to talk or admit anything, and trying to act as if everything was normal and as usual. When they were out on the field, they had thousands of fans looking at them, watching every play they made, cheering for Cleveland to win, wanting them to play badly, and suspecting them, doubting that they were doing their best.

Morning and night, the newspapers told of witnesses, reported that more of the story of the Series had been spread out and unfolded before the grand jury They reported new rumors of involvement or alleged involvements with gamblers in other cities all of the way from Des Moines to Boston. There would be indictments. That was predicted. More witnesses would be called. This all was only a beginning, and the lid had scarcely been lifted. This was the sense of what the newspapers said.

It made you afraid as hell, and you began to think that many more were involved besides the players on our club who had already been named and Gandil who had quit at the end of last year. It almost seemed that before this whole ugly business was ended, there would hardly be anyone in baseball who wouldn't be dragged into it. The seven players were hardly talking to us and they stuck pretty much together and ate together. Buck was friendly and talked with the rest of us as if nothing had happened or was happening, but he stuck with them also.

Of course we knew for sure. We were certain and it seemed that we had been certain for a long time, even for the whole time since the Series when they had made their great mistake and had gone ahead and done the thing. And we knew that the number was up for them. Too many things had been said and printed, and too many people were talking about the scandal. Something was going to happen. It had to happen. It had to happen and it would, some kind of big revelation, something big and dramatic. It was hard to see how they could save themselves and not be thrown out of baseball, even if they didn't go to jail. The possibility or prospect that they could go to jail kind of puzzled me because I didn't see where they had committed a crime. But then, of course I didn't know the law and I was no lawyer, and the papers mentioned indictments, conspiracy of some kind.

In the clubhouse before the second game in Cleveland, Ray said, "It's a crying shame that this ball club ain't at least five or six games ahead in first place."

"If we hadn't had bad breaks," Cicotte said, not to Ray but just talking, to himself, to the wall, to us his teammates, to anybody who heard him.

"Can't cry over spilled milk. We got to go and win every last god-damn game we have left to play," Buck said.

Things like that were said. But it was all coming to an end, and as it was, it was beginning to seem all along, it had been a nightmare.

The judge presiding over the grand jury said that Chicago was the hotbed of baseball gambling. And Ban Johnson, after he appeared before the grand jury, admitted that he knew there had been an attempt at fraud. These were in the papers, in the headlines, and everybody read them in Cleveland. And I remember, too, however, that the Old Roman said that the White Sox would clean up in Cleveland. He mentioned holding up the World Series checks of eight players, but I, and others on the ball club, already knew that.

On September 21st, here were the standings:

Cleveland	90-52
Chicago	90-55
New York	89-57

And compare that with the standings on September 17th:

Cleveland	86-52
New York	88-54
Chicago	86-55

The newspapers also spoke of the spirit of the club. One of them said we "came here today," to Cleveland, that is, "with a fighting spirit seldom seen on a club." And that's true, too. We played hard, hard as hell, with all of this going on. Joe Jackson got booed, like I said, even after he hit a home run. That's the atmosphere in which we won two out of three from Cleveland.

And it was reported that Gandil and Williams might be called before the jury. Then, it was reported that other players would be subpoenaed. Ray was asked by Jim Cruisenberry what he thought of it and what the players ought to do.

"It's up to every player himself," Ray said.

But he had a talk with several of the players and I heard him talking with Red. We sat alone eating breakfast and had the morning newspapers with the big black-type headlines.

"I'll go before that jury, Red, if they're going to drag me into this."

"I guess they'll make everybody go," Red said, eating his eggs and acting very calm.

"The two of them, goddamn it, they didn't pitch right all season. I told you of times when they crossed me up. I've been suspicious of them since early this season."

"Yeah," Red said.

"How does it look to you, Donovan?"

"Hell, I don't know—not right," I said.

"Damn right it's not right."

And when a writer was talking to Lefty Williams, Lefty just said, "I'm in no position to say. Some of the folks on this team maybe are, but I'm in no position to say."

But that gives you an idea, and I don't have to give you too much of a blow-by-blow account.

We left Cleveland one game behind and returned to Chicago. Things were already happening fast, and it couldn't go on much longer. It was beginning to seem clear that the scandal couldn't go on in the same way until the end of the season. It was a lousy ride back to Chicago.

The Chicago papers carried the news that the foreman of the grand jury said that there had been a crooked World Series.

"They know it all, Red—more than we do," Ray said in the railroad station to Red Faber, under his breath. And he told a reporter that he would go before the grand jury, since his name was being dragged in, and he'd tell all he knew. "But the accused players can tell more about it than I can."

"Who are the guilty players, if any, Ray?"

"I don't think it would be right at this time for me to tell names that I'm going to submit to the grand jury. The ballplayers themselves have got to protect the decency and the integrity of baseball."

Yes, it was all up. And I supposed I would be called, too, and asked to testify. But as I have said, I only knew by hearsay and seeing plays on the field that didn't look right.

II

We played Detroit and beat them the same day we came back from Cleveland. Dick Kerr pitched, chalking up his twentieth victory for the season. Going to the White Sox ballpark seemed in advance like going into a den of tigers. You didn't know what was going to happen, and what the fans would do. The Cleveland fans had booed, but the Chicago fans might be worse because they had been the ones who had been let down and betrayed, not the Cleveland fans. I wished I didn't have to go and play ball that day. I knew that once I was on the ball field, I'd feel different, and the fans could yell or jeer and I would still do my best. But it was the thinking, the worrying, the uncertainty of everything.

I was completely unprepared for what the ball club, what baseball, was experiencing, as well as what I was going through. The whole baseball world was unprepared for the scandal. And what could a young player like myself think when the men who ran baseball were themselves pretty much at a loss. The Old Roman and Ban Johnson were feuding like cats and dogs. And the Old Roman and the Little Skipper hadn't been able to do anything even though they were suspicious as early as the very first game of the World Series onward.

I went to the ballpark as usual. Everybody knew the jig was up. It had to be. The newspapers had printed the story that Ray and others were going to testify. The accused players were quarreling among themselves, although this didn't become known until a couple of more days. Risberg was keeping them in line, telling them that so long as none of them talked then nothing could be proven.

Not much was said about the scandal. There wasn't much talking in the clubhouse. Red was pitching, and he and Ray talked about the Detroit batters.

"Hell, I ain't afraid to pitch to him," Red was saying just shortly after I came in.

"I know you aren't. But he isn't afraid to bat against you either, Red."

"I'll break the balls into him and I'll throw him spitters."

"The last time you threw him spitters in different speeds, Red, he made three hits."

"He won't today. I'll be a son of a gun if he will."

They were talking about Ty Cobb, of course.

If we won all of our remaining games, we still had a chance to win because Cleveland could lose a ball game or two.

"We can still win this pennant," the Little Skipper said.

"They have a doubleheader next week with Detroit," Eddie Collins said. "If we're pressing their heels, they might easily blow one of those games. Don't forget that they'll be playing Cobb for two games and closing the season against him."

"I'd like to play against the Giants instead of the Dodgers," Buck Weaver said. "The Giants ain't out yet in the other league. You never can tell what will happen in baseball."

Some of the players looked at Buck but said nothing.

We were getting dressed, then, to go out on the ball field, and we didn't know how the fans were going to greet us, and especially, of course, the accused players. But as I came into the ballpark and the clubhouse, it seemed to me that we were going to find the fans loyal to us and rooting for us. And once at the ballpark, the situation seemed different from what it had in anticipation. And as usual we got some cheers when we appeared on the field. The fans hadn't turned, not even on the accused players. We went through the practice session.

When Ty Cobb came on the field, some of our players tried to flatter him and butter him up as they always did, because they didn't want him mad. He went up to Buck and they talked near the batting cage. Cobb liked Buck and thought him the greatest of all third basemen. Cobb and Weaver talked about hunting, and they laughed.

Then he talked with Joe Jackson, who was a simple soul. I heard Joe saying, "They done went and booed me in Cleveland."

"They didn't like your home run when they want Spoke to win the pennant."

"I'd be helping them win a pennant if they hadn't done gone and sold me."

"With you and Speaker in the lineup, what team would have a chance in the league."

"They done went and sold me here. And I play there, they boo me."

"It didn't strike you out."

"No, I teed off on the ball."

Cobb looked at me. I stood near the cage, holding a bat. "I'm taking an extra base on you today, busher. I'll hit to you and take the base."

"Go ahead and try it."

"If you get fresh with me, I'll do it to you all afternoon."

He was testing me and trying to mix my thoughts up. I saw him about five or six years ago, and he said, "I always tried to split another man's thinking." That's what he was trying to do to me.

We won that ball game. There were about 10,000 fans watching us. The sword was hanging there over us. But it was still hanging on that Saturday night. Nobody's head had been cut off by it.

III

Eddie Cicotte was scheduled to pitch the next day. It was a warm but muggy day. Nothing had changed overnight, and we had a good Sunday crowd, maybe 15,000 or a little more. Like the crowd the day before, it was with us. We were cheered, and the accused players were all cheered.

Just think, five of them were in our lineup, Jackson, Felsch, Weaver, Risberg, and Cicotte. Eddie was breaking under the strain, even though he didn't show it outwardly. He didn't say anything to Ray before the game, but Ray had caught him so many times that he knew what Cicotte would be pitching. Eddie knew the batters as well as Ray, and the two of them had been a White Sox battery for eight years.

Joe Jackson had begun to talk of the end of the season and of going home. Sometimes, he said, he didn't like the cities, and maybe he would soon be retiring from baseball. When he had first come to the big leagues, years before, with Connie Mack, he had gone home twice, and that was the reason why Mr. Mack had not kept him on his baseball team. He liked it at home, sitting around and talking, hunting, and even though he had his business down there, he often thought of farming.

He was a simple guy, easily led, and he was all natural ability as a ballplayer. If you asked him to watch your hitting and tell you if you were off in some way, he'd do it, but he'd have nothing to tell you. He couldn't explain how he did anything and he never seemed to study the game very much. He didn't seem to care what was pitched to him. He stood back in the box, took a step forward and swung. He had the best swing in baseball. He was, like I said, having one of his best years with our club. He hit right to the end. His batting helped us win that Sunday game against Detroit.

Cicotte had Detroit under control from the first pitch until the last. How different a pitcher he was from that first game of the World Series in Cincinnati. And what a different ball club it was during those last September days of the 1920 season. How much better the club played with the black clouds getting thick over its head than it had against Cincinnati when it was recognized as the best team in baseball and was expected to win the World Series almost without making the effort or in any way extending itself.

In that final series against Detroit, the team was all class, and the Sunday game Cicotte won was just easy. None of us had a hard play in the field. We bunched hits, scored our runs, four or five, and Cicotte had Detroit hitting the ball straight up or in the dirt. Hell, it was almost like fielding practice. The fans cheered us, at the beginning of the ball game and at the end of it when we ran in from the field carrying our gloves at the end of the ninth inning. And it was all like a mechanical operation.

Eddie Cicotte was the master of the ball game, an artist on the mound. His funny pitch wobbled in front of the Detroit hitters and they seemed almost to be hitting a feather ball instead of a baseball. He had a book on the hitters in his head and pitched to them making them do what he wanted. He went out inning after inning, going to the mound and coming from it with that funny walk of his, taking short steps, dropping his black glove on the field by the base line in foul territory between third base and home plate, coming on to the bench, taking a blue sweater from the bat boy and getting into it, sitting, crossing his ankles a lot, and staring out at the ball game in progress, sitting mostly silent.

How could anyone have known what was going on in him, how he had sweated and thought and lived with all that guilt he felt because of the Series? But he did. Even as late as that Sunday when something came up, something was said that pointed to the scandal, something I forget now, Eddie said, "I didn't give a damn." He did give a lot of damns.

And Felsch said on the bench, "There'll be good hunting in Wisconsin next month."

"We got a pennant to hunt," Ray said.

Cicotte, a big guy and a great ballplayer, liked to play cards and he played a slow, careful game, never letting himself be rushed. He and Joe palled and roomed together. They dressed alike, and in 1920 they had gotten flashy in their dress and owned sporty new cars. I remember them sitting side by side on the bench during that Sunday ball game and I remember Felsch talking about his foot hurting.

Well, like I said, we won and were still in the race, and the team looked perfect. We were then going into the last week of the season. Everybody was getting tired without knowing it, or knowing at least how tired they really were. You talk about giving everything you got in a pennant stretch right down to the wire. But that season it wasn't just a matter of giving everything you had but of having it pulled and drawn and sucked out of you.

You couldn't relax after a ball game. The ball games were more relaxing than afterwards, because in the ball games you could forget everything that was tearing at you. We were winning most of those games and so you weren't suspicious about them, but when you won then, your doubts and suspicions came back, and then, you didn't know what was happening, what was going on, how it was going to end. You had nothing to hold on to.

I didn't want to stay long in the clubhouse after that Sunday ball game. I wanted to get away. In those days, the players didn't rush out from the clubhouse like today. You sort of cooled off and let yourself down, let yourself relax. You didn't have as much to do as modern baseball players. There wasn't television or radio or all of the questions from the writers about what kind of pitch you had hit or you hadn't hit.

I wanted to get away after that game because it was oppressive in the clubhouse. You felt that you were with strangers. The accused players began to seem like that, strangers. And in everybody's mind there was the question, what was going to happen to you in all of this mess and scandal? Would you be with the White Sox again next year, or where would you be? What was going to happen was something unknown, and that uncertainty kept threatening you.

You knew that for the good of baseball, the scandal had to come out and something would have to be done. But many times you didn't want anything to be done, anything to happen, and you wanted the club to go on the way it had been, hoping that no more ball games would be sloughed. I knew I could be a regular on that ball team, and I could play in the World Series, get my World Series money, and that I could be set as a baseball player engaged in the work I wanted, my life work. But everything could blow up like a bomb right in your face. And you didn't see the bomb.

When I left the clubhouse that Sunday, I was a few feet behind Shoeless Joe Jackson and Happy Felsch. They both were dressed up sportively, with white duck pants and fancy sport shoes and gray silk shirts. They were big fellows, and they looked like they were men in the best of all possible worlds, prosperous and famous. More fans were waiting near the clubhouse than usual. There must have been maybe two hundred, and they stared at Jackson and Felsch as the two of them walked slowly down the clubhouse steps.

I can't say that I remember now the faces of many of those men and kids, but I know that at the time I was struck by their faces. Those fans were watching the players come out of the clubhouse like people who had been hurt by something. They seemed almost solemn. Joe and Happy turned to the right and started walking away. First a couple of kids followed, and then more, and then almost the whole crowd.

"It ain't so, Joe," a kid called out.

This was taken up like a cry. Joe and Happy just walked on, not looking back, and the crowd took up the cry and kept calling out, "It ain't so, Joe, it ain't so!"

I got caught in the crowd, and I choked up at the sight of them and at hearing the men and kids calling out, "It ain't so, Joe!" I could see how they didn't want it to be true. They wanted to believe Joe and all other accused players were innocent.

Like I said, Joe and Happy didn't turn around. And the crowd tagged behind them. The kids didn't run up to walk alongside of them and talk. They, like the men, straggled after the two big fellows, with those in the front of the crowd keeping, oh, three to five yards away. They just straggled and called out, "It ain't so, Joe."

I drew back and followed behind because I didn't want to get caught in the crowd and have to face them or have any of them ask me questions. I felt almost like I was one of the crowd instead of a teammate of Joe Jackson and Happy Felsch, and I suddenly felt like they did. I thought that I had been waiting, waiting for a long time, waiting since that first World Series game of 1919, for Joe or one of the other players to say, "It ain't so."

Of course they had and had denied throwing games every time the subject was raised in their presence. But none of them had really said it so as to make you believe it and put away all your doubts for good and all. None of them could respond to that cry of the fans, "It ain't so, Joe."

A few of the fans noticed me and spoke of me or said I had played good, but it was Joe and Happy, principally Joe, who attracted them.

Joe and Happy walked at that same steady pace all of the way under the stands to the exit on the 35th Street side of the park, and then they walked along on 35th Street as far as the soccer field behind the right field bleachers. The fans following them got mixed with others on the street, the tag end of the crowd that had seen the game. They didn't call out on the sidewalk. But a lot of fans stood waiting by the exit from the soccer field to watch Joe and Happy drive off in their sporty, snazzy gray automobiles.

I thought of going across the street to Ma Kelly's but I didn't. I went home. That incident stuck in my mind, of course. The fans felt the scandal. But they didn't want to believe it. I thought of this and how the scandal was an awful disillusionment to the Chicago fans. They were proud of our ball club. They felt like I did when I was a kid and before I got signed up by the Sox. Of course I hadn't lost all of that feeling, but I wasn't just a fan anymore.

With the fans behind the players, maybe they could save themselves. That thought came to me riding home on the El that Sunday. I walked over to the 35th Street El Station between State and Wabash and took the El instead of going by streetcar.

I might say the scene I described isn't the famous one that's gone down in history, the "Say it ain't so, Joe, story." That was supposed to have happened outside the courthouse a couple of days after the Sunday I'm talking about here. Some baseball players claim it never happened and is a legend, and I don't know if they're right or wrong because I wasn't there. But it could have happened because I saw the same kind of thing happen as I have just told. And that was the way many, many people felt. They wanted to say, "It ain't so, Joe." "It ain't so, Buck." "Say it ain't so."

And I wanted to do just that. "Say it ain't so!" That's what I wanted to say and what I had wanted to say for a long time.

The sun had come out late in the afternoon and the sun was still shining when I got off the El train at 51st Street. In those days ball games didn't take as long as they do now.

It was the tag end of a Sunday afternoon, warm, a fine day. Soon the sun would go down. The baseball game was over. The White Sox had won. It was like there was the echo or the roar of the crowd sounding in my head or like I could still hear the echo of that roar from far away. I always would have a good feeling at the end of a Sunday, thinking the Sox had won. Usually you wouldn't know in those days unless you had been to the ball game or met somebody who had seen the game. There were no Sunday afternoon newspapers and few people would telephone to get the results. Saloons were all closed because it was already Prohibition.

If I hadn't become a big leaguer, I would still have been playing ball over in Washington Park at the time that I came out of the 51st Street El station on that Sunday in September 1920. And I was tempted to go over to the Washington Park ball field. The Rocks had disbanded but Joe Hines and some of the fellows were playing on another ball team. I would have seen them and wanted to very much. But I didn't go because I didn't want to face them and have them ask me questions. There were a few people on the sidewalk, passing by or some men just standing around. A couple of people said hello to me and I said hello. I was glad they didn't stop me and talk. Lots of people began saying hello to me on the streets around my neighborhood after I became a White Sox player.

I didn't have the right feeling of satisfaction after a ball game that we had won. It is obvious why, the scandal and the scene I had witnessed of the fans following Joe and Happy. The ball game we won didn't mean as much as it should have. And I was kind of afraid that the game we won could have been taken away from us, although of course it couldn't have been. It was in the records forever, I thought. And so was the 1919 World Series. You couldn't erase it from the records. You couldn't say it ain't so. Nobody ever could say it ain't so. I told that to myself.

I had other things on my mind, the coming wedding with Mary and the preparation for it. It was all scheduled and final plans had been made for our honeymoon in California after that big Saturday massacre of the Yankees. Now, I didn't see how I could afford it, because I wasn't at all sure of that World Series check. My salary would stop at the end of the season and I'd have to get back soon on my political job because I needed the money. Helping my mother and the young brother and sister and being a married man supporting a family wasn't going to leave me loaded with dough. I got hit with a sudden panic over all this on 51st Street as I walked the half-block from the El station to Prairie Avenue.

As I was turning the corner onto Prairie Avenue, Freddie McGinnis called to me. He lived at 51st and Calumet and I'd known him for years. We'd played indoor ball together, and Freddie used to have a ball game with little ball bearings for balls and a little bat right on the board and we'd play the game, imagining that were big league teams.

We both wanted to be the White Sox, but since it was Freddie's game and we were playing in his home, he was usually the White Sox. But I generally beat him. His father was well-fixed and Freddie was spoiled, so he never amounted to much. At that time, he wasn't doing anything but hanging around the pool room on 51st Street, taking girls out and using his father's Chalmers, and he was starting to drink. But I always liked Freddie and am sorry he didn't turn out better in life. He's dead now, and I think drinking shortened his life.

"Is the ball game over already, Mick?"

"Yeah, Freddie."

"Who won?"

"We won 5-1."

"Who pitched?"

"Cicotte," I answered, feeling peculiar in pronouncing the name.

"Did you get any hits, Mick?"

"I got two singles and scored a run, but one of my hits was a lucky scratch hit."

"Swell, great stuff. Hell, people are always talking about you and how you made good, Mick, and they're saying they knew you when you were just a kid playing ball in Washington Park. I even brag about knowing you."

"I was lucky to get my chance, Freddie." Normally I would have enjoyed a chance meeting like that with Freddie. I was embarrassed and nervous.

"What are they going to do with them ballplayers, Mick?" Freddie asked me.

"Gee, I don't know, Freddie."

"What is the inside dope? Christ, I'm dying to know, and cross my heart, on my word and kick my ass, I won't spill it to a soul."

"I don't know," I said, embarrassed as hell.

"Oh hell, Mickey, seeing them every day and playing with them you must know. Did they throw them ball games?"

A few fellows gathered around, and I just wanted to get away.

"Of course they're crooks, everybody knows they're crooks," a fellow said.

"Who told you? What proof have you got? Where's your evidence?" another said.

"Don't you read the newspapers?"

"But that ain't proof. Didn't the Little Skipper say its all hearsay?"

"Here's the boy who ought to know, Mickey Donovan," Freddie boasted, pointing at me.

"Yeah. Mickey, what the hell is the real lowdown?"

I just said I didn't know and got away quick, leaving them arguing on the street corner. I went home feeling lousy. My kid brother tried to talk baseball with me. I told him to shut his goddamned trap and I went into my bedroom. I sat on the bed and tried to think. I couldn't think of anything. I lay down and I still couldn't think of anything, and it was like I heard the echo of the baseball crowd far away somewhere.

"It ain't so," I told myself suddenly.

But I knew different. It was obvious that I could do nothing about it, and I just wished that I could make it not so.

CHAPTER ELEVEN

I

Of course I see those days and those men from now, when it is years afterward and time has mellowed me. And as I tell about the scandal, I realize that I didn't quite get over my attitude at the time, but I also don't have it anymore. I did get sore at the accused players. I blamed them. I remember when I woke up that Sunday after we beat Detroit, it was just getting dark, and Ma was calling me for supper. I thought of the scandal, of the accused players again, and I burst out in my room, "The dirty bastards, the son of a bitches."

I felt they were robbing me as well as the other honest players on the ball club, and that it didn't matter that they were veterans and some of them were stars and were great ballplayers. And when I picked Mary up that night to take her to a movie, I talked to Jack a minute.

"They ain't any damned good to do what they did, Jack."

"They really did it, Mick?" He still had held to some doubts even though I'd told him the accusations were true and the newspapers by then had also printed enough to make anyone understand that the World Series had been thrown.

"They can ruin baseball for all of us."

"I hate to think of that, Mick."

"We'd be in first place now, ahead of the league," I said.

"Do you really think so?"

"Yes," I said without thinking, even though from that day to this I could never prove it one way or the other about the 1920 season. I don't know for sure if some of the games were or weren't thrown.

"I think people are beginning to think that way."

"Are they?"

"They can't help but do it. But what's going to happen, Mick?"

"I don't know."

"I guess it depends on the grand jury and the evidence they get. But they must have the evidence. It looks to me as if the jig is up for them players."

"Yes, maybe it is."

And as everybody knows, it was, and the players themselves were beginning to know it. They stood it longer than a lot of fellows would, I guess. After all, they played a whole season up to the last week while under suspicion, and they knew this. They knew the Old Roman and the Little Skipper were suspicious, and that most of the baseball writers were either suspicious or else believed out-and-out that they were guilty. They had what they did, and knew on their minds more than I might have guessed or suspected.

I met Jack Fournier, who played first base and the outfield for the White Sox for several years but was let go in 1917. He came back to the big leagues with New York in 1918 and then played six or seven years or so in the other league. He and Buck were friends, and after the 1919 Series Buck and Jack went hunting together. Jack said Buck was not at all himself. There was something on his mind. He wasn't saying much and was all frozen up, and he looked really troubled. That's what Jack said.

When they were eating lunch about the second or third day, Jack asked Buck what the hell was on his mind. Was he having woman trouble? What was eating him? Buck at first didn't want to say anything. But then he poured it all out. He told Jack that the Series was sloughed, that the players had made a deal with the gamblers and that he knew about it but hadn't been a part of it. He hadn't played to throw any games. But he knew about it. Of course Jack or no one could have told Buck what to do, and by the time that Buck had told Jack, a lot of people were pretty sure that the Series had been crooked, including the Old Roman and the Little Skipper. Buck thought the whole thing was crazy but the players went through with it, and they didn't seem to think that the fix could ever be found out. They seemed to have felt pretty confident about getting away with it.

Eddie Cicotte talked about how he wanted to win one game because of his contract the next season. He told that he spent nights of torture after the games, and I guess he did. Of course he was more intelligent than some of the others, like Joe Jackson and Lefty Williams who were easily influenced. He seemed to have some good years of pitching left, but in 1919 he was thirty-five or thirty-six. I guess it was thirty-five. And he was worrying about his future and his family and saw a chance to get some easy money. He took it.

He must have been making at least $6,000. Some said it was $10,000, but I don't think so because the Little Skipper was only getting $7,200 and Ray about $1,000 a month and Joe Jackson's salary was $6,000 and was raised to $8,000 in 1920. They all felt they should be making more money and should have. Lefty Williams was only getting $2,800 a year. I don't know that that was the reason for them doing it, and I don't think it was. Most people think Gandil was the ringleader. He brought in Risberg, and Cicotte said the two of them and Fred McMullen, who was a tough young fellow, hammered at him until he joined with them.

In 1917 after they won the world championship, there were salary cuts, and when I was with the club in 1918 there was a lot of griping about salaries. And in 1918 baseball was disrupted by the war and the season closed early, leaving the players to go find jobs or go into the armed services. That was on account of the famous work or fight order. Baseball came back strong in 1919, but the players didn't have too high a morale. They were a rougher, tougher bunch in those days, with less education than ballplayers nowadays, and the gamblers got to them. Other players like Chase had been throwing ball games. One got the second and he got the third, and then the players who were weak, like Jackson, could be easily influenced, and they saw a pot of gold.

With all of the talk and gossip and rumor, they seemed safe until the grand jury started its investigation. And then, like I guess I've indicated, everything moved fast. It was then that they felt the pressure, and they didn't know what to do.

Joe Jackson and Lefty Williams wanted to break and say something, and Risberg said if they did, every honest ballplayer would be against them. Once the heat was kept on them, they couldn't stick together, but most of them began to get afraid. I guess Risberg didn't. He was the toughest of them and didn't give a damn, no more than Gandil, who had a bad reputation. With the scandal all over the newspapers and the threat of indictment, and important men getting worked up, they all got worried and afraid and didn't know what to do. They didn't have lawyers and didn't seem to go to anybody for advice. Maybe they couldn't have done it. They weren't like the gamblers who could stick together and who didn't lose anything when they promoted a fix. There's no gamblers league to be thrown out of for a fix.

The players seemed like big men to me and to many others, too. Some of them were heroes to the fans. But they were weak and foolish, and you would have thought that they could have seen that they couldn't get away with it when so many knew of the plot. I guess more than anything else, I finally came to think of them as poor fellows who did an awfully dumb thing. I don't mean that I don't think it was wrong for them to do it, because it was. But it was dumb and stupid.

Cicotte was breaking even when he pitched such a beautiful game against Detroit that Sunday. That was his last big league ball game. I don't know if he ever pitched again, but I think he did some weekend pitching in 1921. The next day, Dick Kerr beat Detroit. Felsch showed up with an infected foot and couldn't play. He sat in the stands. Nemo Leibold played center field. We won again and then had only three weekend games to play in St. Louis, and if we won them and Cleveland lost one game, we would have had a tie. Our pennant hopes were fading, but we talked of fighting right to the end and tried to convince ourselves that we'd fight and win. But it was all over. We beat Detroit mechanically.

A newspaperman, Mike Gallagher, asked Cicotte about a story, and Eddie told him to phone that night. That was Monday, and during the game it came over the press wires that a Philadelphia newspaperman had gotten a full confession from Maharg, the pal of Bill Burns. That was the end.

"He's a liar," Cicotte said in the clubhouse after the game, but he was pale and nervous. His lips trembled.

"Goddamn it, I don't know him. I never heard of him," Buck said.

It was solemn, and most of the players were kind of stunned. Ray was. He would just look, press his lips tight, and say nothing.

Later he said, "They got to talk now."

"I had nothin' to do with all that," Joe Jackson said.

Outside the ballpark, newsboys were selling extra papers about the confession of the Philadelphia gambler.

I saw Buck walking by the newsboys. He didn't buy a paper. I did, and read the whole thing. I felt sick and hurt. And I was sore at them. Now how could we win the pennant? I was cheated out of my World Series money, maybe over $5,000. And I'd lost $700, $800 in 1919 because they were crooks. Goddamn them, I thought. They deserved whatever they got. I wished I'd been left all season with San Francisco in 1919. I wished I was with another ball club, the Cubs, any other club. And I wondered what would come next.

The players' first reaction was that of denying everything. But day by day, the noose was getting tighter. Day by day, the world had been closing in, and more people were bound to talk. It was a snowball rolling down hill and it was getting so big it had to knock over whatever it hit.

And now I would have to testify, too, along with all the other players, and that worried the hell out of me. I was doubly worried because I was innocent. The uncertainty was worse than it had been. I wanted to talk and didn't know what to say. I didn't know who to talk to. Of course there was Mary.

"Mickey, dear, don't you be so worried. It doesn't affect you, you're innocent."

"Yeah, but what's going to happen?"

"No matter what happens, it won't harm you. It can't. You had nothing to do with it."

"Yes, I know," I said, but I was still distracted. We were sitting alone in her parlor. I hadn't wanted to go any place or even take a walk.

"They'll punish the guilty players and that will be the end of it."

"Yes, I guess so," I said. I froze into silence for a while. She tried to distract me by talking about our wedding and our plans. Suddenly, I said, "I can't understand why they did it."

"They wanted money and saw a way of getting it easy. But cheating doesn't pay, Mickey."

"Some of them are some of the greatest players in the game today," I said.

"But they weren't honest."

"They all deny it. Maybe they'll deny it, and what can be done to them then?"

"Mickey, you must stop worrying and fretting about all this scandal."

"I'm not worrying."

"Then what are you doing, darling?"

"It just hits you, and you don't know what to think. Maybe we can still win the pennant."

"There's worse things that can happen than losing the pennant."

I looked at her, dumbfounded, I guess. I tried to say something but, for a few seconds that seemed a long time, I couldn't. Winning the pennant had naturally been uppermost in my mind, and nothing counted next to it.

"My heart was set on it," I said weakly.

I was confused, all confused. Mary kissed me, and told me not to think, and we sat quietly in the dark, holding hands. And I felt rotten, rotten as all hell, but this was all calming and it sort of helped me to get my perspective and to realize that I couldn't be hurt, and that I still had my own future with all of its promise of good things and love and success and fame and happiness. And the fate of those players, well, in the last analysis, what business was it of mine?

It was wonderful sitting there with Mary.

II

Eddie Cicotte was alone that night in the hotel. Mike Gallagher went to see him with the paper containing the confession, and Mike later, some years later, told me of this.

"I went to see Eddie," Mike said. "He was pale and harassed. I showed him the newspaper."

"'It's a lie,' he said. "But his hands were trembling as he grasped the paper. And I noticed the ashtray on his dresser. He had been chain-smoking them. He read the newspaper, and his hands were still trembling. Then he said to me, 'Mike, it's not true. It's all a lie. There's no evidence here. It's my word against his.'

"'Eddie, don't you want to give me a story?' I asked him.

"'I've got no story. I say it's a lie, Mike.'

"But God, he was in such shape. I could see that he was shaken to hell and terribly worried. He knew I knew that he was guilty. He didn't know what to say. He lit another cigarette and sat down, trying to calm himself. He was silent for a few minutes. I felt sorry for him. Hell, he was one of the most intelligent ballplayers I ever saw on the field. And there he was, looking wrecked and ruined. But I was out to get a story. That was my business. And I knew that he was in that mess because of his own doing. He looked at me, trying to tell me things he couldn't say.

"'My wife will read this,' he said, pointing to the newspaper.

"He dropped the newspaper on the floor. Finally, he told me to come back and see him in the morning and he'd give me a story. As I left, I felt sorry for him, Mick. I felt sorry as hell for him.

"'So long, Eddie. Good luck,' I said.

"'So long, Mike,' he said.

"You know, I haven't seen him from that day to this. That's the last time I saw Eddie Cicotte. You know the rest of it, Mick."

Yes, I guess I do. Eddie Cicotte didn't sleep that night. He paced the floor and walked in his room all night, smoking cigarettes, and thinking. All those nights before that when he suffered tortures with his own conscience must have come back to him. His self-respect was gone, and he was afraid and ashamed and like a man in a trap. And think of it. He was about thirty-six.

After his long career, he had become one of the best in the game, next to Walter Johnson in our league. He'd been that kid, small and skinny, who'd gone to Detroit from Augusta, and with Ty Cobb. He had spent all those hours and hours and hours to learn control. And he'd learned control. He'd learned everything there was to learn about pitching, including tricky pitches. He never would tell anyone just how he did it, how he doctored the ball to make it wobble like it did so that the hitters just couldn't connect. Of course that was what's called cheating, but plenty of pitchers were doing it. There was only one Walter Johnson who could rear back and throw.

And then, after reaching the top, there he was in his last years but still good, still with more seasons in his arm, and he knew that he couldn't deny his crookedness anymore. He knew that he was caught. And all over the country millions had read that Eddie Cicotte had thrown World Series games and that he had been one of the players in the organizing of it. What else did he have but his fame and reputation as a pitcher? And that was gone. And he'd let his friends bet on him and they'd lost their money. There was Pal. Pal hadn't come around all that season, but the paper said that he'd gone before the grand jury of his own free will.

So there he was, alone, and just thinking all night. And he would have to face men he'd lied to. He'd maybe have to face the rest of us on the ball club, Eddie Collins and Ray and Dick Kerr and the Little Skipper. And maybe he would be sent to jail. The ballplayers had been double-crossed by the gamblers during the Series, but Cicotte had insisted that he be paid, and he had told his brother that he didn't give a damn because he had gotten his. But now he was giving a damn and sweating a damn. Yes, it was like a man going to hell before he died.

Anyone who has had sleepless nights or been a hypochondriac can guess how Cicotte suffered that night. And there he was when the dawn started to come. Those hours just before dawn and as dawn comes are the longest. But then when you haven't been able to sleep, and at last it's really dawn, and the new day has begun and the sun has come out, then you feel better. You are relieved. It's a new day. You're tired. You're like a wet rag, like a sopping towel thrown on the wet bathroom floor. And that's all you are, tired. And it's daylight. But daylight was worse for Eddie. He was all broken up inside and he couldn't deny it anymore.

And he'd been by himself. He hadn't gone to the other players. He hadn't consulted them. There had been no meeting like the meetings they had in the Ansonia Hotel in New York and the Sinton in Cincinnati. Not for Eddie.

He was broken. All he could do was give up and ask for mercy.

And he was the pitcher who stood out there on the mound, looked at Ray's signals, at the batter, rubbed the ball on his pants, or drew his hands to his lips, drew back his arm and threw, and Babe Ruth couldn't connect off him. And thousands would watch him and cheer. He pitched like an artist. He was just all broken up and all he could do at last was say it, say, "I've been crooked."

I was worried, like I said. I was down in the mouth and down in the guts that night. But I kissed Mary good night.

It was one of those fall nights. I passed that vacant lot at 50th and Calumet Avenue where I played ball as a boy and dreamed baseball. And there was a mess and a scandal, but I was still dreaming baseball. I was hitting .310 and, hell, maybe we'd still win three straight, Cleveland would lose one or two, and, if they lost one, we'd have a play-off and I'd hit and run and we'd win. And then I'd star in the World Series. I would hit a home run. I would hit a home run with the bases full. That was one of my great dreams, to hit a home run with the bases full.

I was tired that night. My dreams and Mary carried me above the scandal. I was tired and glowing with my dreams, out of this world and in that wonderful daze of happiness, like I used to be dreaming myself asleep in baseball as a kid. And I fell asleep on that Monday night, dreaming baseball.

III

After that Monday, Shoeless Joe Jackson stopped off at Ma Kelly's and sat in her parlor, silent while he drank a few beers. She always said of him, "He was a good man. He'd sit and say very little."

He left and drove off in his big car. Joe was getting frightened by that time. He had already spoken to Risberg and some of the other accused players about talking, and Risberg had said, "If you talk no one will believe you and every honest ballplayer will turn against you."

This had checked Joe, but he was feeling the pressure and getting frightened. He spoke again of talking, and someone, apparently Lefty Williams, said that Risberg threatened to bump him off if he'd blow. He didn't know what to do, and what was happening was getting way over his head. He didn't know clearly what it was all about and he couldn't read the newspapers. Maybe by that time he could make out a little, but that was the best he could do.

Jackson had already begun to talk a lot about back home, and several times during the season he had mentioned retiring and maybe farming. He also had some little business. I think it was a store. With the scandal on the front pages of the newspapers, Chicago might just as well have been a foreign city to him as a part of the United States. All he could think of was to get away from the trouble and save himself from harm or jail, or whatever might be done to him.

"I was dumb," he said. Some years later, around 1938 or maybe later, Tim Farley, the Chicago sportswriter, interviewed him and he said that to Tim. So after the Monday game, Joe went out and got himself teed off.

Happy Felsch gave a confession to a newspaperman but later denied it. But he denied having gotten any money. He did draw some money out of a Chicago bank right after the World Series and it was thought he won something betting. Lefty Williams was the fourth who confessed, and Risberg must have talked to him, making cracks about Williams having worked in the shipyards during the war. Risberg said that he'd been a slacker. He and Jackson seem to have had a falling out then, although they made up quickly and left Chicago together. Like Jackson, Williams was easily influenced. He got $5,000 and he sacrificed good years as a star. That night for him must have been a bad one too.

Chicago was Buck's home and he was married and had many in-laws in the city. I don't believe Buck thought that anything would happen to him. I think he really believed that he was safe because of his World Series play and record.

Cicotte went down to the ballpark early the next morning to confess to the Old Roman. The Old Roman was at his office around nine that morning. Cicotte went in to see him and said to the Old Roman, "I don't know what you'll think of me, but I came here because I got to tell you that I double-crossed you. I did and I'm a crook. I got $10,000 for being a crook and double-crossing you."

All the Old Roman said was to take him down to the grand jury. The Old Roman's lawyer took Cicotte to his office on La Salle Street.

It was a dull gray morning with some rain. What an awful dreary ride that must have been. And then Cicotte was left alone in the waiting room. They deliberately made him wait, and he sat there nervous and sweating, for maybe fifteen, twenty, thirty minutes. Then the lawyer talked to him and he was hustled over to the grand jury. He confessed with tears in his eyes, and when he left the grand jury room he was crying.

"Did you get a bath, Eddie?" That meant immunity. He'd asked the lawyer for immunity, and no promises had been made, but he'd been told that his confession might be taken into consideration.

And Eddie told the reporters, "I did it for my wife and the kiddies."

That broke the whole story and brought the tension and suspense to an end. And Eddie Cicotte left Chicago right after he confessed. He went home saying he didn't know what his wife, his friends and neighbors, and, also, his children would think of him.

But Cicotte and the other players didn't think to consult or hire a lawyer who could have helped them and told them about their rights. I don't believe that they even thought of hiring a lawyer. They were just demoralized and afraid. He went to the Old Roman, his boss, to confess, and then, helpless, he was shunted into the grand jury. It was pitiful.

Cicotte told the story everybody knows. The players had met with

Burns and Maharg in the Ansonia Hotel and agreed to throw the Series. He got $10,000, which was left under a pillow in his hotel room. He spoke of the accused players as "the eight of us."

Joe Jackson was still a little stewed the next morning, and he phoned the Old Roman and said that he was innocent. He was told he'd better hurry to the lawyer's office and that Cicotte had confessed. Joe appeared at the office of the White Sox in a hurry, still teed off and frightened of Risberg's shadow. He was afraid that he was going to be bumped off and had to have two bailiffs go with him for protection. He wanted to know if he would be able to escape jail by a confession. No deals would be made. Then he wanted to know if he could leave Chicago. The White Sox lawyer thought so, and later the judge said he could go any place he liked. Joe went to the County Building accompanied by two bailiffs and confessed, mentioning the meeting in the Ansonia and a meeting in the Sinton in Cincinnati. He told of getting $5,000 in dirty bills from Lefty Williams. He didn't quite know what he signed when he put his name to his confession.

I went to the ballpark that morning. It was damp and I felt damp inside. When I heard that Cicotte and Joe Jackson were confessing, I felt tired. I wanted to go home and go to bed. I wanted to sleep. There was a notice announcing the suspension of the seven ballplayers, "each and every one of you" as the notice said, and it was tacked up in the clubhouse. That was our ball team and that was our last chance at the pennant. But I didn't think much of that. I wanted to know more of what was going to happen, and how much farther the scandal would be carried. And I was kind of numbed, I guess. I couldn't or didn't think of things very clearly. One of the players, I think it was Shorty Bowman, said the man responsible had been Gandil, and he wasn't around to take his medicine. And of course there was talk of Cicotte coming to the ballpark and being shipped to the lawyer's office and the grand jury, and of him crying when he confessed. And there was more talk of Joe Jackson, and we wondered how much poor Joe understood of what it was all about.

"This damned thing had to happen," Eddie Murphy said.

"This did, but the cause of it didn't," Collins said.

"What do you mean, Captain?" Murphy asked.

"The original deal with the gamblers," Collins said.

"Them poor fellows were took and double-crossed," Shano said.

"They don't seem to have gotten much, and now they're through in baseball," Collins said.

"They didn't care about us," Dick Kerr said.

"They seemed to hate us before this whole thing blew up," Collins said.

"I'm not wasting sympathy," Leibold said.

"I guess they have it coming to them," Shano said.

"Yes, they'll be getting their desserts. But they were victims," Collins said. He shook his head as he went on. "How in the name of hell they ever came to think this wouldn't get out, I don't understand. That was the dumb thing. Joe Jackson, yes, I can understand him. He's weak. He's weakest, and he was more easily influenced than I ever realized."

"Gandil's the man who was behind it. That's the way I figure. And he didn't care if it was found out or not," Red said.

None of the accused and barred players except Buck showed up at the ballpark. Felsch left town that morning. But Buck showed up and went in to see the Old Roman. Buck was asking for his reinstatement. He went to explain that he was innocent, to say that he had not helped to throw any of the games. And he believed that he would be reinstated, not only on that morning but for a long time afterward. I believe it, too, that Buck didn't try to throw the games by making any misplays. I don't think he would have known how to do it. His instincts wouldn't have let him. Hell, he loved baseball as much as I did or just about as much as any player I've ever known.

Of course he knew about the fix, and I guess he must have been at least at one of the meetings. But he didn't know what to say or to do, and he wasn't the only one who didn't. I don't know that he was or wasn't given a fair deal, and I guess maybe he had to be banned along with the rest of them. I won't say I know the answer here because the judge who came in as baseball commissioner after the scandal had to think of the good of the game of baseball. But it was tough on him, and I was in his corner during his last years.

Anyway, Buck came down to see the Old Roman. He came out of the office pale, and he came into the clubhouse pale and silent. I guess he didn't know how we would greet him. It must have been hard on him, harder to walk in the clubhouse and face us than to face the Old Roman. He didn't like the Old Roman and sometimes called him "an old bastard" and a "tightwad bastard." And he went to see the boss believing he was innocent and would be reinstated. But he was in the office a half-hour, and he talked but the Old Roman wouldn't budge. The Old Roman told him to go before the grand jury. Buck told the Old Roman that he had nothing to say. He didn't have anything to tell. The Old Roman told him that some of his teammates, Cicotte and Jackson, told a different story and that he expected the other ones would also. They said he was one of the guilty players. Buck said he wasn't and that no man could say or prove he was. The Old Roman told him he ought to go before the grand jury. Buck said he had nothing to tell the jury about the nature of the investigation going on.

That's the way it went. And so, like I said, Buck got no satisfaction. He came into the clubhouse right after that. He was sore. But he was more shocked than sore, and more hurt than shocked.

He walked more than halfway across the room toward his locker. No one spoke. Then I did. I don't know why I spoke but I did. I said, "Hello, Buck."

He turned and smiled at me, and that smile was pathetic.

"Hello, Donovan."

"You drove by my Hupmobile comin' down, Buck. I tried to catch you but I couldn't," Red said.

"Oh, I didn't know I passed you, Red," Buck said. He went to his locker. "I came to get my things," he said, opening the door of his locker.

He bent down and picked up his black glove and put it on his left hand. He looked down at the glove and at the pocket on it. "I saw the old man."

"Yes, we heard you were seeing him," Red said.

Buck pulled a small black suitcase out of the bottom of his locker and began dumping his things into it. Although there had been a brief exchange of conversation with Buck, the atmosphere remained constrained. Most of us were sitting there, waiting for Buck to collect his belongings and leave. Buck was slow and noisy. He pulled the dirty pants of his baseball suit off the locker hook and looked at them. He slowly dropped them in the black bag. Then he did the same with the top of the uniform. He bent down for a second glove.

We sat waiting for Buck to leave. His presence was embarrassing. Buck straightened up and looked around.

"I'll be back here. There's nothin' on me." He walked out.

We were quiet for a moment. Seeing Buck walk out that way made an impression. It was the farewell of a great ballplayer.

"He acts like he's innocent," I said.

I had begun to speak out more around the team by this time.

They didn't agree with me. He had stuck with the other players and had hung around with them rather than with the rest of us. Right along, Buck had been held just as much in suspicion as the other players.

Harry Grabiner came in and talked to us a minute or two, telling us that the Old Roman found comfort only in the honest players he had, the ones who had not been crooks in 1919. He had envelopes for all of us who were on the club then, with checks giving us the difference between a losing and a winning share. This lifted our spirits. There was a nice statement to us by the Old Roman, and after Harry left, we signed a joint statement of appreciation. It was written by Eddie Collins.

There was nothing to keep a player in the clubhouse, but we hung around a while feeling glum, and then we left. I went home and did nothing. I got the afternoon papers and read about the confessions of Eddie Cicotte and Joe Jackson.

I read that a number of the players were being subpoenaed, Eddie Collins, Ray, Red, Shano, Nemo, Eddie Murphy, and a couple more, as well as the Little Skipper. My name was not mentioned. I was glad, but only for a few moments. Then, I began to worry for fear that people might think I was guilty or involved since I hadn't been subpoenaed along with the honest players.

Now it was all over. Maybe there would be more revelations, but the big ones had come out, and we knew for sure. And these players were gone. I'd never play ball with them again. They'd never play ball in the big leagues. I found myself feeling glad. I was not glad only because they were punished for wrongdoing. I was glad, that's all, glad because I was glad. I wanted to see them go. I hadn't realized this before, and a little later I felt differently, but sitting at home on that afternoon, that's the way I felt. It was a little like feeling that you had won over them. It was also a little like they might have died, and you were launched on your own now, without them. They had of course died to baseball.

And I began to think of the last three games of the year in St. Louis. It was only Tuesday. On Thursday we'd go to St. Louis and play games

Friday, Saturday, and Sunday. We could win those three games and maybe still get a tie or even come out ahead of Cleveland. If we did that with a patched-up team, that would be one of the most dramatic achievements in baseball. And I could star, become the hero. I started imagining myself winning the pennant for the White Sox, starring at shortstop in place of Risberg. I guessed I would be put in at shortstop and I was right. That's where the Little Skipper put me in that St. Louis series. But I knew that I was only having daydreams.

There was more news later that day. Lefty Williams was said to have told a reporter, "I'll tell whatever I got to the grand jury, if they call me. Nobody has the goods on me. My word's as good as Cicotte's or Jackson's. I got no yellow streak. I gave Joe Jackson $5,000. Did I? Ask the police on the corner. I'm not stampeded and talking for publication." But the next day, he confessed and the eight players were indicted for conspiracy.

But on that Tuesday night, the telephone rang. My mother answered it and called to me to say I was wanted by Mr. Collins. As I went to the telephone, I was nervous. I thought it had something to do with the investigation. I didn't associate the name. It was Eddie Collins and you could have knocked me over I was so dumbfounded. He asked me to come to his place that night. A number of the players were coming.

It was a party got up on the spur of the moment. "The honest players," as we were called, were all there. Ray had driven out of town to see friends in Gary, Indiana, but Eddie Collins got him and he raced back to come to the party. There was plenty of beer and sandwiches and everybody was so excited that you might have thought we were having a victory celebration party. Nemo Leibold slapped me on the back and I slapped Eddie Murphy and he slapped Eddie Collins and Eddie slapped Shano.

"God, it's a great day," Eddie said.

"I just sank back with relief and told myself it was all over now," Shano said.

"I don't know how you fellows stood it," Eddie said.

"We're not standing it anymore," Murphy said.

"I knew for a long time, something has to happen, something has to give," Red said.

"Jesus Christ, I used to get so mad, and then I'd become so depressed," Shano said.

"I'm not depressed. They only got what they deserve," Ray said.

We drank more beer and pounded each other on the back and sang. We talked. We shouted, rather than talked. Everybody raised his voice. Ray's voice was booming loudest of all.

"And I had to catch them two fellows and I knew they weren't throwing the way they can throw," Ray said.

"Some of those games this year looked terrible to me," Collins said.

"Why can't we win the pennant? I'll pitch two ball games in St. Louis if the Skipper tells me to go twice," Red said.

I drank about four or five glasses of beer. It was potent and I felt a little woozy.

"Well, Donovan, how do you like it?" Ray asked.

"Swell."

"That's the kid."

We went on. Really, we were maybe a little hysterical. We were really celebrating our escape from that awful situation more than the downfall of the banished ballplayers. Until the names were mentioned, everyone on the club was suspected, and we played with some people, and quite a lot of them at that, thinking we were crooks. And we had to go out on the field not knowing but what they were going to double-cross us again. All of the other players had felt it just like I had. And everybody wanted to celebrate because that kind of an ordeal was over. But it was kind of grim, considering why we were having that celebration.

The next day I didn't care so much when I read the newspapers. The investigation was still going on, and Buck was supposed to have seen a friend of his in the DA's office, a young fellow named Owens, in order to arrange for him to go before the grand jury and tell his story. One newspaper said that it would be the same as the story told by Cicotte, Jackson, and Lefty Williams when they confessed. And there was a little bit about Gandil.

"It's all bunk," Gandil said. "Somebody is trying to pin a bum rap on me. It's all bunk and I don't care what Cicotte or any of those players say."

I was relaxed when I went to the station to take the train for St. Louis. I got the train at 63rd Street, and the rest of the ballplayers were on it in our special car. As I walked into it and saw their faces, I suddenly felt ashamed. It wasn't because of our little celebration, but I don't know why it was. I just felt ashamed. I saw the faces of all the players but I missed the banned players. The newspapers had already started calling them "the Black Sox."

This was the first time that I really felt the full effect of the meaning of their suspension. I realized how much I had come to love the life of a big league ballplayer, the traveling, the hotels, the excitement and importance and limelight and all that went with being in the big leagues. And those fellows had been big leaguers much longer than I. Now, all they had was gone. Already the baseball writers and the newspaper editorial writers were beginning to attack and denounce them, to call them crooks and thieves, dishonest ballplayers, and to treat them as though they were just about the biggest criminals in America. At the same time as the scandal, the newspapers were full of headlines about a governor who was supposed to have gotten something like $1 million in graft, but he wasn't treated the way those ballplayers were.

I was used to seeing them, and they had become a part of my life as a ballplayer. Making my first trip after they were gone, kicked out of the game, I missed them. And I began to think all over again about the scandal and to ask myself new questions. Maybe what they did deserved the punishment of blacklisting, but were they as rotten and as no-good as the day's newspapers described them, and wouldn't it be more right to give them a second chance? I didn't know how to answer that question, but I did know that I was sorry about what happened to them. I wasn't the only one.

It was a quiet and subdued bunch of White Sox ballplayers who took the trip to St. Louis to finish off the season and make a last desperate effort to win the pennant. We had gotten everything off our chests drinking those few beers and talking loud and slapping each other on the back at Collins's two nights before. I thought of things about the blacklisted players, and of how they played, and I just wish—hell, I wished that it all hadn't happened. It was like we were all coming home from a funeral.

And we went out and played with a patchwork ball club, with Murphy on third base and with Birdie Lynn in right field. We lost all three games and Cleveland won the pennant. The season was over for us with the confessions and suspensions, and we were all of us off our form.

I came back to Chicago with most of the players. I was coming back to get married. I hit .305 for the season and my own future seemed certain. I thought there was a good nucleus for a new team, one that could be built up to become greater than the one that had just been broken up. That team wasn't anymore, I told myself. But I was disappointed, and every day when I read about the World Series games between Cleveland and the Brooklyn Dodgers, I was disappointed and sore. We should have been playing that Series, I told myself. We would have been but for those players. I was the loser because of them. That made me sore. But I still felt sorry for them at the same time that I cursed them.

I thought of the next season, 1921. I thought that the 1919 Series, the scandal, the ball team I had broken in with, was all a dead letter. It was all history. It would be covered over with time and forgotten.

And in the happiness of my honeymoon and of those first months of the off-season with Mary and I living together in our first home, I did forget. The whole episode was fading away in my memory. I had the future to look ahead to. I was still only twenty, and on my way to becoming a star. It was tragic what happened, but it would give me a bigger and better chance. I was expected to become one of the mainstays of the new White Sox. Like I said, it was as if those fellows died. The dead were buried, and the living went on. I was young and one of the living. That's how I came to think and feel during the winter.

CHAPTER TWELVE

I

Did you ever read the box scores of old baseball games that were played years ago? You read the names of the players in the lineups and remember them all, and for a minute you almost think that time has not flowed under the bridge and that you are reading the box score of yesterday's ball game.

You wish it was just that and all those old players, Cobb and Speaker and Ruth and Eddie Collins and Walter Johnson, were all back there in their prime. And you keep looking at the score, the runs and hits, and you think that this player is dead, and this one and this one. It's a sad feeling. There they once were strong and young and healthy, and now they are old or are six feet under the ground. Nobody can ever see them play again.

And if you are an old ballplayer yourself, you think about when you were young. You can never play again. I sometimes look through my scrapbooks and read about myself and read the accounts of games in which I played and box scores with my name in them. I think of the days I played and of all those players. Well, that's what it all is now, old box scores. And I look at young players, ones I'm scouting, and I wonder, "God, did I look as young as that?"

I had a pretty fair career. It wasn't anything like what I dreamed it would be, and I never became the star I dreamed of becoming. In 1920, when I went into right field and played right up with those players on the greatest ball club ever assembled, everybody thought I was a coming star. Great predictions were made for me. I batted .305 and did everything right. I had guts and good baseball instinct. I remember how the pitchers would knock me down and I'd get up and stand right there, waving my bat, and if they knocked me down again, I was up again. All I seemed to need was polish and experience.

Well, I ended up a lifetime .300 hitter and I played seven positions. I think if I had stayed put at one position, shortstop or second base, I'd have developed more. But I think of those years and they were a climax to 1920. All those years we finished in second division. One year we were fighting for the pennant and went into Yankee Stadium full of fight. Eddie Collins was managing us then. He broke his leg. We lost five straight to the Yankees and sank back into second division.

So after being called up in midseason 1919 to become a member of a pennant winner and then going through 1920 on the club that should have won, I was never again on a good ball club. I have no complaints. I'm glad for all my years in baseball, my experiences, the friends I made, the memories I have carried away from the game, and I'm proud to have an association with the game today.

But I still cannot help thinking that it would have been much different but for 1919. It's not the same being a .300 hitter on a pennant winner and contender and on a second-division club, and neither is the salary the same. I always fought hard and tried, and I don't say that I would have played any better, because I wouldn't have. But it wouldn't have been anything like what it was back in the twenties, playing year after year on losing ball clubs, hoping for something better the next year, seeing a lot of dummies come and go, although I must add we had some mighty good ballplayers on our club.

But we played under a shadow and the fans saw us under a cloud. They didn't see me that way because I was part of their memories of better days. The way I played during the September stretch drive made me very popular, and I was thought of as one of the old White Sox. But a ballplayer was often playing with a ghost beside him, Joe Jackson, Buck Weaver, Eddie Cicotte, Happy Felsch, and Lefty Williams. And we had many a Humpty-Dumpty in their place.

We went to Texas for spring training in 1921, determined to forget and start anew. And there was Eddie Collins and Ray Schalk to build a new team around, and Red Faber and Dick Kerr as the stalwarts for our pitching. I was scheduled for shortstop. It looked like we had a good ball club and that it was the basis for another great one, and the fans came out and supported us enthusiastically at the beginning of the season. But we went nowhere, and some of us had good records. I hit .315 that season and my pay was up to $350 a month.

With the winter, the blacklisted players kind of faded a little from memory, although you couldn't help remembering them. During the first days of spring training I kept expecting something to happen, and I didn't believe we were fully under way. What I was expecting was for Joe Jackson, Buck Weaver, and that contingent to arrive. The veterans didn't like to talk about them or the scandal. They wanted to forget, and so did I. I felt almost like a veteran myself.

We made a fair beginning but lost a lot of games we ought to have won. Red had a terrific year, and with a good ball club like the 1919 or 1920 teams he should have won thirty or maybe thirty-five ball games. He had won twenty before the end of July, but then only got five more for the rest of the season. The trial of the eight players didn't cause us to go down, but it was a painful thing. It was like an anticlimax, or like bringing dead people back to die all over again. The trial was for conspiracy and it came up in July.

They all came back to Chicago for the trial and it started while we were on a home stand against the eastern clubs. There we were, going to the ballpark every day, and there were those fellows in court with the story of the court proceedings printed in the news every day. They were standing trial as criminals and could have gone to jail. The way the trial turned out, they didn't, and it looked worse to me than it was. But that was a hard thing to understand, the banished players on trial as criminals, charged with conspiracy to ruin the Old Roman's business.

You got to be an old ballplayer to know that feeling of the first year after you've hung up your spikes, the feeling of loneliness and disappointment that comes when it's spring training time and the ball clubs go south or west to California, and you aren't going. You feel nervous and restless and old, older than you are. You're the same as you always were physically for all the purposes of ordinary living, but you're no good for baseball. You miss it.

You think of how you went away a year ago and didn't think it would really be your last time. It had been harder the last years and you ached more and used to feel pooped out and tired at the end of the day. It took you longer to get into condition. But you thought you still had enough left. And so you are out of it. It's all over. Your baseball life is finished.

You won't be there on opening day, except perhaps in the stands. You won't be drawing that first paycheck. You won't be going on trips to other big league cities, seeing ballplayers on the other clubs and asking them what kind of a winter they had, kidding a little, feeling yourself one of that kind of fraternity of ballplayers. In my time, the big league clubs didn't play so many exhibition games with each other. You didn't see so many of the players on other clubs until the season opened.

But you feel all of this. You aren't playing. You aren't making the same money you did. You aren't in the limelight. You don't have as many people telephoning you and wanting to see you. You aren't in demand. You walk along the street and maybe aren't recognized, and you feel that. You had become used to people recognizing you. It made you feel more important and you came to expect it. You had gotten separated from people and lived in baseball so much of the time that you were a part of baseball and other things weren't important.

And you only then begin to realize that other things are important and that the whole country isn't waiting to know the results of the ball games, and that many people don't care about baseball or what happens on the ball field. You've given the best years of your life to baseball, and you were somebody, a ballplayer. And that's finished, and you're not so important anymore. There are lots of things people talk about besides baseball, but you haven't got much to say and you feel out of the picture. You aren't used to that either, because a year ago you weren't out of the picture. But you didn't get as much education as you could have, and you don't know very much, and you've got to start learning a little of what others learned a long time ago while you were in there playing ball and not thinking of much else.

And after you started earning a good salary, you didn't work much in winter but went fishing and hunting and played golf, spent some time in Florida loafing, and you enjoyed it and miss it all right. But you think of how while you were doing all this, others were getting ahead of you in the race of life. You weren't Babe Ruth or Ty Cobb, and you didn't pick up a job in baseball, and you're just out of it, that's all. You get lonesome and dissatisfied and bitter, too. You have bitter moments, and begin to think that people in baseball don't want to see you coming around. You forget that in your own playing days, in your heyday, you didn't pay too much attention to all of the ex-ballplayers who came around in spring training or at the ballpark or at your hotel when you were on the road. You never thought how they felt or even imagined it, and you got bored when they talked too much about how it was in their time.

Of course all of this must have happened, and it did to those fellows who got barred from baseball. And the seven of them were kicked out before they were washed up. They left baseball in disgrace. They were sorry as all hell, and Buck kept proclaiming his innocence until he died. They couldn't go around and see old friends or former friends, and they didn't know if they still had many of their old friends. Most ballplayers are like everyone else. They don't like to write a lot of letters. And when players retire, they don't hear much from old friends or write. And of course few ballplayers wrote to those fellows. They couldn't write. They were out of it worse than I was or felt I was when I retired, or than the average run of ballplayers are in their first and second year away from the game.

Well, think of all that, and then think of them coming back to Chicago the next summer to stand trial. There they were again in the limelight. But what kind of a limelight? The spring training season had come and gone and the baseball season had passed the half-way mark. And with the Babe, baseball was getting into a new period of popularity. Ty Cobb was still a terrific ballplayer and had been made manager of the Detroit Tigers. He only hit .334 in 1920 but went back up to .389 in 1921. Somehow or other, baseball was the same, and it would go on forever like that with Ty Cobb still in there.

I didn't know much of what had happened or was happening to those fellows. Gandil was playing outlaw ball, and a couple of them were picking up a little money, $50 or $100 playing a little ball. Buck, I knew, got a job with some company but wasn't playing ball in 1921 because he wanted to get reinstated, and he expected to. Back the year before when Cicotte and Jackson and Williams had confessed, the newspapers printed that story, saying that Buck was seeing his friend Owens in the DA's office and was going to testify. Then, the story was that Owens told him he could never get his story believed, and then there was an item that he had retained a lawyer.

Joe Jackson and Lefty Williams had gone south to Joe's hometown in North Carolina and had been put out of the first hotel at which they registered, but then they had passed out of the news. Felsch had gone back to Milwaukee and had some job or other. Later, he got his own saloon. And Jackson had his business but I don't know what Williams was doing. Risberg was playing some ball, I believe with Gandil in an outlaw league, and he was on a farm in Minnesota or North Dakota, somewhere in that region. Eddie Cicotte had a job as a guard with one of the automobile companies. I don't know what Fred McMullen was doing.

And a year before, they were members of the greatest baseball team going.

We were playing at home. I was going so good at shortstop that the baseball writers said Risberg wasn't missed, and I was a better hitter than him. But the ball was livelier and he would have probably had a higher average had he been able to go on playing. I had a pretty good arm but nothing like his. But what shortstop had an arm like that fellow's? Eddie Collins was still a great ballplayer and he was hitting pretty good. He finished about .337 or .338 that year but I think he was up on that in July. I don't know what his new contract called for, but I know it was above the $15,000 he'd been making on his other contracts. And there we were, floundering around sixth place, and with them we'd have been battling the Yankees.

The Old Roman was bitter. I haven't said too much about him so far except to mention him. I always say in public what a fine man he was and that he always treated me fair and square, and I did respect him. I still do. But I don't think I really liked him. I was kind of afraid of him. He didn't mix much with his ballplayers and, after all, they were working for him. He didn't want to pay more than he had to, and he let Dick Kerr go out of baseball rather than pay him something of what he was worth, and think of how Dick pitched in 1919. Joe Jackson said that Dick won that first game he pitched when they were trying to lose it for him.

He never went bankrupt with what he paid me, and I tried to get $600 a month in 1922 and held out but finally signed for $480. I went up though and my highest salary was $9,800, like I said. But he liked to entertain big and spend money entertaining and have plenty of drinks on hand for the newspaper writers on the White Sox Special when we went to spring training, but he didn't pay much. He wasn't a good man to work for, and I used to wish I'd get traded, especially to the Yankees. But what ballplayer wouldn't have wanted that to happen to him, in my day or now?

I never could understand why he didn't do something fast and quick and rough after that first game of the World Series. It seems to me he was the man who should have done something, and that might have saved the whole situation. Why hell, look at what happened to the players when the heat was put on them, and how some were led by the others. But that's all past and I don't want to speak ill of the dead. But he would just as soon have let them go behind bars, or that's the way I felt at the time. And I thought that they had been barred, and their living had been taken away from them. Their names were smeared all over the newspapers, and Cicotte had broken and cried. None of them could be happy about what they did, so I thought they ought to have been left alone. They ought to have been left to sink away where they would be forgotten.

I'd read the *Chicago Tribune* in the morning during that time when the trial was on, and I'd go to the ballpark. It was like it was full of ghosts of the year before. The other ballplayers were interested, too.

"My God, they ought to let them fellows alone," Ray said.

"I don't see why they have to be put on trial like this," Red said.

That was the way nearly all of us felt. The Little Skipper said, "They can't be convicted."

I hoped not.

Dick Kerr never said he wanted to see them in jail, but he didn't like the others none. He was sore at them for trying to lose for him because he was a busher.

The Old Roman was put on the stand, and one of the lawyers for the ballplayers got under his skin by saying that he got players to jump contracts when the American League was founded. The signed confessions of the players had disappeared. They were stolen from a safe in the DA's office, I guess, for the big-shot gambler in New York who was supposed to have been the real evil genius of the plot, and there wasn't much new testimony given. Joe Jackson got laughs in the courtroom when he was put on the stand.

We went on an eastern trip, and the trial was still in progress, but it wasn't looking so bad for the players. The judge had said that if Buck Weaver and Happy Felsch were convicted, he'd overrule the verdict. There was no evidence against them. We were playing in Washington, and those of us who had been on the 1919 World Series club had to take the train back to Chicago to testify. That left us with as bad a club as when we played the last three games of 1920 in St. Louis. The Washington ball club wanted the easy victories it could win against our makeshift lineup and came in for criticism because of bad sportsmanship. I guess it was that. And there is sportsmanship in baseball. It wouldn't be the game and the sport it is and occupy the place it does in American life if there wasn't sportsmanship. But you play to win, don't you? And it wasn't Washington's fault that we had to go to Chicago to testify.

Anyway, we took a train during a heat wave and couldn't sleep all night. It was a brutal, punishing trip. We got into Chicago in the morning feeling wrung out, and it's good we didn't have to play ball that day. We knew that our testimony wasn't going to be difficult, or so we'd been told. But how could you be sure? The mere idea of having to testify can make you nervous. When any smart lawyer gets you on the stand, he can throw curves at you that you'll never hit. The scandal had cost us enough money and trouble and it had wrecked our ball club. Christ, was it going to go on troubling us? Most of us were not in a good mood when we went to court.

We walked into the crowded courtroom. It was packed with fans. Something happened to me, and to the others, too, the Little Skipper, Eddie and Ray, Red and Dick. We were glad to see the players. We smiled, shook hands with them, and asked, "How are you?" It was really like meeting friends.

"It's damn good you're playing shortstop, Mickey. If you were playing third, you'd be out of luck, because I'm comin' back to take over my old job," Buck said.

"We sure could use you, Buck," I said.

"You're looking good, Eddie," Ray said to Eddie Cicotte.

"You're the same yourself."

And Eddie Collins talked to Joe Jackson. "Well, Joe, you look good, in good shape."

"Ah, yes, Ah'm in good shape," he drawled.

But it was all cordial. It was brief, of course. We testified, but that was very brief. We only had to state a couple of facts, like Eddie Collins stating that he had ridden in a cab with Buck to the races over in Kentucky on the day before the 1919 Series started.

Dick Kerr was asked hardly anything. "I made this lousy trip all these goddamn miles for one minute. What the hell is this?"

We took a train to Philadelphia and resumed playing.

The players were acquitted.

"Everybody knows I'm innocent. I did nothing to lose that Series. I believe I'm entitled to have my old position back and I'm going to fight for it," Buck said.

"I'll stick to semi-professional ball," Lefty Williams said.

"I'm through with organized ball. I got a store. I'm going to play ball with Williams in Oklahoma for a while this summer and I'm contemplating a position as coach in Japan. And I had an offer to go before the footlights," Joe Jackson said.

"I'm going home. I'll never talk again," Eddie Cicotte said.

There were cheers in the courtroom. Cicotte pounded Joe's back, and they celebrated that night. It turned out that the jurors celebrated in the room next to theirs some place on the West Side. The acquittal didn't prove them innocent, although it didn't prove Buck guilty, either. It merely acquitted them of the charge of conspiracy. And in 1920 the Old Roman made more money than in 1919, so the conspiracy charge would have looked raw if they had been found guilty. That was the last time they were together, and the last time I saw any of them except Buck. I think it was the last time most of the others saw the blacklisted players except for Ray and Red who saw Buck also. The Little Skipper and Eddie Collins never saw them again. Dick Kerr walked into a hardware store in Detroit to buy some nails one day. This was long after he was out of baseball. The man behind the counter put out his hand. "Give me the goddamn nails." The fellow behind the counter was Eddie Cicotte who had some interest in a hardware store for a while, along with one of his relatives.

During the time the players were on trial, Red won his twentieth game. I hit my first major league home run.

II

The trial of the players and their acquittal was like an end, as happy an ending as they could have. I remember when I walked out on the field at the ballpark in Chicago when we returned home, I thought of this. "It's all over now," I told myself.

I felt a sense of relief about this. I was glad the players weren't put in jail, like I already said. But I had enough of the whole damned business. And at the same time I wished them all as much good luck in life as they could possibly have, I just didn't want to think anymore about the whole business. I'd been thrown close to it because I was on the ball club. It caused me agony and made me break in under one hell of a set of conditions. And the players had cost me money, the World Series cost of 1920 as well as my chance to play in a World Series. I'd have at least alternated with Nemo Leibold against left-handers like Marquand and Sharrod Smith if we'd have been in the Series with our full ball club. I forgot to mention that Nemo and Shano were traded to Boston after the 1920 Series. And Eddie Murphy was released early in 1921, before the trial.

We finished seventh in 1921, but I played my first full year and proved myself a big leaguer over the course of a season. I was in 146 games and I was one of the most popular players with the Chicago fans. I was four years in the majors and only twenty-one. The scandal was the tragedy of those fellows, not of myself. Now and then, I'd have some thought of them or hear their names mentioned, but that was all. Sooner or later, one of them would have had to make way for me anyway, and I got my chance sooner, I guess.

Toward the end of the 1921 season they were mentioned in the clubhouse. "Oh, for Christ sake, the hell with them," I said, blowing my top.

Just about every player close to the scandal wanted it buried. It hurt every one of us. It wrung most of us out. Just as you forget sickness when you convalesce and get well, so we forgot 1919. Or thought we did. In those early years of the 1920s, it was pretty much forgotten.

Now and then, there was something in the newspapers or you heard a player say something about one of those fellows. Buck got a settlement out of court on his contract. Joe Jackson sued in Milwaukee and got a verdict but the judge overruled the jury and threatened to hold Joe and Happy Felsch for perjury. Some of them started an exhibition tour from Chicago in May 1922, but I don't think it made much money. Joe Jackson could still hit the ball, however. That's what the reports were. Buck was turned down in the first and maybe the first and second of his appeals for reinstatement.

And there I was on my way. I had learned the ropes. I was different from the kid who was shy about eating in a big hotel in 1918, and I thought of myself as a real big leaguer. I just wanted the team to be better and to make more money. We were getting along, and the family was comfortable and our first boy, Johnny, was born.

And there's a lot I never did find out about the 1919 scandal.

III

Almost every year I hoped. I hoped the team would be better, or that I'd be traded, and of course I hoped that I'd have my biggest year. We climbed from seventh to fifth in 1922, just behind Cleveland by a game or so and about seven percentage points. That was kind of ironic to find us battling Cleveland for fourth place when two years before we were fighting Spoke for the pennant and our two ball clubs were such powerful ones. Because that 1920 Cleveland team was a honey of a club with plenty of fight. But that's baseball.

I got off to a bad start in 1922, and I guess I was too cocky and confident. I had a couple of lousy slumps and was benched twice. I didn't get going until about the Fourth of July. I was on the bench but went in to pinch hit in the first game and hit for two bases. The Little Skipper thought I was hot and I was. He played me in the second game and I went four for four, and from then on I hit my stride and wound up batting .292. But that was a big disappointment, because I had the ambition to bat .300 or better in every season.

And I didn't get a raise until 1924. In 1923, the club was bad and I was .321. But my record is in the books, and who wants to hear an old timer like myself talk about how he hit .292 and .321 and .300 when, what the hell, look at what Eddie Collins hit and look at Ty Cobb's record, a lifetime average of .367?

In 1925 I was a damn fool. I was drawing $6,500 and I had some gay times on the road, and I did some skirt chasing. Something happened to me and I didn't understand it. I began to think I was pretty goddamned good, and I thought I'd missed something in life. Other young fellows had had plenty of babes, and I'd been a pretty faithful husband and a clean-living ambitious young baseball player.

The team was going nowhere that season, and I'd been fighting year after year for seven years and always on a team going nowhere. The Little Skipper was gone and another couple of managers, and Eddie Collins was at our helm. He was still a great ballplayer but he was slowing up, and Ray was getting closer to the end than he realized. But Red was still a mean pitcher. I was a veteran at twenty-five and I had a good year but went haywire and sowed wild oats all around the league.

I went out on one party with Babe Ruth and a couple of Yankees and that was quite a party. I thought, then, that I was really big stuff. Mary had a pretty good idea of what I was doing, and to this day I feel pretty rotten because of the nights she was red-eyed with crying because of me. But she was a saint and smart, too, and she gave me enough rope so I could use it to pull myself back to her instead of hanging myself with it. I don't know what really got into me but I saw the same thing happen to other ballplayers, and some of them ruined their careers. I thought I was above ruining my career and that I could carouse and hell around and still play big league ball. Eddie Collins called me to turn, and I laughed at him behind his back. He was a college man, and as great a ballplayer as he was, what the hell did he know about living? He always took good care of himself.

"For God's sake, you goddamn fool," Ray told me.

"What the hell you talkin' about?"

"You know goddamned well what I'm talking about."

"Mind your own goddamned business, you old Arab," I told him, and we almost had a fight. We didn't speak for about three weeks, but we shook hands and have been friends ever since.

Late in August, Eddie called me into his office. I can remember him sitting there in his uniform, and I felt a sudden awe of him, the way I did when I was still a kid and dreaming of starring and he was then a great star on the White Sox. Sitting down and talking to him, that was the same as talking to Ty Cobb.

"Mickey, you're a smart ballplayer, and you haven't been playing up to your full potential."

"I'm hittin' over .300."

"I'd rather have a .260 hitter who's good for the ball club."

I felt like telling him to trade me, and the words were on the tip of my tongue, but something told me or kept me from saying it.

"You know goddamned well why I'm talking to you."

I sat there and my sulkiness was just melting away. I was really ashamed of myself and it was a defense I threw up.

"You're twenty-five. I was your age in 1918 and I batted .368. I batted .368 the year before. But do you think I'd be here now if I had started friggin' around the way you are? This is my twentieth year. You were six years old when I began in this league. A lot of ballplayers were good for a few years and what the hell happened to them? And a lot of great ballplayers didn't mature. Look at poor Joe Jackson."

"You can't say I done that."

"I'm not. I know you haven't, or you wouldn't be playing on my ball club. But he didn't mature, and he was easily led. If I had only realized how he was a weak fellow, I might have talked more to him and we'd still have him on our ball club. And we damned well could use him."

I was really beginning to be ashamed of myself.

"And look at Buck Weaver. Buck never liked me. He had no use for me. He hated my guts. Buck used to think that I was only thinking about myself. I was. I wanted to get all I was worth and play up to my full potential. Buck didn't like me because I made more money than he did. But I was worth it, and I knew it and I was going to goddamn well see that I would be worth it for a long time."

He let these words sink in.

"I don't know how far Buck was in on that stupid deal those fellows made. He played a hell of a lot better baseball than I did in that Series. You were around then. You were with us then. You remember, because you were just about as studious a young busher as we ever had on this ball club, at least in my time."

"Did you know that?"

"Listen, Mick, I was already an old-timer then. But my legs were better than they are today. But Buck didn't take care of himself. He didn't go helling around like you've been doing." I opened my mouth to speak. He tapped the table. "Don't kid me. I know and I didn't have to have anyone to tell me or hire a gumshoe to find out."

I could have crawled through the floor. And I thought that this was Eddie Collins who was talking to me. And I had dreamed of playing alongside of Eddie Collins and I was. Donovan to Collins to ——. We had so many first basemen in those days, the name is like a dash. I was a friggin' fool.

"Buck was a good fellow in his way and he's where he is today because he thought of being a good fellow and going along with his friends. He knew what a ballplayer he was. He was one hell of a ballplayer, a great player. You heard Ty Cobb talk of him. You should hear Mr. Mack. But he just didn't use his head and he thought no one could say anything against Buck Weaver. You haven't developed into the ballplayer he was, but you started better than he did. He began to reach his peak after he was twenty-five. I remember when he first came up from the Pacific Coast League. He used to say, 'I was a goof then.'

"Now don't you be a goof. I could fire you and I have reason for it. I could bench you or suspend you and I have damned good reason for such actions. Instead I'm talking to you. I'm telling you to quit being a goof. You weren't until this year. Even if this ball club isn't going anywhere this season, you can be going somewhere, much farther than you've gone."

I was too much in awe to speak right away. And I was now feeling pretty rotten. "Yeah," I said, thinking.

I remembered how I had often wished it were back in 1919 before the first discussion of the World Series fix and that something had happened so that there never had been a beginning to it. I remembered things I'd heard in grammar school and high school. I thought of how I had loved to play ball since I was about seven years old.

"Yeah, Eddie, I was more than a goof. I've been a goddamn fool. Hell, thanks for talking to me like this. It's been like a father talking to me."

"All right, let's see what you can do."

As I left the office, he gave me a slap on the behind. That helped straighten me out.

I remember the next Saturday night, I said, "Dear, let's go to confession."

Mary was quite surprised, because I'd fallen into the habit of making my Easter Duty and going to confession on Christmas Eve. She guessed, too, but said nothing. And then I felt that lift and freedom like I was almost walking on air, and I straightened myself out pretty well. I might have backslid now and then, but it was only now and then. I stopped sowing wild oats like a goof.

I often thought of that talk with Eddie Collins. And it helped me in many ways, especially since I got back into baseball as a scout. And I thought of what he said of Joe Jackson and Buck. Buck was loyal to his friends when they were wrong. At least I would like to think he was. Cicotte said that he wanted more than $5,000, and there was that story of the package delivered by Fred McMullen. But there was what Jack Fourier told me, and so I think that Buck went along and didn't think of his own interest when he should have. And I thought of Jackson.

Eddie spoke of being mature. He meant to grow up and act your age. I thought I had and that talk made me realize I hadn't fully done that.

And that talk gave me an idea. Why couldn't I be a manager someday? I hadn't thought very much of that angle before. I began thinking a lot of it after that. The ambition to become a manager was planted in me.

I don't know for sure, but I think my goofing around might have hurt me with the Old Roman. Because while he didn't like to give me a big salary no more than he did his right arm, he had seemed to be warm in his feeling toward me and he'd stop and talk to me. And Ma Kelly told me he liked me. He knew about my wild oats. He knew about his ball club, which is another reason why I would sometimes puzzle about 1919 and wonder why he didn't step in. Anyway, it might be because of that year and my hell-raising that I didn't get to manage the club. I don't know if it's so but I have often speculated about it.

IV

After the 1926 season there was a near-scandal in baseball. The pitcher, Dutch Leonard, and he was a good one, started it by producing a letter of Ty Cobb's concerning Cobb and Speaker betting. It looked bad for them in the newspapers, but they were cleared. And that brought some charges from Gandil. I hadn't heard about him for a long time. He charged in an interview that the White Sox had made up a pot to pay Detroit pitchers for letting the club win a series in 1917, and he involved all of the players on the club and Clarence Rowland, the manager.

The players denied it and said that the pot was made up to reward the Detroit pitchers for beating Boston in a series. The Red Sox were the contenders with the White Sox that year. The judge who was baseball commissioner held a hearing and Gandil testified and then Risberg. Risberg had been working on a farm in Minnesota or somewhere around Minnesota. It's not big league territory and I don't know that part of America well. The big fellow said he was too muscle-bound to play any more baseball.

About twenty-five or thirty players and former players testified at the hearings, Detroit and White Sox players of 1917 and others. None of them gave any evidence to support what Gandil and Risberg said. Also they charged that Detroit had thrown a series to us in early September of 1919. I remember those games and Detroit played rotten baseball. Our players ran wild on the bases but I never thought there was any dirty work.

The players got sore and called Gandil a liar, and Eddie Collins showed a checkbook stub about his check, which he hadn't at first wanted to give. That helped vindicate the players.

And Risberg said that during the grand jury investigation of 1920, he met Clarence Rowland on the street and Clarence said, "I hope they don't bring up that 1917 Detroit series."

Rowland got sore and called this a lie. And the Old Judge vindicated the players, and Risberg and Gandil left Chicago with no one believing them.

Buck testified, and he didn't support Gandil and Risberg. He had a broken wrist at the time and wasn't with the club, but he had given a valise to his friend on the Tigers, Lester Tapp. But they were friends from Buck's days in the Pacific Coast League and Buck used to go hunting with Lester and stay at his cabin. They were real good friends. Buck told the newspapers he expected to be reinstated and he asked the Old Judge for reinstatement at the end of the hearings.

"Write me a letter," the Old Judge said.

I mention all of this, but the money involved in all of this was small potatoes. A suit of clothes or $100 went to some of the Detroit pitchers and a catcher. That used to be done the same as the players used to trade hits, especially when the results of games toward the end of a season didn't affect the standings. I never traded hits and there's no good purpose served in my naming those who did, but I could name them. I went down around the hearings and saw some of the players. I saw Buck and we had a talk over a cup of coffee. This was a little bit unusual because Buck avoided being seen in restaurants with ballplayers. He did this even more so when he got older. He was ashamed, I believe, or he would get embarrassed if strangers recognized him and came up and talked to him.

He was thirty-six then, and had looked in good shape and was at about his old playing weight.

"Yes, he says, 'Write me a letter.' I'll write him a letter. Then I suppose I'll be asked to go see him in his office. So I'll do that. And he'll put his jar in front of me and say 'Have a chew of tobacco, Buck.' And I'll have a chew of tobacco. I been to see him and that's what happened."

"Well, maybe he'll be different this time, Buck."

"John McGraw wanted me to play with him. He would have given me more than I ever made with the White Sox. But I couldn't get my reinstatement. Goddamn it, kid, if I'm good enough for John McGraw I ought to be good enough and honest enough for that sour-faced Old Judge. He can't refuse me now. I wasn't accused of no more, not one goddamn thing more, than all them fellows were, and there was no evidence against me. Why in hell ain't I as good as Eddie Collins?"

I didn't know what to say to Buck. It wasn't up to me, and so far as I was concerned, we still could have used him.

"I want to go back to playing my old position, center field. I played center field in my first game in the Pacific Coast League."

Then we talked baseball and Buck got excited. But I could see how he had missed playing ball all those years, six of them. He was hurt, and bitter, too.

"Why do I get life?" he asked, coming back to his own case.

"I don't know, Buck. I don't know any players who aren't for you."

"I know the ballplayers, yes, but it's the bastards on top. He had to give me my salary and I was acquitted, wasn't I? What are our courts for? The judge says he'll not allow me to be convicted because there's no evidence. He advises me to separate my case from the others, but I don't because they tell me it will jeopardize the other fellows.

"Why, goddamn it, what can I tell them? When I saw the Old Judge he told me to tell him. But what can I tell him? That's what I say, I say 'Judge, I ain't got nothin' to tell you.' What am I gonna do, be a goof? Look at Risberg and Gandil. They talk and what are they now? They're goofs. I'm going to fight. I have a right to be reinstated. That's my bread and butter."

I wished strongly that he would be reinstated after sitting with him and talking like we did. But what was I to do? I was only a player and I couldn't have said anything. If I should have said something in public, where would I have been? And I believe most of the players would have been glad to see Buck reinstated.

I asked Buck what he was doing.

"I'm getting' by. I'm going to manage a team and play with it up in Wisconsin, that's if I don't get my reinstatement."

That's about all he was doing, getting by. He'd had another job and he'd played ball wherever he could, and for all those years, he'd been hoping for and trying to get his reinstatement. I thought maybe he could play a year or two or a couple of years if he did get back, but he couldn't be the same player. He'd lost his best years just when he was at his peak.

He was nervous, too, and finally left. He wished me luck and was glad that I had developed so well. "But get what you can, kid," he advised me. Then, he had a puzzled look on his face. "I mean honestly," he said. He shook hands with me and left.

Hell, I thought, it had been tough on Buck. But I also thought that he wouldn't be able to get back. And so, I guess he'd have some tough, sad years ahead of him.

V

Before those hearings, Eddie had resigned as manager and Ray had been appointed his successor. Only him, Red, Bibb Falk, and I were left of the 1919–20 ball club. Bibb had been a rookie and had become a good hitting outfielder. Dick Kerr had held out, like I said, after the 1921 season, and the Old Roman let him go. That was a raw thing, and Dick wasn't making much money, no more than $400 a month at most. He was a damned good little pitcher. He was out three seasons and tried a comeback in 1925 but he had lost his stuff.

Eddie went back to Connie Mack, and he was the only other member from 1919–20 still actively playing major league ball. And Ray was getting near his end. Eddie had slowed up but he stayed on the active list for about four more years. But a number of the veterans had gone or were on their way out.

It was time for me to blossom out. And I had a couple of good years. That's how I got salary raises. I hit .330 and .344, and when it looked sure that Ray was on the skids as manager, I began to hope that I would become his successor. I was pretty dumb about it because I didn't do anything. I didn't try to get it by asking or hinting or maybe trying to get one of the baseball writers to write something about me as a possible or potential manager. I just hoped to be named, and when Ray was dropped, I was more disappointed than I had a right to be.

In 1929, I began to slip, and I hurt my knee sliding into third in a game in St. Louis. The next year, I slipped and hit only .240, and my knee was gone. I went to spring training in 1931 and wrenched my knee again. I got my unconditional release with no ceremony at all.

That was a black day. It was much worse, of course, than any of the days during the scandal or the 1919 World Series.

It was my worst day in baseball. My knee was swollen. I couldn't get on with any other ball club until it got better. I went home to rest it. It seemed all right about June, and the team was one of the worst of all since 1920. It was a last-place team. I asked the Old Roman to take me back and he did, but with my salary cut down to $5,000. I hit .220 and was slowing up.

I got my unconditional release at the end of the season and no major league club wanted me. I was finished. I could have played minor league ball but I had no heart for it. So my baseball career was over. I was thirty-one. I had had all I dreamed of and wished for as a boy. And it was gone. It seemed so short to me. It couldn't have been thirteen years.

I had reached my height and that had been far below my dreams and expectations. I felt that I had failed. It was an awful feeling and I almost became an alcoholic. And that was during the Depression. Jack Collins lost most of his money and then he died of a heart attack. A political job saved us. And since then, the years have gone fast, so fast that I don't know where they went to.

I already have told about what it's like right after you retire and the next season's spring training starts. It was awful, and then, gradually I got used to my new life. I played about four or five years of semipro ball, playing with the Morgan Aces along with Buck. We were an old man's keystone combination, but Buck was still pretty good, better than me, although I was pretty fair as an aging semipro.

Buck was getting more bitter in those days. It was too late for him ever to play again in the big leagues but he thought that he could be a coach or a scout. He still played a fair game of semipro ball, although he was nothing of what he used to be. Some thousands of fans had signed a petition asking for his reinstatement and he had applied for it again and maybe more than once, but the ban on him stuck and for good. When he was too old to play any more ball, he managed a girl's baseball team for a year but he couldn't have made much money at it. And then he got work at a pari-mutuel window at the race track.

The war came and time just slipped by on all of us. I don't know how the last fifteen or sixteen years have gone by, and I don't remember too clearly what happened in them. One day passed into the next until suddenly you realized that you are starting to get old. Why, 1919 and 1920 seem so far away, and still there are many times that they seem to me like yesterday.

And that 1919 Series now doesn't seem so important as it was then, and few of the writers who saw those games are even around. Why, there are now a lot of writers who never saw me play. But 1919 did affect us. It made my career different. I would have played on better ball clubs and made more money, and maybe I would have stayed in the game after my playing days were so suddenly over.

Hell, I would have maybe hit better, because you got a better chance when you're in the lineup with a gang of hitters. If I had had Joe Jackson and Happy Felsch and Buck in the lineup with me in 1921 and 1922 and 1923, I couldn't have missed hitting better and having a higher average. And if I had played on a team up there at the top, I'd have gotten more attention and publicity. Like I say, I'm not complaining or eating my sour grapes on State and Madison in the rush hour, but what I say is obvious enough and it's true.

Or if I had been traded, that might have been a good thing for me. Because I was associated with that 1919–20 ball club it cast shadows over me. Some of the fans would come to the ball game and watch us and think of the players who were out.

"You know, Mick, when I go the ball game now, I look at you fellows and I can't help but think of them other fellows, and I think, 'Now, what would happen if old Shoeless Joe Jackson was stepping up there to the plate with that black bat of his, Black Betty?' And I ask myself, 'Now suppose Buck Weaver was out there, and the rest of 'em, what would this team look like?'"

Hell, I played some games at third base in those years and I'd catch myself thinking that I was playing Buck's old position. Then I'd say to hell with that gang, Mickey Donovan's playing here now. My playing wasn't affected, I'm certain of that. But you were playing ball in shadows, and with the teams we played, you had to keep fighting just to be fighting. It was different in games like that one when we beat the Yankees and Eddie Cicotte pitched against Babe Ruth for the last time. It was electric that day. Few games were really electric after 1920. A lot of ballplayers never played in a World Series. Look at Sisler and Lajoie. They're in the Hall of Fame. And Harry Heilmann. But a hitter like myself, well, I'd have seemed better with a good ball club. I somehow sort of think I'd have lasted longer, too.

I tried not to let all this gnaw at me, and I do now because, hell, it's too late, and, all things considered, life and baseball have been good to me. But I can't help thinking of it and I couldn't help having thoughts like these when I was playing. I'd walk out on the field, maybe on a day when I knew there would be hardly anybody in the stands, and I'd wonder what it would have been like if that Series hadn't been crooked.

I didn't like to think of that. As I said, I wanted to forget it. I wanted to forget it for other reasons, too, because it was just an unhappy memory. That was the worst thing that ever happened to baseball. I never liked to talk about it with others, especially with people who weren't in baseball. It brought everything back, and made me wish it had never happened, and made me think of how things would have been different but for it, and of how we felt, and it just was a hell of a thing to remember. Why torment yourself with unhappy memories? But like I have already said and have often said, it comes up every now and then, and you felt something like a stab of pain.

None of the players connected with it ever tried to make any money by signing their names to articles in the magazines telling the inside story of it, except that Gandil gave an interview not long after Buck was dead. He was bitter and said they were all in it, and Buck was and that when Buck first heard of the plan he said to get the money and double-cross the gamblers, and he wanted more money than was being offered. Buck was dead and couldn't answer, and I know me and Ray and a lot of others were sore at Gandil.

I remember when the first players were installed in the Hall of Fame I thought of Buck. I told myself he would have someday been eligible for it if he got reinstated. And Joe Jackson might have been one of the first to be elected. And Eddie Cicotte and Lefty Williams and maybe Happy Felsch all might have been there in Cooperstown along with Eddie Collins and Ray Schalk and the other baseball greats. That's what they gave up without understanding it or caring at the time, their immortality.

And maybe I shouldn't admit this but I am. I was as disappointed as I was glad about the Hall of Fame. It was a natural and every fan carried around his own private hall of fame in his memories, and the baseball writers used to write about "the mythical Hall of Fame" way back even before I broke in. And that's what I dreamed of, the Hall of Fame. And when it was established, I knew that Mickey Donovan would never be elected to it. I wasn't good enough. I guess I wouldn't have been good enough even if I had been on a succession of championship ball clubs.

It was a bitter pill for me to swallow even though I never told this to a soul, not even to Mary. I brooded by myself and I got drunk and sat in my home, drinking beer and brooding, and with my head full of beer. I blamed those fellows and cursed them out and wondered why I hadn't punched some of them on the nose. I got over that, and now I'm resigned. I had hoped one of my sons would have become a ballplayer, but they want no part of the game and they long ago became tired even of hearing me talk about baseball.

It was 1938 that the first five members—Ty Cobb, Babe Ruth, Christy Mathewson, Honus Wagner, and Walter Johnson—were elected. Sometimes I've thought I was as good as Maranville or would have been if I had lasted as long, or as Tinker or Evers. And if there hadn't been the scandal, I might have played on an infield combination with Eddie Collins and Buck and maybe some great first baseman the club might have acquired, but there's no use in thinking of this now.

But the Hall of Fame must have added to Buck's torment because he knew he was eligible if he only got reinstated. Around that time he made still another try at reinstatement and was turned down again. It was always for the same reason. He had "guilty knowledge," the Old Judge told him. Everybody had some guilty knowledge from that first game on and was afraid to say anything in public and was paralyzed, and we were all a little like Buck, even the Old Roman.

Buck, as he got older, became bitter and cynical. He didn't go to any old-timers meetings or dinners, and he avoided most people in the sports world and newspapermen. That was not like him, because he was gregarious and friendly. He was obviously ashamed and embarrassed.

We formed a little organization to help old-timers in a quiet way, Ray and Red and a lot of old-timers, and Buck's best friend, Marty Bleeker, who owns a tavern and has been a baseball fan all of his life. One of the members is Bill Stanton, who tried out with me in 1918 and got the gob of tobacco juice in his face. Bill became a baseball statistician. Well, anyway, there was a proposal for us all to go on record as appealing to the baseball commissioner to reinstate Buck. That was about 1950 or 1951 or sometime in there. But there was still opposition. Marty loved him and talked of what a swell fellow he was and how we knew he was a great glove man and what it would mean to Buck if his name was cleared. That's all Buck wanted, to have his name cleared and to take care of his wife, who was crippled.

I didn't think much about it, and I suppose I would have gone along with this idea, but Stanton suggested that we find out more about it before we took any such step. After all, we had members who were old ballplayers and some of them would one day be in the Hall of Fame where they belonged, and we could offend the powers that be without very good cause. We ought to find out about it before we did anything that went to the office of the baseball commissioner and got into the newspapers.

"That's the only sensible thing we can do. I don't want to do anything to hurt Buck Weaver, but on something like this, we got to find out what the score is," Bill Stanton said, getting up and addressing his remark toward Ray, who was in the chair, since he was president of our organization. Ray was wearing a gray suit, and he was, of course, gray-haired. For some years he'd worn glasses. His face was quite round and his cheeks were full, and he had quite a bit of width and girth.

I looked at him for a few moments and I remembered Ray when he had been with the White Sox and was considered by a lot of people as the greatest living catcher. He had been so slim, weighing 150 or 155 pounds at the most, and he'd looked so young. Even at about thirty he looked like he might just have passed twenty-one.

And others in the room, they were old and looked it. Red was sitting near me, and he's gray, but he's in good shape and is erect. You'd have taken him maybe for sixty instead of sixty-seven or sixty-eight. He sat with Walt Hunt, who had been let go just before I reported from San Francisco in 1919. Walt was another big fellow, but he was fading, and you could see that he was. His hair, what little he had of it, was turning white and he was thin and didn't have much strength. Hell, when I was a kid just starting in high school back in 1914, Walt was a big, strong young pitcher. And there he was with not much more time to spare. Walt was up there in his last innings. But we were all getting into our last innings, I thought.

Like I said, the question had come up as to our appealing to the baseball commissioner to reinstate Buck, and Bill Stanton had suggested that we ought to find out the score before we took any action. That seemed to be sensible to me, too.

Big Marty Bleeker got up. He's fat and has a rough, loud voice and a heart of gold. "What the hell, we have Buck's old teammates here, and they can tell us the score because they know it. They were all around then, Ray, Red, and Walt over there and Mickey Clover Donovan."

I just knew that Ray, standing at the table up front, didn't like what Denny said. After all, I played on the same ball club with Ray for a number of years, over ten.

"I've said and I say it again that I'm in Buck's corner. Every man here knows that. But I have nothing more to say than that. Those fellows suffered the tortures of hell and I won't say anything to make them suffer any more. I'm not going to say any man was guilty or not guilty in that Series. That's all I got to say. I won't get involved in no discussions pro or con about those games."

At first, I thought that Ray was letting Buck down, and then I suddenly realized that I felt just about the same as Ray did. I didn't want to get myself involved either so that I'd be way over my head. I wanted Buck to get his vindication, and I couldn't see then, no more than I can now, how it would hurt baseball any if Buck had gotten his reinstatement, or even if he was to get it now, posthumously. But we were only old baseball people with a few, like Marty, who were fans, and we weren't official in any way. I didn't know if it was right or a good thing if we were to go sending appeals to the baseball commissioner saying that Buck Weaver had been innocent.

Walt Hunt stood up and spoke in an old man's voice, "Ray, I don't know about all this. No, Old Walt don't know. He ain't sure. I wasn't there at the end of that season, only the beginning. Old Walt was too old to finish that season with the White Sox. He was let out. And Buck Weaver—and Ray, you know this, and maybe young Donovan over there knows it—Buck Weaver took charge of the meetin' when the players voted shares of the World Series money. All they gave Old Walt was $750. They could have given Old Walt more. Old Walt was with the White Sox before any of them players, even Ray here, except Shano. Old Walt joined the White Sox in 1911 when Buck Weaver was still in the Pacific Coast League. They could have given Old Walt a better share, but it was Buck Weaver who stopped them. I was there that day and waiting while the meeting was held, and then I went into that clubhouse and I knew, I knew just as sure as I know I'm Old Walt, that it was Buck Weaver who had seen to it that Old Walt, was not given a better and fairer share of the World Series money. There you are. I don't know about Buck Weaver."

Walt sat down, tired and breathing heavily, and nobody could think of anything to say for maybe a minute or two. What Old Walt had to say kind of took us aback because he had said it with spirit and he meant it. Of course his words had no bearing on what we were discussing, but none of us would have gotten up and said that out of deference to Old Walt because he was really pathetic. He was feeble, and hearing him talk with his voice cracking, you just knew that you weren't going to be seeing much more of him.

Then Red got up. "Heck, I don't remember that. Son of a gun if it ain't gone clean out of my mind. I can't say anything against Buck in that Series as I can remember it, sitting there on the bench. I don't know that there's anything we can do to help him. If we do send a letter to the office of the baseball commissioner, they'll put it in the file and that's about all that will happen to it."

Bill Stanton said that he would get some information to give us the score. All Bill got was a story about Buck giving a Gladstone bag to Lester Tapp, Detroit Tiger third baseman, but they were good friends. But anyway, our little organization never did anything about Buck.

It was because of this that Marty Bleeker held a Buck Weaver Night in his tavern. There's nothing fancy about Marty's tavern. It's just a corner tavern, that's all, and fellows go there for their beer and stronger liquor and to talk. They're rabid about baseball and talk baseball a lot. Marty is always pulling out the baseball encyclopedia to settle some question or argument. Almost all of those who go there know one another and they all look up to Big Marty. They don't much take to strangers, though.

I like to stop out there now and then to see Big Marty. He's just a grand guy with a big warm heart. Marty organized a collection to give a pot to Buck and newspaper people came out that night. I went, and so did Ray, and Red and Old Walt came. The tavern was crowded, and pictures were taken. Big Marty and Ray and the rest of us said a few words, praising Buck and saying that we were in his corner. Buck didn't show any emotion but he liked it very much. It warmed his heart, and meant a hell of a lot to him.

Buck was thinner and gray. He didn't look too well. Others besides myself noticed this and commented on it.

"They'll never do anything," Buck said. "The Old Judge wanted me to tell him something I didn't know. I can't accuse you and it comes back on me, and then what am I? I'm a goddamned goof. That makes sense to me. I didn't have any evidence to give. I can't give what I ain't got.

"All we got is our judges and juries, and if they acquit a man, that's enough to go by. And they even pardon or parole murderers. But I got life.

"All I did in that Series was field 1.000 and I hit something like .336. I'd have hit .600 if I had any luck. There wasn't a game that they didn't spear one or two line drives. I says the only thing we got left in the world is our judges and our jurors. I was acquitted in court. The judge even wanted to throw my case out.

"I sent a letter to the commissioner. I say the Old Roman settled for my 1921 contract. But that shows that they're wrong and I'm right. But still they paid it and I can't do nothin' about it. I never threw a ball game in my life."

That's the way he talked, and that's just about all he had to say on the Series.

But fellows kept crowding around him and shaking his hand, praising him and telling him how happy they were to see him and asking for his autograph. Buck was sort of embarrassed and a little overwhelmed.

Most of the crowd, there except for those of us who'd been in baseball and the reporters, were fans and fellows in that neighborhood. They were just ordinary fellows, working men, fellows who came to Marty's tavern for a few glasses of beer and some talk. And they all meant it when they said to Buck that they wanted to see him reinstated and that they remembered him as a player and that he had been the greatest third baseman who ever wore a glove.

"Buck, it's an honor to shake your hand. I'm Pat Cline."

"Hello, Pat."

"I saw you play. There's never been another like you."

"Thanks, Pat."

"But Buck, man, you're not drinking. Hey Marty! Marty, what the hell kind of a shindig is this when the guest of honor doesn't get a drink? Buck, man, let me get you a drink."

"What did you say, Pat?" Marty called in his booming voice.

"No, no, no, I don't want one," Buck said.

"Why, man? Buck, this is your night."

"I don't drink," Buck said.

"Say, you're Donovan, ain't you?"

"Yes."

"Mickey Donovan, Clover Donovan, well, I'm glad to shake the hand of another great old-timer. I'm Pat Cline."

We shook hands. "Thanks, Pat."

"Buck Weaver, Clover Donovan, Ray Schalk—who would ever have thought that I'd ever be standing talking to them right to their face, just like this?"

"Congratulations, Buck," an old man said.

"We owe this to Marty Bleeker. Marty's a grand guy. The greatest guy I ever knew," Pat Cline said.

Others crowded around Buck. "We're cheering for you, Buck."

"Thanks, fellows," Buck said.

"If it was up to us, there'd be no question about you, Buck. You're our boy, Buck."

They milled around and talked, and Marty's voice would boom out. "Buck Weaver is the grandest guy and the best glove man who ever played third base. Go and shake hands with him, Long, don't be bashful."

I had a few words with him in a corner. "You're looking pretty good, Buck."

"Me, I'm in good shape. I'm the same weight as when I was playing."

"Are you going to be working out at the racetrack again, Buck?"

"Yeah, I'll be back there at one of them windows. You still got the same job, Mick?"

"Yeah."

"Things goin' okay, kid?"

"Yeah, pretty good. Say, Buck, why don't you come and have dinner with us some night."

"No, Mick, but thanks. I go home every night to take care of my wife. She's sick. She had a stroke. I take care of her. But she was a good hairpin."

Ray joined us. Buck smiled kind of sheepishly at Ray.

"This is a nice night for you, Buck."

"Yeah, it's okay."

"Look at 'em. There was a lot of baseball value," Marty said.

"Not in the game today. We wouldn't fit up there now, Marty," Ray said.

"You two guys would fit up there any goddamned time. And so would Clover."

"All they think about today is money. We had three Cubs out to make a personal appearance for some Little League kids and their parents. We were doing it for baseball. But every damned one of them, do you know what he asked for? A hundred dollars. For kids. It wasn't like that in my day. Was it, Buck?"

"Goddamn right it wasn't."

"We went out and spoke if we were told," Ray said.

"I see the ball games now and then on the television. I see the night games. Jesus Christ, them announcers say, 'Now here is a slugger, battin' average .229.'"

They burst out laughing.

"Hell, I could hit .229," Ray said.

A crowd of course gathered around and listened. Some of those fellows hung on every word. We talked baseball. The name of Ty Cobb came up.

"He liked you. You were his boy, Buck," Ray said.

"There'll never be another like him. But I told him, 'bunt on me and I'll throw you out.' I could pick up the ball and throw it without bending down."

"He didn't bunt on you, Buck."

"He better not have. But he wasn't dirty. All them goddamn things they write about him. Take Baker." Buck was referring to an incident when Cobb spiked Home Run Baker, and there was a lot of criticism of him. That was long before my time, but I'd read about it.

"Say, for Christ's sake, I got it right here in the book. Baker wasn't hurt. Look at the games he played in every year. He wasn't badly hurt by Cobb," Marty said.

"That's true," Ray said.

"Baker is slow. And I always say that base line belongs to the runner. That base line belongs to the runner, and if you are in his way and you get spiked, you damn well deserve it. I'd take the ball and I'd spread my legs." Buck showed how he used to tag a runner spreading his legs out sidewise as he bent down.

"That's where I learned how to tag a runner, Buck, from you," I said.

"Yeah, kid. Baker was slow and he was in the base line," Buck said.

"Look at them, couldn't the White Sox use 'em today. Hell, they'd give this town a team that'd whip the Yankees and Casey Stengel," Marty said.

We were all enjoying it very much, and Buck was spirited, his old-time self. That dispirit of his was gone. I looked at him and Ray and Red and I told myself that all of those years couldn't have gone by. For a minute I had the strange feeling that they hadn't gone and that all of us would be going to the White Sox ballpark the next morning and putting on our suits to go out for morning practice.

Walt Hunt joined us. "Buck, I was telling a fellow I beat you and Ray to the White Sox by one year, 1911."

"I was just a kid in grammar school then," I said.

"Yes, Old Walt pitched for the White Sox in 1911. I won three and lost two. Buck, Old Walt hasn't seen you in years."

"I know, Walt. You're looking good."

"No, Old Walt's pitchin' his last innin', his last innin'."

"For Christ sake, Walt, you'll bury all of us," Marty said.

"I lost Walt some ball games when I first came from the Pacific Coast League, a busher. Jesus Christ, I don't know what was the matter with me. But put me at shortstop, and I'd throw that friggin' ball. Christ, I don't know what it was," Buck said. He was referring to how in his early years he made many wild throws from shortstop.

"There's the man who made the wild throws," Ray said, pointing to Lefty Sullivan, who had also shown up for Buck's night.

"I threw myself from the White Sox into semipro baseball," Lefty said.

That night was real good. And it was for Buck's morale. But it was pathetic. It was pitiful. Because you could see how hurt Buck was. He was hurt right clean through. He never would have come except that it was Marty who arranged it. And Marty got up $1,000 for the purse. That must have helped Buck, because he only got along.

I heard Marty Bleeker say to Buck, just before it ended, "We'll do something about you yet, Buck."

"I can't do nothin' about it, Marty," Buck said bitterly.

That was the last time I saw Buck. And it was his only public appearance in years. Buck used to go to a saloon over at 63rd or 64th and Cottage Grove every day and he'd sit in the back room and play pinochle with his cronies. He stayed home with his wife almost every night, taking care of her. She was all crippled up with arthritis. He made enough in the racing season to support the two of them. He was a broken man. He was haunted by his fate. Ray was 100 percent— 1000 percent right when he said, "Those men suffered the tortures of hell."

As I said, I never saw any of the others. Fred McMullen died about 1951. He was the paradox in that whole chapter. Fred was asleep in the clubhouse one day and he woke up, hearing Risberg and Gandil talking about how they could work a fix and clean up on it. He demanded in on it and he was let in and out. Joe Jackson tried to get reinstated in the 1930s in order to manage his hometown team down in South Carolina, and the citizens of his hometown all appealed to the Old Judge, but Joe didn't get nowhere on that. He interested himself in Boy Scouts and kids playing baseball, or so I was told.

Happy Felsch runs a saloon in Milwaukee and I always have thought I'd go in and see him sometime when I drove up to Milwaukee to see one of the Milwaukee Braves games. Eddie Cicotte, like I said, is in Detroit. I read he was retired and living on a little farm with him and his wife getting old-age pensions. There was a young reporter from Chicago named Benton who saw him somewhere about ten, twelve years ago when he was a plant guard for an auto company.

"Mick," Benton said, "that Cicotte was funny. Do you know he's sore as hell at baseball. He didn't say one word about the crooked World Series. He said he won 211 games and he's sore that they haven't put him in the Hall of Fame."

And Lefty Williams is somewhere around Chicago, working at one job or another, but nobody has seen him. A couple of years ago, two kids were bumming a ride on a Sunday afternoon up in Michigan. They were in baseball uniforms, and an old fellow picked them up. They were going home five miles away.

He asked them, "Are one of you fellows a pitcher?"

One of them said that he pitched.

"I used to be a pitcher," the old fellow said.

The kids thought that he was just some old duffer who had maybe pitched for one of the small towns in that region a long time ago, before they were even born.

"How'd you throw a curve?" the old fellow asked.

The young kid showed him.

"Got a ball?" the old fellow asked. The young fellow handed him a ball. The old fellow gripped it with his two fingers bent and his thumb and said, "I threw it this way."

The two kids got interested. "Where did you pitch?" one of them asked.

"Oh, I pitched in the American League."

"What team did you pitch for?"

"Chicago."

"Say, what's your name?"

"My name's Williams."

Lefty Williams would have been just about the greatest of all the south-paws except maybe Rube Waddell and Eddie Plant and Lefty Grove.

Stanton, I might add, told me that story.

The whole story will never be known. Some of it is lost in the grave. That's where it belongs. Some baseball people think those fellows got what they deserved. Don Blake, the best manager in the National League and one hell of a guy, was asking me about the 1919 Series about two years ago. I said those fellows suffered a lot.

"Hell, Donovan, they were thieves," he said.

Well, plenty worse has been done in the world than they did. And the gamblers who bought them didn't pay any price. But the more I think of that Series, I just can't figure out why the Old Roman and the Little Skipper just didn't move in and break it up after that first game. Maybe the whole situation could have been saved if they had. But just think, I had been a kid, dreaming baseball like any American kid. And then, and mainly because of the war, I broke in young. I would have broken in anyway but maybe not as fast. And I was on the ball club with all those players who were heroes of my boyhood. And that's what they did. And what they did changed my whole baseball career. But I want to forget it.

Thirty-seven years have gone into the record books since then. I was down in the front office at the ballpark yesterday, and the Old

Roman's grandson, Billy Comisky, happened to say, "I wasn't born then. I don't know anything about it. My grandfather ran this ball club his way. Now, I want to run it mine. I just want to take care of my kids and have them grow up good Americans and I want a world championship team."

Billy is only twenty-nine. It's all different now. And those days are gone. But it's like that ballpark is full of ghosts. And it's not only the ghosts of those players who are gone from the scene of baseball and some of them from the scene of life. It's also the ghosts of my own dreams.

And every day I'm working, looking at kids, those ghosts and those dreams are with me. And I'm hoping that on that day I'll find a kid, a prospect who will make good and help make the team that will drive away those ghosts, a ball club that will be greater than my old ball club of 1919 and 1920. And I think, too, I'll find a kid who will do what I wanted to do and never did, become the great star I never became, a kid who will be in the annals of baseball where Ray and Eddie and the immortal greats are—in the Hall of Fame at Cooperstown.

That's what my life has been and that's what my life is—it's just dreaming baseball.

AFTERWORD:
JAMES T. FARRELL AND
THE BLACK SOX
Ron Briley

Unlike many fans of James T. Farrell, I did not initially encounter the novelist through his Studs Lonigan trilogy. Instead, I discovered Farrell's *My Baseball Diary* in 1959, when the Chicago White Sox appeared in the World Series. While I was a young fan of the "Go-Go White Sox," Farrell opened my eyes to the players of an earlier era. Although a serious novelist, Farrell never apologized for his boyish love of baseball. As he wrote in his Introduction to *My Baseball Diary*, "I have always loved the game. I don't care whether it is childish. Long before I possessed any capacity to examine myself or the reasons for the game's appeal to me, I loved it."

With *My Baseball Diary*, Farrell was returning to his boyhood love for baseball during a troubled time in his life and career. During the 1920s and 1930s, Farrell was disillusioned with the United States and moved to the far political Left. Later, during the early years of the Cold War, Farrell rejected Marxism and embraced the anticommunism of the American Committee for Cultural Freedom. This political transformation led many former associates to denounce and ostracize him. In response, Farrell produced his Bernard Carr trilogy, about a writer attempting to break with his radical past. The Carr novels were a critical and commercial failure for Farrell, who was increasingly in difficult financial straits following the collapse of his marriage in 1957.[1]

In addition, his relationship with his longtime publisher, Vanguard Press, was troubled after James Henle sold the firm to Evelyn Shrifte, whom Farrell distrusted. Accordingly, Farrell asked Vanguard to release him from his contract so he might place two baseball books with

A. S. Barnes, who published numerous sports titles. Vanguard agreed
and allowed Farrell to pursue the baseball deal with Barnes.

The first book, *My Baseball Diary*, was published by Barnes in
late 1957. The volume included interviews with players, pieces of
sports journalism, excerpts from novels, and personal reminiscences
of Farrell's youth in Chicago, spent attending White Sox games and
playing baseball in Washington Park. Farrell had great expectations
for this nostalgic volume, but problems arose when he inadvertently
libeled a former American League umpire, provoking the threat of legal
action against Barnes and limiting distribution of the book. Despite
these problems and a change in ownership at Barnes, the publisher
continued to express interest in the second book, a baseball novel about
the infamous Chicago Black Sox.[2]

By May 1958 Farrell had completed a second draft, a substantially
shortened version, of the manuscript and delivered it to Barnes. Publisher John Lowell Pratt was disappointed with the story and said that
the novel's world seemed two-dimensional. Farrell asked to be released
from his contract with Barnes and attempted to place the book with
Vanguard. His old friend Henle found the baseball novel promising
but was not ready to issue a contract. Farrell needed money though,
and he was losing interest in the project. *My Baseball Diary* had not
sold well, and he felt he needed a serious work to bolster his literary
reputation.[3]

It is surprising, however, that Farrell never completed and published
the baseball novel, for he made the Black Sox scandal of 1919 the focal
point of his baseball fiction. As was made evident in *My Baseball Diary*, the fixing of the 1919 World Series was a disillusioning experience
for the young Farrell, who grew up idolizing the Chicago White Sox,
the World Series champions of 1917. Farrell did not seem to question
that the accused White Sox players conspired with gamblers to lose
the 1919 World Series to the underdog Cincinnati Reds. Ironically, the
players were acquitted in a 1921 jury trial, but the newly appointed
commissioner of baseball, Kenesaw Mountain Landis, banned the players for life. Farrell did not debate their innocence or guilt. Rather, he
saw the entire episode and its aftermath as a tragedy.

Reflecting on the Black Sox in *My Baseball Diary*, Farrell wrote:
"My interest in baseball changed after this. For years, I had no favorite
team. I was growing up, and this marked the end of my days of hero-

worshipping baseball players. Many fans felt betrayed. I didn't. I felt sorry. I wished it weren't true. I wished the players would have been given another chance."[4] Perceiving the Black Sox story as a tragedy, Farrell was unable to muster much enthusiasm for the campaigns to clear the names of Joe Jackson and Buck Weaver. In reviewing Donald Gropman's *Say It Ain't So, Joe!* which made the case that Jackson was not involved with the gambling conspiracy, Farrell expressed some reservations regarding Jackson's innocence, but he concluded that Gropman's book and Jackson's story would "appeal to anyone interested in the human condition and to the reaction of people to their destinies." In a similar vein, when commenting on his last interview with Buck Weaver, his childhood hero, Farrell observed that the White Sox third baseman "was caught in a net of circumstances as are many characters in tragic novels. For to him, baseball was a way of life, and his barring was a supreme defeat."[5]

And, indeed, the Black Sox scandal served as an inspiration for such literary works as F. Scott Fitzgerald's *The Great Gatsby* (1925), Bernard Malamud's *The Natural* (1952), W. P. Kinsella's *Shoeless Joe* (1982), Harry Stein's *Hoopla* (1983), and Brendan Boyd's *Blue Ruin: A Novel of the 1919 World Series* (1991). The story of the 1919 World Series has remained a staple of American literature, according to cultural historian Daniel Nathan, because "how people have thought about and depicted the Black Sox scandal reflects something revealing (and sometimes important) about their identity, their values, and their historical moment."[6]

Although his novel on the Black Sox remained unpublished, Farrell certainly left his mark on how the eight banned White Sox players would be remembered. In the 1960s writer and former baseball player Eliot Asinof decided to pursue the story of the 1919 World Series. His interest was piqued in 1960 by his work on a proposed television drama on the Black Sox, which was opposed by the baseball commissioner, Ford Frick, as being detrimental to the interests of the sport. Asinof, however, continued to pursue the subject, and his labors resulted in *Eight Men Out* (1963), which most scholars perceive as the definitive study of the scandal.

Asinof informed Farrell biographer Robert K. Landers that he considered abandoning his project when he learned that Farrell had prepared a manuscript on the Black Sox. Farrell intervened and encouraged Asinof to continue his research. In fact, he invited Asinof to his New

York apartment and spent several hours sharing his knowledge of Chicago and the Black Sox. Asinof told Landers that Farrell had a phenomenal memory of the 1919 Chicago White Sox and that the novelist was a good friend who read parts of his manuscript and suggested revisions. In his introduction to *Eight Men Out*, Asinof credits Farrell with imparting his valuable insights into the Black Sox: "Above all, he encouraged me to pursue a central theme that gave the work its real reason for being: the story of the 1919 World Series scandal must be centered around the lives of these eight men. Why did they do it? What were the pressures of the baseball world, of America in 1919 itself, that would turn decent, normal, talented men to engage in such betrayal?"

According to Asinof, the actions of the players must be understood within the context of the times. Gambling in baseball was rampant; players were throwing games, and the White Sox players were underpaid and taken advantage of by White Sox owner Charles Comiskey. In fact, Comiskey emerges in Asinof's account as one of the villains for his unfair labor practices. While earlier journalistic histories of the scandal simply blamed crooked players and gamblers for the fix, Asinof presented a more nuanced argument in which the baseball establishment, the judicial system, and media were at least as responsible as the players for the scandal.

The editors traveled very different paths in arriving at *Dreaming Baseball*. I was preparing a paper on Farrell's *My Baseball Diary* for the Farrell Centennial Conference in Paris in the summer of 2005, when Marshall Brooks, the coordinator of the conference, informed me that Farrell had an unpublished baseball novel in the Rare Book and Manuscript Library at the University of Pennsylvania. Nancy Shawcross, the curator of manuscripts, sent me the 650-page copy of the manuscript. I changed the topic of my presentation and talked about the unpublished baseball novel.

My paper was well received. Farrell's son Kevin and Farrell's friend and companion Cleo Paturis, executor of his estate, encouraged me to continue my exploration and study of the manuscript. Also supportive were Farrell scholars Dennis Flynn and Donald Yanella, who play major roles in this story. Shortly after my return from the conference, Dennis Flynn contacted me with the news that Ms. Paturis had given him permission to share with me two other versions of the baseball novel that she had sent to him in the late 1980s.

Meanwhile, Jim Barbour had read about the James T. Farrell Centennial Celebration hosted by the New York City Public Library, chaired by Don Yanella. Jim remembered an evening some twenty-five years prior when he was discussing Melville with Yanella, who shifted gears and said, "I hear you are interested in baseball" and then proceeded to tell him of Farrell's novel of the Black Sox, a book "full of gamblers and smoky dark hotel rooms." Jim decided that now perhaps the time had come to attempt to publish the manuscript. When he contacted Yanella, Don told him that I had the manuscript.

Everything fell in place. Jim and I have known each other for long years through literature and history circles at the University of New Mexico. Jim walked into my office early that summer before the Paris conference, and within fifteen minutes we agreed to work on the manuscript together. Jim's wife, Margaret, joined the enterprise when he took the manuscript home and the editing conversations began. Thus was born *Dreaming Baseball*.

When we began to edit *Dreaming Baseball*, we had three versions of Farrell's novel in our possession. Two of the manuscripts were identified as second drafts (typed at the top of the first page) and were virtually identical but for a few significant differences.

1. The first draft, sent by Dennis Flynn, was some 900 pages in length and has a working title of "Baseball Novel." The principal character in this version is named Mickey Dennison. The story is not a first-person narration. This draft focuses considerable attention on Mickey's courtship of his wife, Mary, and includes more on the White Sox players and gamblers in 1919.

2. The second draft, still designated "Baseball Novel," is 615 pages in length. It was sent to us by the University of Pennsylvania and was the manuscript we primarily used in editing the book (hereafter 2:UPA). The draft contains two chapters designated as "Chapter One": one of these chapters begins with Mickey Donovan as an old scout for the White Sox at a winter instructional camp in Florida; the other begins with Mickey as a young boy in love with baseball and the Sox and follows him around his south Chicago neighborhood.

3. Another second draft, a duplicate of 2:UPA, was again graciously supplied by Dennis Flynn. This draft (hereafter 2:DF) does not include the opening chapter set at the Florida camp. This duplicate manuscript was especially helpful in editing the book, for it is complete and contains the information we found missing from 2:UPA (anywhere from a few missing paragraphs to a four-page gap).

There were three major editorial decisions we made. The first involved the beginning of the book, for Farrell had two Chapter Ones and a Chapter Two that begins very much as one of the Chapter Ones. He clearly had trouble beginning the book. He typed the following note on a sheet attached to the front of one version of Chapter One, dated "Jan. 13/58": "Section three of this chapter goes on too long. It has got to be slashed down, possibly to the bone. I wanted to catch a sense of the two kids as friends, although what they say to each other is commonplace. I can see back to cut this when I get further along. And after I've finished the novel" (2:UPA). Again, on the next page, about Chapter One, Farrell writes, "I am not sure but that the whole or almost all of the first two chapters of the second draft could be cut" and notes that the indications of character could be inserted as he went along (2:UPA).

Farrell did not revise the second draft, but he did write a significantly better opening chapter—one that was probably written later to cure the rather flat beginning—that begins with the older Mickey Donovan, now a scout for the White Sox, watching kids playing a ball game at a baseball camp in Florida. Mickey hears the news that Buck Weaver has died of a heart attack, and his past rushes through his mind, thus introducing readers to the centrality of Buck Weaver in the novel and the importance of innocence as depicted in the enthusiasm of the young men and the game of baseball—the innocence that young men lost in the contaminated environment that surrounded the Black Sox. We chose to begin *Dreaming Baseball* with this, the Florida chapter, and move then to Chapter Two (2:UPA). As Farrell anticipated, Chapter One (2:UPA) was eliminated in favor of the more dramatic and thematic beginning.

Farrell also had not made up his mind about Donovan's diction, whether he speaks correctly, grammatically, or expresses himself in more informal, colloquial street language. At times he offered both styles, one in parentheses. We decided that Donovan should speak correctly. After all, Mickey had graduated from Catholic high school; he had also married an intelligent and educated woman and was concerned with impressing her parents. And Mickey's vocabulary, too, made correct—but never stilted—grammar and diction the better choice.

We also had to decided how to handle the proper names that appeared in the second draft (2:UPA). For the ballplayers, Farrell employed both fictional and historical names, with the historical in parentheses. He also gave fictional names to the reporters who covered the team and to the team officials. For instance, the eight banned players are referred to as Will Wiggins (Joe Jackson), Paul Gilson (Ed Cicotte), Spunk Ellis (Buck Weaver), Hank Dunham (Chick Gandil), Oscar Eckhart (Swede Risberg), Lefty Hilton (Lefty Williams), Frankie Zeller (Happy Felsh), and Danny Connelly (Fred McMullen). Many of these people were still alive in the late 1950s when Farrell was writing the novel, and he was no doubt mindful of the threatened libel suit by the umpire on the publication of *My Baseball Diary*.

We decided that since none of the personalities mentioned in the book are living and since the story Farrell tells is factual, historical, it would have been a mistake not to use the characters' real names. Accordingly, we revisited Asinof's *Eight Men Out* and dug around in old issues of *The Sporting News* and read ancient box scores and kept a baseball encyclopedia at hand in order to establish the identity of the Sox fringe players, the gamblers, and the sportswriters.

Interestingly, there is no direct reference in Farrell's writing to any model for Mickey Donovan, but a good case can be made for Freddie Lindstrom, a boy wonder who came from the sandlots of Chicago.[7] Like Donovan, Lindstrom was the best player in Washington Park. He signed with the New York Giants and came up to the majors at a young age. Like Donovan, he played the infield, and his lifetime batting average is comparable to Donovan's. He, too, was the heir apparent to be manager, but, also like Donovan, he never got the job. But it can also be argued that Donovan is simply the fulfillment of Farrell's youthful ambition: to play second base for the Chicago White Sox.

We were careful to maintain Farrell's wording and phrasing and corrected his spelling only occasionally and deleted very few repetitions. With the novel's readability in mind, however, we did standardize the spelling and regularize the punctuation and usage. This is neither a critical edition nor a facsimile edition of Farrell's work but, rather, a new work of fiction we are introducing to a contemporary audience.

Farrell never chose a title for the novel: he typed simply "Baseball Novel" at the beginning of each draft. *Dreaming Baseball* was our choice. It suggested itself, really. It is a phrase that is repeated throughout the novel to capture the fantasy, longing, and ambition of the players and the game as well as Donovan's own reverie. And suggesting his own title, Farrell ends the book with Donovan ruminating on his life as a scout looking for the kid who will drive away the ghosts of the Black Sox:

> And I think, too, I'll find a kid who will do what I wanted to do and never did, become the great star I never became, a kid who will be in the annals of baseball . . . in the Hall of Fame at Cooperstown. That's what my life has been and that's what my life is—it's just dreaming baseball.

NOTES

1. For an overview of Farrell's work, see Edgar M. Branch, *James T. Farrell* (New York: Twayne, 1971).

2. Robert K. Landers, *An Honest Writer: The Life and Times of James T. Farrell* (San Francisco: Encounter Books, 2004), 357-61.

3. Ibid., 366–74.

4. James T. Farrell, *My Baseball Diary* (New York: A. S. Barnes, 1957; reprint, Carbondale: Southern Illinois Univ. Press, 1998), 108.

5. James T. Farrell, "Replaying the Black Sox Scandal," review of *Say It Ain't So, Joe!: The Story of Shoeless Joe Jackson*, by Donald Gropman, *Chicago Tribune*, Sept. 2, 1979; and Farrell, *My Baseball Diary*, 186.

6. Daniel A. Nathan, *Saying It's So: A Cultural History of the Black Sox Scandal* (Urbana: Univ. of Illinois Press, 2003), 2.

7. Farrell wrote a chapter about Lindstrom in *My Baseball Diary*, "From Washington Park to the Big Leagues" (259–76).

The editors acknowledge the contributions of Donald Yanella,
Dennis Flynn, and Cleo Paturis, whose support helped bring
Dreaming Baseball *to fruition.*

OTHER WORKS BY JAMES T. FARRELL

Studs Lonigan trilogy: *Young Lonigan* (1932), *The Young Manhood of Studs Lonigan* (1934), *Judgment Day* (1935)
Gas-House McGinty (1933)
Calico Shoes (1934)
Guillotine Party and Other Stories (1935)
A Note on Literary Criticism (1936)
A World I Never Made (1936)
Can All This Grandeur Perish? and Other Stories (1937)
No Star Is Lost (1938)
Tommy Gallagher's Crusade (1939)
Father and Son (1940)
Decision (1941)
Ellen Rogers (1942)
My Days of Anger (1943)
Bernard Carr (1946)
Literature and Morality (1947)
The Road Between (1949)
An American Dream Girl (1950)
The Name Is Fogarty: Private Papers on Public Matters (1950)
This Man and This Woman (1951)
Yet Other Waters (1952)
Reflections at Fifty and Other Essays (1954)
French Girls Are Vicious and Other Stories (1955)
A Dangerous Woman and Other Stories (1957)
My Baseball Diary (1957)
It Has Come To Pass (1958)
Boarding House Blues (1961)
Side Street and Other Stories (1961)
The Silence of History (1963)
What Time Collects (1964)
Lonely for the Future (1966)
When Time Was Born (1966)
A Brand New Life (1968)
Childhood Is Not Forever (1969)
Invisible Swords (1971)
Judith and Other Stories (1973)
The Dunne Family (1976)
The Death of Nora Ryan (1978)